For CARYL BRAHMS, who always insisted, quite
inaccurately, that she only provided the occasion for wit in
others.

First published 1984
© Ned Sherrin 1984

This book is set in 11 on 13 Linotron Sabon by
Inforum Ltd, Portsmouth
Printed in Great Britain by
Richard Clay (The Chaucer Press) plc, Bungay, for
J.M. Dent & Sons Ltd
Aldine House, 33 Welbeck Street, London W1M 8LX

British Library Cataloguing in Publication Data

Sherrin, Ned
 Cutting edge or 'Back in the knife-box,
 Miss Sharp'.
 1. Wit and humor
 I. Title
 808.8'017   PN6151

 ISBN 0–460–04594–6

CONTENTS

ACKNOWLEDGMENTS

I should like to express my thanks to the following writers, publishers and literary representatives who have kindly given their permission for the use of copyright material. Every effort has been made to trace the owners of copyright material, and the publishers apologize for any omissions.

Jonathan Cape Ltd. for extracts from *Brief Chronicles* by James Agate.

Woody Allen and Random House, Inc. for extracts from *Side Effects* by Woody Allen; and Woody Allen for remarks by him printed in *The Standard* and *The International Herald Tribune*.

Robert Hale Ltd. and Random House, Inc. for an extract from *On Wine* by Gerald Asher.

Faber & Faber Ltd. for some lines from 'New Year Letter' in *Collected Poems*, extracts from *The Dyer's Hand* and a line on opera from *Secondary Worlds* all by W.H. Auden.

The New York Times for extracts from *Champion, Beat Thy Typewriter, Magazine Rack* and *Anti-Anglo-Saxonism* by Russell Baker.

The Guardian for permission to reprint extracts from Nancy Banks-Smith's column of television criticism.

The Standard for permission to reprint an extract from a theatrical review by Felix Barker.

The New Statesman for permission to reprint an extract from Julian Barnes's column of television criticism.

Lady Shirley Beecham and Hutchinson Books Ltd. for a few lines of verse and other extracts from *A Mingled Chime* by Sir Thomas Beecham.

Granada Publishing Ltd. for an extract from *Around Theatres* by Max Beerbohm; William Heinemann Ltd. for an extract from *Zuleika Dobson* by Max Beebohm. Harper & Row, Publishers, Inc. for extracts from the theatrical reviews of Robert Benchley originally printed in *The New Yorker*.

The Estate of E.C. Bentley and the Oxford University Press for permission to reprint 'The Art of Biography', 'John Stuart Mill', 'Columbus', 'Sir Christopher Wren' and 'George the Third' from *The Complete Clerihews of E.C. Bentley* © 1981.

The Spectator for an extract from the 'Low Life' column of Jeffrey Bernard.

The Guardian for permission to reprint extracts from the theatrical reviews of Michael Billington.

Michael Joseph Ltd. for extracts from *No Bed for Bacon* and *Six Curtains for Stroganova* by Caryl Brahms and S.J. Simon.

Acknowledgments

The Spectator for permission to reprint an extract from a theatrical review by Alan Brien.

International Creative Management and Random House, Inc. for extracts from *Restaurants of New York* 1982–83 edition by Seymour Britchky.

Michael Joseph Ltd. for an extract from *Loose Talk* by Tina Brown.

A.D. Peters & Co. Ltd. for extracts from *The Road to Oxiana* by Robert Byron.

Irene Josephy for an extract from *The Coarse of Events* by Patrick Campbell.

Longman Group Ltd. for an extract from *Cricket* by Neville Cardus.

Deborah Rogers Ltd. for permission to reprint extracts from *Previous Convictions* copyright © 1958 by Cyril Connolly, *The Unquiet Grave* copyright © 1944 by Cyril Connolly and *Enemies of Promise* copyright © 1938 by Cyril Connolly.

The Observer for permission to reprint an extract from an article by Peter Conrad.

Punch for permission to reprint extracts from articles by Alan Coren.

Weidenfeld & Nicolson for extracts from the *Diaries* of Noel Coward.

Davis-Poynter Ltd. for a line from *Design for Living* by Noel Coward.

Radala and Associates and Fontana Paperbacks for extracts from *The Naked Civil Servant* by Quentin Crisp.

The Observer for a line from a theatrical review by Robert Cushman.

The Daily Telegraph for an extract from a theatrical review by W.A. Darlington.

A.J. Hubbard for extracts from *Bernard Shaw and Mrs. Patrick Campbell: Their Correspondence* edited by Alan Dent.

Laurence Pollinger Ltd. Watkins Loomis Agency Inc. and Victor Gollancz Ltd. for an extract from *Comfort Me With Apples* by Peter de Vries; and Little, Brown and Co. and Victor Gollancz Ltd. for an extract from *The Glory of the Humming Bird* also by Peter de Vries.

Chappell Music Ltd. for part of the song 'That's Entertainment' by Howard Dietz © 1953 Chappell and Co. Inc.

Citadel Press, a division of Lyle Stuart, Inc., for extracts from *Wit's End* by Robert E. Drennen (titled *The Algonquin Wit* in the United States.) Copyright © 1968 by Robert E. Drennan.

W.H. Allen plc for an extract from *Music Is My Mistress* by Duke Ellington © 1974.

Methuen London Ltd. for permission to reproduce the poem 'Not Quite Cricket?' by Gavin Ewart, reprinted in *Summer Days* edited by Michael Meyer.

David Higham Associates Ltd. and Hutchinson Books Ltd. for extracts from *The Shakespeare Scene* by Herbert Farjeon.

Hutchinson Books Ltd. and London Management for an extract from *Ackroyd* by Jules Feiffer.

The Field for permission to reproduce an extract from a theatrical review.

Acknowledgments

of Double-Dactyls edited by Anthony Hecht and John Hollander. Copyright © 1966 by Anthony Hecht and John Hollander.

The Spectator for permission to reproduce a piece from Richard Ingrams's column of television criticism.

Clive James for four lines of verse reprinted in Godfrey Smith's column in *The Sunday Times*.

A.D. Peters and Co. Ltd. for permission to quote extracts from *Unreliable Memoirs* by Clive James.

Jonathan Cape Ltd. for permission to quote a piece from *Visions Before Midnight* by Clive James.

The Observer for an extract from an article by Clive James.

The Times for extracts from articles written by Frank Johnson.

Curtis Brown Ltd. for permission to include lines from *Nude Descending a Staircase* © 1956, 1958, 1959, 1960, 1961 by X.J. Kennedy.

Anthony Shiel Associates Ltd. and Miles Kington for permission to include extracts from the 'Moreover' column written by Miles Kington, which first appeared in *The Times* © Miles Kington.

Chappell Music Ltd. for part of the song 'Hymn to Him' by Alan Jay Lerner © 1956 Chappell and Co. Inc.

Bernard Levin for permission to quote from articles he wrote in *The Observer* and *The Sunday Times*.

Jonathan Cape Ltd. and Bernard Levin for extracts from *The Pendulum Years* by Bernard Levin.

Chappell Morris Ltd. for part of the song 'Hound Dog' by Jerry Lieber and Mike Stoller © 1952 Lion Pub. Co. and Elvis Presley Music.

Carlin Music Corp. for part of the song 'Three Cool Cats' by Jerry Lieber and Mike Stoller.

W.H. Allen plc for extracts from *Every Other Inch A Lady* by Beatrice Lillie © 1973.

University of Washington Press for an extract from *Men of Destiny* by Walter Lippman.

Chappell Music Ltd. for part of the song 'Adelaide's Lament' by Frank Loesser © Frank Music Corp.

A.D. Peters & Co. Ltd. for extracts from *Personal Pleasures* and *Crewe Train* both by Rose Macaulay.

Weidenfeld & Nicolson for an extract from *The Privilege Of His Company* by William Marchant.

Doubleday & Co. Inc. for an extract from *Sun Dial Time* by Don Marquis, © 1936 by Don Marquis.

The Executors of the Estate of W. Somerset Maugham and William Heinemann

Ltd. for permission to reproduce extracts from *The Summing Up, The Moon and Sixpence, A Writer's Notebook* and *Cakes and Ale* by W. Somerset Maugham.

Little, Brown and Co. for permission to reproduce 'Epitaph on a Waiter' and 'To a Certain Most Certainly Certain Critic' (first) appeared in *The Saturday Review of Literature* and from *Odds Without Ends.* © 1945 by David McCord.

Alfred A. Knopf, Inc. for extracts from *Prejudices: A Selection* edited by James T. Farrell, *Minority Report, A Mencken Chrestomathy* and *H.L. Mencken's Notebooks* all by H.L. Mencken.

Chappell Music Ltd. for part of the song 'Blues In The Night' lyrics by Johnny Mercer © 1941 Harms Inc.

Methuen London Ltd. for extracts from pieces written by Harold Pinter and Thomas Keneally which are reprinted in *Summer Days* edited by Michael Meyer.

A.D. Peters & Co. Ltd. for an extract from *The Pursuit of Love* by Nancy Mitford.

Robson Books Ltd. for extracts from *Frank Muir Goes Into . . .* by Frank Muir and Simon Brett.

André Deutsch and Curtis Brown Ltd. for permission to reproduce the poems 'The Song of the Open Road', 'The Turtle', 'Genealogical Reflections', 'Reflection on Ice-Breaking' and 'Lines to a World-Famous Poet Who Failed to Complete a World-Famous Poem; or Come Clean Mr. Guest!' by Ogden Nash, printed in *I Wouldn't Have Missed It* (1983); and for an extract from *The Old Dog Barks Backwards* also by Ogden Nash (1973).

Sports Illustrated for lines on baseball by Ogden Nash © 1957 Time Inc.

Mrs. George Jean Nathan and Ms. Julie Haydon Nathan for extracts from *The Theatre Book of the Year 1942* and *The Theatre Book of the Year 1953* by George Jean Nathan.

A.M. Heath and Co. Ltd., the Estate of the late Sonia Brownwell Orwell and Martin Secker & Warburg Ltd. for an extract from *The English People* by George Orwell.

David Higham Associates for extracts from *A Better Class of Person* by John Osborne, published by Faber & Faber Ltd.; and for permission to reproduce a letter written by John Osborne to Michael Billington.

National Association for Advancement of Coloured People and Andrew D. Weinberger, Sheridan Square, New York, 10014 for extracts from *The Portable Dorothy Parker* (Viking Penguin) © 1973, originally published in *The New Yorker*.

Duckworth and Co. Ltd. for the poems 'The Flaw in Paganism', 'News Item', 'Comment' and 'Resumé' in the *Collected Dorothy Parker* by Dorothy Parker.

Liz Darhansoff Literary Agency for extracts from *Vinegar Puss* by S.J. Perelman printed by Simon & Schuster. Inc.

Chappell Music Ltd. for part of the song 'I'm a Gigolo' by Cole Porter © 1929 Harms Inc. and part of the song 'The Tale of an Oyster' also by Cole Porter © 1929 Cole Porter Music, Inc.

Acknowledgments

Granada Publishing Ltd. for an extract from *The Theory and Practice of Gamesmanship* by Stephen Potter.

William Heinemann Ltd. for an extract from *All About Ourselves and Other Essays* by J.B. Priestley.

Private Eye for extracts from its 'Colemanballs' column and 'The Diaries of Auberon Waugh'.

Anthony Quentin for an extract from a piece he wrote for *The Sunday Telegraph*.

A.D. Peters & Co. Ltd. for extracts from *Cricket Prints* and *More Cricket Prints* by R.C. Robertson-Glasgow.

Weidenfeld & Nicolson Ltd. for permission to quote from four letters by Henry Root in *The Henry Root Letters*.

Constable & Co. Ltd. for extracts from *Runyon à la Carte* by Damon Runyon.

Macmillan Publishing Co. Inc. for extracts from *The Life of George Gershwin* by Robert Rushmore © 1966 by Macmillan Publishing Co. Inc.

Harcourt Brace Jovanovich, Inc. for lines from *The Complete Poems* of Carl Sandburg.

Carlin Music Corp. for part of the song *Little Tin Box* by Stephen Schwartz.

The Society of Authors on behalf of the Bernard Shaw Estate for permission to reproduce extracts from the music criticism of George Bernard Shaw and from *Our Theatres in the Nineties* also written by him.

New York magazine for an extract from an article by John Simon entitled 'May, Bogdanovich, and Streisand: Varieties of Death Wish'.

Random House, Inc. for extracts from *Singularities: Essays on the Theatre 1964– 1973* by John Simon.

The Daily Telegraph for an extract from an article by Peter Simple.

Carlin Music Corp. for part of the song 'Little Things We Do Together' and for the song 'Uptown, Downtown' both by Stephen Sondheim.

The Spectator for an extract from a theatrical review.

Random House, Inc. for an extract from *Major Campaign Speeches of Adlai E. Stevenson, 1952*, by Adlai E. Stevenson.

Pelham Books Ltd. for an extract from *At Random Through the Green* by John Stobbs.

Alfred A. Knopf, Inc. and Penguin Books Ltd. for extracts from *The I.F. Stone's Weekly Reader*, edited by Neil Middleton.

Faber & Faber Ltd. for an extract from *Dogg's Hamlet, Cahoots Macbeth* by Tom Stoppard.

The Guardian for an extract from an article by Tom Stoppard.

Candida Donadeo and Associates for extracts from *George S. Kaufman – An Intimate Biography* by Howard Teichman.

FOREWORD

Defining wit is an irresistible temptation, especially for those who have little. Those who can, do, those who can't, define. What did Nietzsche think he was up to when he called wit 'the epitaph of an emotion'? How far did George Herbert take us by describing it as 'an unruly engine'? Even wittier souls spar with the word and concentrate on those facets which most nearly match their own style.

Truth, wisdom, insult, humour, satire, sexuality and madness have all been held to be essential ingredients in the recipe. The proportions may vary with the chef. Long-winded Polonius identified brevity as 'the soul of wit'; but to say less is no guarantee that you mean more and Shakespeare, who put those words in the old man's mouth, was happy elsewhere to report that 'when the age is in the wit is out'. In this case, of course, he meant those wits on which we live or which we keep about us, not the kind that gets itself collected between more or less hard covers.

The responsibility of being a wit can be heavy; Pope knew about that:

> You beat your pate and fancy wit will come
> Knock as you please; there's nobody at home.

So did Caryl Brahms and S.J. Simon in *Don't Mr Disraeli*:

> . . . A rainy day. The cobbles of the Haymarket look like toffee but taste like mud. Max Beerbohm, overshoed, umbrella'd and meditating an epigram, is hurrying towards Piccadilly. Oscar Wilde, meditating an epigram, overshoed and umbrella'd is hurrying towards Trafalgar Square. Mr Greville, overshoed, umbrella'd, and in no hurry whatsoever, pops behind the pillars of the Haymarket Theatre. What material for his diary! He pulls out his notebook and stands damply, pencil in hand, ready to record the masterly ripostes of the two wittiest men in town.
>
> 'Good morning, Max,' said Oscar Wilde.
> 'Good morning, Oscar,' said Max Beerbohm. They looked

1

at each other. They thought furiously. They hurried on.

Under his porch at the Haymarket Theatre, Mr Greville looked at his material. He shook his head . . .

The public reputation of wit leans heavily on people like Wilde, Beerbohm, Shaw, Coward, F.E. Smith and Dorothy Parker. Sometimes the strain tells:

Oscar Wilde: I wish I had said that.
Whistler: You will, Oscar, you will!

Gore Vidal echoed it in 1978 when I asked him on an American TV Quiz Show who that week had said, 'The possibilities of heterosexuality are very nearly exhausted.' The correct answer was a mournful pornographer, but Gore did not know the correct answer. 'Did I?' he asked, hopefully.

Dorothy Parker, required to specify the essentials of her trade, settled for truth: 'There's a hell of a difference between wisecracking and wit. Wit has truth in it. Wisecracking is simply callisthenics with words'.

Aristotle wanted insolence, 'cultured insolence', with his idea of wit. Falstaff talked of being 'not only witty in myself, but the cause of wit in other men'. And there is a group of people, almost as valuable as the wits, who attract insolent comment.

The American actress, Sylvia Miles, is one such. As rumour tells it, after a disastrous affair with a homosexual, Miss Miles was understandably distraught when he left her. Nightly, she drowned her sorrows at Joe Allen's Restaurant in New York. One night, a large, witty, black waiter, asked her solicitously if she would like some coffee. She would. How would she like her coffee? Miss Miles looked him up and down and rolled out another old chestnut, 'Like my men!' The waiter's voice went up a register, 'Oh! Miss Miles, we don't serve no gay coffee here!' At a party also attended by many actresses younger and more svelte, Sylvia is said suddenly to have proclaimed in a loud voice, 'I've got the best body in this room'. 'Why didn't you bring it with you?' inquired one of the others. Early morning previews are held to be the only time an average man can go to the movies and find Miss Miles looking better than he does.

Noel Coward doubted if he was really witty – acknowledging that there was a certain quality of truth and surprise about 'women should be struck regularly – like gongs'. Coward was a prime victim of another of the occupational hazards of the wit. It is convenient to ascribe any sharp remark to an acknowledged wit, rather than bother to find out who really said it. Coward hated the inference that he had said of the huge Queen of Tonga's tiny companion, in the Coronation procession, Haile Selassie, 'That's her lunch'. Very reasonably, he pointed out that she was his good friend and would have been hurt. Coward's apocrypha is also popularly assumed to include every hoary, dirty limerick, and most additional verses to Eskimo Nell.

A nervous retailer of another man's wit gains confidence from giving a remark impeccable credentials. For our musical, *The Mitford Girls*, Caryl Brahms and I found a witty line of Evelyn Waugh's. Advising Nancy Mitford to ditch her first lover, Hamish Erskine, Waugh said, 'Save your money, dress better and catch a better husband'. The attribution of the remark to Waugh before it was delivered had the audience sitting forward, relaxed, happy and primed to receive a witticism with laughter.

Much of F.E. Smith's wit proclaims him an apostle of Aristotle in his 'cultured insolence'. His answer to the Labour politician, J.H. Thomas, who as a new MP did not know the way to the House of Commons loo, was direct, his instructions succinct: 'First left, go along the corridor. You'll see a door marked Gentlemen, but don't let that deter you'. Somehow, Smith and Thomas stayed friends and soon, when Thomas complained of 'an 'ell of an 'eadache', Smith prescribed 'a couple of aspirates'.

The Irish connection, Congreve, Swift, Wilde and Shaw, fall easily into the top ten list of wits. It is ironic that the Irish joke should be at the expense of a nation which has produced an unusual number of sharp minds. Oliver St John Gogarty is not perhaps as widely quoted as those fellow-countrymen, but I relish his reply on the occasion of a campaign to ruin the look of the Liffey. Gogarty had some ministerial responsibility to answer a question about the prostitutes who entertained their clients against the trees that lined the river. There was a motion to cut them down. Gogarty put a stop to it in one sentence. 'Surely', he argued, 'the trees are more sinned against than sinning!'

The Liffey brought out the best in Gogarty. When a gift of swans was bestowed upon it, he swam across alongside the birds. The

Liffey at that time was notorious for the sewage which poured into it, and Gogarty was asked if the experience had not been unpleasant. 'Oh no', he dismissed it, 'it was no more than going through the motions'.

Quick wit, in this case, and not unlike the non-Irish Provost of King's, Cambridge, who was showing Queen Victoria across a new bridge over the Cam. Suddenly, he saw the miniature monarch peeping over the balustrade, her eyes fixed on small scraps of paper floating beneath. It was another question of sewage. 'What,' she inquired, 'are those?' 'Those, Ma'am,' he replied, 'are notices prohibiting bathing.'

To return to the Irish counter-attack, it is not only the famous who achieve a quick-witted response. W.B. Yeats once delivered a speech of intoxicating eloquence which lasted an hour and a half. He was followed by a country senator who knew how to get himself off the hook. 'Mr Yeats has talked the very words out of my mouth', he said. Not, I suppose, quick wit, since he had an hour and a half to prepare it; but highly commendable.

Dryden knew how demanding the job could be:

> Great wits are sure to madness near allied,
> And thin partitions do thin bonds divide.

Shadwell went along with Dryden:

> And wit's the noblest frailty of the mind.

Which did nothing to improve Dryden's opinion of Shadwell's wit:

> Some beams of wit on other souls may fall,
> Strike through and make a lucid interval.
> But Shadwell's genuine night admits no ray
> His rising fogs prevail upon the day.

Pope, perhaps, puts it as nearly and completely as anyone:

> True wit is nature to advantage dressed.
> What oft was thought; but ne'er so well expressed.

Molière wanted a sterner test — immediacy — 'The true touchstone of wit is the impromptu'. A well-earned laugh can be a saving grace when it turns away wrath from a remark which would otherwise be no more than rude; but La Rochefoucauld may have been over-

4

stating the case when he suggested that 'Wit enables us to act rudely with impunity'; on safer ground he suggested, 'If it were not for the company of fools, a witty man would often be greatly at a loss'.

Every seventeenth- and eighteenth-century wit was ready to stand up and be counted on the subject. Wycherley, in *The Country Wife*, thought wit more 'necessary than beauty; and I think no young woman ugly who has it and no handsome woman agreeable without it.' Congreve's plays are studded with wit and reflections upon it. 'Wit must be foiled by wit: cut a diamond with a diamond', he wrote in *The Double Dealer*: and, in *The Way of the World*, 'A wit should be no more sincere than a woman constant; one argues a decay of the parts, as t'other of beauty.' While Vanbrugh in his preface to *The Relapse* suggested that 'Wit's as slow in growth as grace'. In the *Tale of a Tub* Swift was similarly gloomy. 'It is with wits as with razors, which are never so pat to cut those they are employed on as when they have lost their edges'.

In the *Spectator* in 1711 Addison addressed himself to the problem of reconciling wit and good nature – a perpetual headache for wit-fanciers. 'It is grown almost into a maxim that good-natured men are not always men of the most wit. This observation, in my opinion, has no foundation in nature. The greatest wits I have conversed with are men eminent for their humanity.' Sheridan disagreed – at least in *The School for Scandal*: 'There's no possibility of being witty without a little ill-nature; the malice of a good thing is the barb that makes it stick'.

Attitudes to wits vary from idolatory through fear and mistrust to contempt. Pope knew that 'fools are only laugh'd at: wits are hated'. And Lord Chesterfield wrote to his son, 'A wit is a very unpopular denomination, as it carries terror along with it; and people in general are as much afraid of a live wit, in company, as a woman is of a gun.' 'What brutes all wits are' was Beaumarchais's sweeping generalization in *The Barber of Seville*. In the contempt corner Sydney Smith lectured on the failings of wits: 'Professed wits, though they are generally courted for the amusement they afford are seldom respected for the qualities they possess'; Benjamin Franklin's penetrating dismissal was more specific: 'There's many witty men whose brains can't fill their bellies. . .', a view endorsed by Hazlitt nearly a hundred years later: 'Those who cannot miss an opportunity of saying a good thing . . . are not to be trusted with the management of any great question'.

The other ever-raging debate is fought over the boundaries between wit and humour. 'To be comic is merely to be playful, but wit is a serious matter. To laugh at it is to confess that you do not understand', wrote Ambrose Bierce in his *Music and Morals* in 1871. H.R. Haweis defined humour as 'the electric atmosphere' and wit as 'the flash'. One dictionary definition makes this distinction: 'Wit is more purely intellectual than Humour and implies swift perception of the incongruous: it is primarily verbal in its expression, and depends for its effect chiefly on ingenuity or unexpectedness of turn, or patness of application. Humour commonly implies broader human sympathies than wit, so that its sense of the incongruous is more kindly, and is often blended with pathos'.

Guy Boas took issue with most of this in introducing his *Anthology of Wit*. 'To say that wit consists in a perception of the incongruous is to ignore Bergson's essay on Laughter in which he credited wit and humour alike with possessing this faculty, and to associate "unexpectedness" with wit is to forget that Hazlitt found surprise to be one of the chief features of humour. Finally, to describe humour as being "often blended with pathos" is to remove humour completely from the sense in which we use it today and to produce that type of verbal confusion which caused Thackeray to lecture on Swift and Pope as "Humourists". "I should call Humour a mixture of love and wit", said Thackeray. But why should humour be a mixture of anything, and above all, why should it be mingled with wit, from which it is the instinct of an enquiring mind to divide it?'

Boas derives humour from the supposition that human nature was once held to be determined by the physical 'humours' and fluids which made up the body. Imbalances of these fluids produce – as in Ben Jonson's plays – conduct which was freakish, absurd or whimsical – provoking laughter at a recognizably humorous situation. The word 'wit', however, stems from the Anglo-Saxon *witan*, to know, which lent itself flatteringly to the Anglo-Saxon approximation to Parliament and implied the exercise of the intellect. So wit is associated with the mind's contribution to what is amusing. 'Humour', to Boas, 'is the funny situation or object; wit is the fun which a particular mind subjectively perceives in the situation or object.'

Foreword

'Experientia Docet . . .' said Mr Micawber, so the following pages are offered in the hope that they lie largely within the boundaries of wit and that if the experience fails to teach a definition of wit it may provide moments of pleasure along the way. The object is to lead the reader through groups of cherished old friends and to introduce numerous new acquaintances. You do not help old ladies across the street by giving them a definition – they either accept the invitation with a smile or, if the approach offends them, beat you over the head with an umbrella. It is devoutly to be wished that this journey will be pleasant and not an incitement to assault and battery.

I should add that I acquired the sub-title to this book while mapping out the trip myself. Two actor friends, Terry Sheppard and Ricky Kirwin, were appearing for the Thames Television Company in an episode of *Jemima Shore* – starring the delightful Patricia Hodge. As extremely good friends often do, they became dazzlingly bitchy towards one another. Eyes burned, tongues flashed and the exchange of wit brought the studio to a standstill. Needless to say the content was ephemeral and neither can remember what he said – but the clinching line was barbed enough to distract three elderly, camp, male dressers from their stitching, bring them erect and cause them to say, as one woman, 'Ooh! Back in the knife box, Miss Sharp!'

Ned Sherrin
February 1984

I
THE WORDSMITHS

'I love being a writer. What I can't stand is the paperwork'
– Peter de Vries

'In the Beginning was the word. . .', and after that it was mostly downhill. Nowadays words fly off the pen into books never opened or into plays or films flung onto stage or screen by ambitious directors with so much sound and fury that nothing signifies; out of the mouths of actors who hold them in scant respect and shed them with relish; onto television channels unheard or unheeded; and into advertisements which debase their currency in the service of unappetising 'new lines' ('Advertising is the rattling of a stick inside a swill bucket', said George Orwell). Edith Sitwell saw it all coming. 'A great many people now reading and writing,' she said, 'would be better employed in keeping rabbits.'

However, journalists, novelists, playwrights, actors, poets and copywriters do, in the course of these frustrating exercises, become practised in the use of words and so, in their off-duty – even occasionally in their on-duty – moments, they harness them in the cause of wit, back-biting or merriment, sometimes as an amusing corrective, sometimes for improvement, and frequently for insult. In the worlds of journalism, advertising, books, showbusiness, everything loosely lumped together under the label of 'The Media', there is room enough, heaven knows, for back-biting, correction, improvement and insult. 'Words can be your friend or enemy, depending on who's throwing the book', says a character in Tom Stoppard's *Cahoot's Macbeth*. 'A flaw in a piece of white jade may be ground away, but a word spoken amiss may not be called back', said Confucius. He also said, 'For one word a man is often set down as wise, and for one word he is as often set down as a fool' (presumably, then, being a man of few words is an admirable trait because it diminishes the chance of the latter verdict?). Words have been said to 'pay no debts', fine words to 'butter no parsnips', fair words to 'cost nothing' and to 'break no bones'.

9

It is new words that are often seen as suspect. In his 'Essay on Criticism', Pope suggests that:

> In words as fashions, the same rule will hold,
> Alike fantastic, if too new or old:
> Be not the first by whom the new are tried,
> Nor yet the last to lay the old aside.

The Earl of Roscommon, translating Horace in 1680, adopted a braver stance:

> Man ever had, and ever will have, leave
> To coin new words well suited to the age,
> Words are like leaves, some wither every year
> And every year a younger race succeeds.

Keith Waterhouse, writing some 300 years after the Earl (and at least 1980 years after Horace) found witty cause for disquiet in many unattractive new words which, though they might suit the present age, did not suit him. He compared the 1980s with the last period of frenzied verbal invention, the 1940s – rejoicing that words like blitz, black-out and evacuee lost their popularity with the cessation of hostilities. He saw no such hope for the new words, 'which, I fear, are here to stay'. Here are some:

> Aggro, additive, Afro, audio. Backlash, bus lane, butter mountain, breathalyser, bionic, battery hen. Computer, confrontation, complex, cheque card, chat show. Decibel, devolution, dissident, discrimination, disposable, digital, drag-queen. Environment, ethnic, ecology. Feedback, full-frontal. Gay, gang-bang, groupie, giro, graffiti. Hostage, hypothermia, hijack. Identikit, inner-city. Jet-lag, junkie. Kilo, keg. Lib., low-tar. Mugger, metricate, militant, motorway, media, multi-storey. Nuclear, no-go, new p. Oil slick, overkill. Punk, pollution, porn, provo, phone-in, postal code, panda-car, photo-copy. Redundant, referendum. Single parent, shopping-centre, sit-in. Tower block, take-away, topless. Up-tight, urban clearway. VAT, vandal, vasectomy. Wild-cat, whizkid. Yellow-line. Zone.

Words may often fall like leaves but we do well to listen to Charles Lamb's advice. 'All words are no more to be taken in a literal sense than a promise given to a tailor', he said, hinting at the power of words to dazzle, confuse, and dismay. 'When ideas fail, words come in very handy', snapped Goethe. In Peter de Vries's phrase, you can be 'a deluge of words and a drizzle of thought'. 'Most of the disputes in the world arise from words', moaned Lord Mansfield, in his judgment in a case in 1773. 'When two men communicate with each other by word of mouth, there is a twofold hazard in that communication', was the verdict of another lawyer, Sam Ervin, during the Watergate hearings. James Callaghan (who was not talking of Watergate) once said, 'A lie can be halfway around the world before the truth has got its boots on.' So there are dangers as well as excitements in words.

Simple words have always been best, but not always fashionable. 'An average English word is four letters and a half', wrote Mark Twain, combining a close fist with a sense of style. 'By hard honest labour I've dug all the large words out of my vocabulary and shaved them down till the average is three and a half . . . I never write *Metropolis* for seven cents because I can get the same price for *City*. I never write *Policeman* when I can get the same money for *Cop*.' G.K. Chesterton had the same idea: 'Science in the modern world has many uses. Its chief use, however, is to provide long words to cover the errors of the rich. The word "kleptomania" is a vulgar example of what I mean.' Churchill once said he liked 'short words and vulgar fractions'. Ira Gershwin brought a scholarly and witty approach to his examination of the simple words most frequently used in popular love songs – taking as his example his own charming lyric, 'But Not For Me', in his book *Lyrics on Several Occasions: A Brief Concordance*:

Excluding two letter prepositions and 'an', I imagine the pro-noun *me* is the most used two-letter word in Songdom. 'I' (leaving out the indefinite article 'a') is doubtless the most used one-letter word (and everywhere else for that matter). 'You' (if the definite article 'the' bows out) is the most frequent three-letter word. 'Love' probably gets the four-letter nod (referring strictly to songs that can be heard in the home). In the five-letter stakes I would wager that 'heart' and 'dream' photo-finish as a dead heat. As for words of more than five letters, you're on your own.

Words undoubtedly fascinate people. They appealed, for instance, to a performer, Eddie Cantor, who gleefully remarked that 'Browsing in a dictionary is like being turned loose in a bank'. Adlai Stevenson was more circumspect: 'Man does not live by words alone, despite the fact that he sometimes has to eat them.' In *Don Juan in America*, Eric Linklater's hero turns nasty on the subject of his wife's vocabulary: 'I've been married six months. She looks like a million dollars, but she only knows a hundred and twenty words and she's only got two ideas in her head. The other one's hats.' In *Back to Methuselah* Shaw wrote: 'Make me a beautiful word for doing things tomorrow, for that surely is a great and blessed invention.' (Perhaps he was unaware of the question posed ages ago to an Irish priest by a Spanish colleague: 'Do you have an Irish equivalent of our word "mañana"?' 'Yes', said the Irish priest, 'but it doesn't have quite the same sense of urgency.')

For centuries more words have appeared in newspapers than in any other form of print. 'The newspapers', Sheridan wrote in *The Critic* in 1779, 'The newspapers! Sir, they are the most villainous – licentious – abominable – infernal – not that I ever read them – no – I make it a rule never to look into a newspaper.' If Sheridan has one thing to say about the press, Oscar Wilde, as usual, has three: 'Modern journalism justifies its own existence by the great Darwinian principle of the survival of the vulgarest', he wrote in *The Critic as Artist*. In *The Soul of Man Under Socialism*, he adopts the historical approach: 'In centuries before ours, the public nailed the ears of journalists to the pump. In this century journalists have nailed their ears to the keyhole.' By 1889 in *The Decay of Lying*, Wilde was more tolerant: 'Newspapers have degenerated', he wrote, 'they may now be absolutely relied upon.' As a newspaper-owner this century, the view of Lord Thomson of Fleet was characteristically idiosyncratic and not too wide of the mark: 'It is part of the social mission of every great newspaper to provide a refuge and a home for the largest possible number of salaried eccentrics.'

Though not a principal inspiration for poets, the press has occasionally caused a pen to scatter a page with verse. In *The Dunciad*, Pope pinpoints the origin of the phrase, 'Gutter Press' – describing muckraking weekly journalists scavenging for their unsavoury subject matter in the sewage-laden waters of the River

Fleet which provided Fleet Street with its name. The goddess, Dullness, presided over these rites from a nearby bridge:

> To where Fleetditch with disemboguing streams
> Rolls the large tribute of dead dogs to Thames,
> The King of dykes! than whom no sluice of mud
> With deeper sable blots the silver flood.
> 'Here strip, my children! here at once leap in,
> Here prove who best can dash through thick and thin,
> And who the most in love of dirt excel,

A journalist, to Byron, was:

> A would-be satirist, a hired buffoon,
> A monthly scribbler of some low lampoon
> Condemned to drudge, the meanest of the mean,
> And furnish falsehoods for a magazine.

A lot later Humbert Wolfe, poet and critic, sold much the same sort of message to *Punch*:

> You cannot hope
> To bribe or twist
> Thank God! the British journalist,
> But seeing what
> The man will do
> Unbribed, there's no occasion to.

J.G. Saxe was less stringent, writing in 1855:

> Who would not be an Editor? To write
> The magic 'we' of such enormous might.
> To be so great beyond the common span
> It takes the plural to express the man.

Elbert Hubbard, who lives on through his *Book of Epigrams* (1922), appears to have been the source of one of Adlai Stevenson's favourite saws on the subject of editors: 'A person employed on a newspaper whose business it is to separate the wheat from the chaff and to see that the chaff is printed.' Just as sadly, but perhaps with more originality, Stevenson observed that 'Writing good editorials is chiefly telling the people what they think – not what you think.' The idea was confirmed by Alexander Cockburn in 1974: 'The first

13

law of journalism – to confirm existing prejudice rather than contradict it.'

'A newspaper consists of just the same number of words whether there be any news in it or not', Henry Fielding argued in *Tom Jones* – or as A.J. Liebling rephrased it in New York in the 1950s, 'People everywhere confuse what they read in the newspapers with news.' Dr Johnson's attitude was more in anger than in sorrow: 'A news-writer is a man without virtue who writes lies at home for his own profit. To these compositions is required neither genius nor knowledge, neither industry nor sprightliness; but contempt of shame and indifference to truth are absolutely necessary.' Equally harsh words came from John Quincy Adams: 'They are hired assassins who sit with loaded blunderbusses at the corner of streets and fire them off for hire or for sport at any passenger they select.' Journalism to Charles A. Dana (the man who made the immortal distinction between the news value of 'dog bites man' and 'man bites dog') was simply the business of 'buying white paper at two cents a pound and selling it at ten cents a pound'.

But, of course, journalists labour under the strain of what Katherine Whitehorn has termed 'Rothermere's Law', by which 'Any journalist may be exchanged for any other journalist without penalty.' In *The Pendulum Years*, Bernard Levin applied it to Cecil King's dismissal from IPC – 'What was unprecedented was that it was the Boss who was sacked; and if King's head could roll, whose would sit firmly on his shoulders?' – and went on to say that 'With time on his hands, King (whose unlucky acquisition of the *Daily Herald* had earned it the nickname 'King's Cross') turned to writing his memoirs – a post as a kind of editorial adviser to *The Times*, to which he had been appointed, clearly not sufficing to occupy his days – and these were presently published. They were not memorable except for the revelations they contained about his family, of whom, it appeared, some had been drunkards, some lunatics and some had laboured under either or both these afflictions.'

Levin was sharp about the changes to *The Times* in the 1960s as well as to its editorial advisers:

Change, indeed, must have been the word for the Sixties, if *The Times* itself, which had resisted so many pressures in its time, and exerted so many more, which had even escaped unharmed from the dreadful embrace of Lord Northcliffe, even when he went raving mad in the proprietor's chair, should fall into the ever-open jaw of the Canadian upstart, Lord Thomson, peering mole-like through his pebble lenses and collecting newspapers with a satisfied chuckle, as another man might collect postage stamps or Post-Impressionists.

He might equally well reflect today upon the decline in *The Times* under Murdoch's unaided eyes.

Americans have always been self-conscious about their newspapers, perhaps because they have always so depended upon them. Anthony Trollope remarked in 1862 that 'the average consumption of newspapers by an American must amount to about three a day'. And Jefferson is often quoted as preferring 'newspapers without a government to government without newspapers'. Those who quote him with approbation are usually journalists who, as Gore Vidal points out, ignore the 'mellifluous old faker's' qualifying phrase, – 'but I should mean that every man should receive those papers and be capable of reading them'.

In *Martin Chuzzlewit* Dickens was vivid and vicious in his visitor's view of the plethora of American scandal sheets:

> Here's the *New York Sewer*! Here's the *New York Rowdy Journal*! Here's all the New York Papers! Here's the full particulars of the last Alabama gouging case, and . . . here's the *Sewer*'s exclusive account of a flagrant act of dishonesty committed by the Secretary of State when he was eight years old, now communicated at great expense by his nurse . . . Here's the *Sewer*'s article on the judge that tried this paper day afore yesterday for libel, and the *Sewer*'s tribute to the independent jury that didn't convict it, and the *Sewer*'s account of what they might have expected if they had.

That picture of New York journalism 130-odd years ago rings as true for a modern visitor to the same city in all but the number of available news-sheets. (It's not too inaccurate for Britain.) The obsession with violence, scandal, score-settling, cheque-book journalism and extravagant overkill on any new subject still lingers; and if there are not as many papers, there seem to be just as many columnists scattered across the surviving broadsheets picking over the same bones ad infinitum.

The heirs and descendants of Mr Jefferson Brick of *The Rowdy Journal* are no more highly regarded. 'I keep reading between the lies', said Goodman Ace, a favourite of American radio audiences. 'The aim of so much journalism', Gore Vidal added, 'is to exploit the moral prejudices of the reader, to say nothing of those of the proprietor.' Rupert Murdoch, a proprietor on the defensive, has complained about the problems of 'competing with double-page spreads of pubic hairs', in an attempt to explain his Page Three papers and to answer the charge that they fail to measure up to Arthur Miller's definition of a good newspaper as 'a nation talking to itself'.

With a nicely judged line in sarcasm, in his *Private Eye* column in 1972, Auberon Waugh sought to arrest the parade of page three nipples:

> Thursday, 1st October. Another 14-inch nude woman in my copy of *The Times* this morning . . . I see Rees-Mogg still asks his women to hide their pubic hair, but I wonder if he is right. Perhaps he is of the opinion that the less explicit the image, the greater the sexual arousal. But is sexual arousal what we are looking for at breakfast time, rather than clarity and truth? His brother-editor, Mr Harold Evans of *The Sunday Times*, seems to have been rather more experimental. A young woman accused of having manufactured petrol bombs in Kensington, explains that she was only following the instructions which she read in *The Sunday Times*. The judge expressed surprise at this and I confess I agree with him. Sexual titillation is one thing. Many people nowadays argue that masturbation is not only harmless but even beneficial in certain circumstances. If Mogg and Evans think they can increase their sales by helping their readers to masturbate, that is a matter for their own judgment, but there is all the difference in the world between this and peddling detailed instructions on how to make petrol bombs and other murderous devices to readers, many of whom may be emotionally immature and unstable.

The Sunday Times, under Harold Evans, pioneered the revival of investigative journalism in the 1960s. Bernard Levin wrote that

'. . . whole pages . . . took on the air of a racily written blue-book . . . *The Daily Mail* got the message . . . *The Sun* caught the prevailing tide.' From the right, in *The Daily Telegraph*, Peter Simple, under the by-line of Jack Moron, was at the same time noisily lampooning the strident voices of the popular journalists. 'Wake up, Britain!' shouts 'Jack Moron':

> Today the People of Britain are hopping mad. Men cannot look their wives and sweethearts in the face. Children eye their parents with mute reproach. Dogs and cats refuse their food . . . [Their anger was aroused by Britain's lack of a space programme] . . . Turf out the dreary pedagogues and dodos who will have the cheek to teach non-scientific subjects in our schools and universities . . . Animals, children and old people should be pressed into service. Women should be conscripted . . . Maybe we can't afford a full-sized space satellite. But surely we can get some representative British object, some symbol of our way of life into an orbit round the earth immediately? Wake up Britain!

Peter Simple's Clare Howitzer is an agony aunt, whose reply to a query from Sandra Cloggie, of Barrow-in-Furness – 'My boyfriend, Jim, is a manic-depressive, one-legged, homosexual dwarf. He wears kinky boots, carries a flick knife, sucks ice-lollies all the time I am talking to him and is very hairy. Do you think this is the real thing for me this time?' is straight to the point: 'I certainly do. You have got a real winner there, Sandra. My advice to you is to write a T.V. play about him right away before some other girl can do it first.' Amongst a rich gallery of characters Peter Simple also has Virginia Ferret ferreting away in the twilight world of drugs: 'There had already been reports from Nottingham and elsewhere of teen-agers smoking their grandparents.'

To return to America, Bob Dylan's attitude to the press is understandable, if defeatist: 'If I don't talk to the press, I'm a hermit. If I do talk to the press, I'm trying to manipulate. I can't win.' John Crosby (whom I will quote on the least excuse, since he once called TW3 'The Best Television Show in the World') was specific: 'Viewing with dismay the conditions in somebody else's backyard is the speciality of the *New York Times*.' Adolph S. Ochs was realistic about his paper: 'If a newspaper prints a sex crime, it is smut: but when the *New York Times* prints it it is a sociological study.' Don Marquis was highly professional: 'The art of newspaper paragraphing is to stroke a platitude until it purrs like an epigram.' Long before the explosion of political exposé writing, James Haggerty, Eisenhower's Press Secretary, was rueful: 'If you lose your temper at a newspaper columnist, he'll get rich, or famous, or both.' Wolcott Gibbs approached the press and particularly the style of *Time* magazine in a mood for parody. 'Backward', wrote he, 'ran sentences until reeled the mind.' There is controversy around the *Washington Post* over the authorship of the famous definition of news as 'the first rough draft of history', which has been attributed, give or take a word, to both Ben Bradlee and Katharine Graham – perhaps editor and proprietor used the same staff writer. Marshall McLuhan was philosophical: 'People don't actually read newspapers. They get into them every morning, like a hot bath.' I.F. Stone, professional iconoclast, was brisk: 'A good journalist is a cross between Sir Galahad and William Randolph Hearst.' James Thurber was tolerant: 'There is of course a certain amount of drudgery in newspaper work, just as there is in teaching classes, tunnelling into a bank or being President of the United States. I suppose that even the most pleasurable of imaginable occupations – that of batting baseballs through the windows of the RCA building – would pall a little as the days ran on.'

Gossip columnists are a favourite target on both sides of the Atlantic – though the American litterateur Louis Kronenberger wrote, realistically, 'It's the gossip columnist's business to write about what is none of his business.' It takes a scandal-spattered disco-star to realise that gossip is rather like a rumour; as Amanda Lear has said, 'I hate to spread rumours, but what else can one do with them?' Or, in the words of the great survivor of American gossip columnists, Earl Wilson, 'Gossip is when you hear something you like about someone you don't.' Tina Brown has collected a good phrase from one of Nigel Dempster's – current doyen of English gossip columnists – would-be contributors: 'He sounded so Byronic and attractive in an awful way' – a sentence which sums up the revulsion and fascination of gossip as well as the gossip pedlar. Ms Brown's perceptive conclusion on Dempster himself is that, 'He has broken down society's reserve to the point where it comes to him and lays its scandals at his feet. Society's pariah has become society's puppeteer.' That was always true of gossip spreaders. In another vignette, Ms Brown captured, more perceptively, Richard Crossman arriving at that haunt of gossips – a *Private Eye* lunch: 'He has the jovial garrulity and air of witty indiscretion that shows he intends to give nothing away.'

'If all men knew what others say of them there would not be four friends in the world', Blaise Pascal wrote in one of the great heydays of gossip, the seventeenth century. Wycherley summed up the technique in *The Country Wife*: 'I have told all the chambermaids, waiting women, tire-women and old women of my acquaintance, and whispered it as a secret to 'em, so that you need not doubt 'twill spread.' Pope versified the refinements of the next century in *The Temple of Fame*:

> And all who told it added something new
> And all who heard it made enlargements too;
> In ev'ry ear it spread, on ev'ry tongue it grew.

'At every word a reputation dies', he added in *The Rape of the Lock*.

Wilde ensured an appropriate nineteenth-century focus on gossip: 'There is only one thing in the world worse than being talked about, and that is not being talked about' (*Picture of Dorian Gray*). Wilde also believed that there was a becoming age for scandal-mongering: 'One should never make one's debut with a scandal; one should reserve that to give interest to one's old age', and, he wrote, in *A Woman of No Importance*, 'It is perfectly monstrous the way people go about nowadays saying things against one, behind one's back, that are absolutely and entirely true.' After Wilde's Lord Mayor's Show, comes Walter Winchell's dust-cart: 'Gossip is the art of saying nothing in a way that leaves practically nothing unsaid.'

Three proverbs sum up the universal taste for gossip. From China: 'If what we *see* is doubtful, how can we believe what is spoken behind the back?' From Germany: 'Little people like to talk about what the great are doing.' And from Spain, the great truth: 'Whoever gossips to you will gossip of you.' Alice Roosevelt Longworth was perfectly frank on the subject: 'If you can't say anything good about someone', she once said, 'sit right here by me.'

However, there are a few more general broadsides against the press to discharge. Yehudi Menhuin reflected sadly: 'Whenever I see a newspaper I think of the poor trees. As trees they provide beauty, shade and shelter. But as paper all they provide is rubbish.' Nick Tomalin, a great journalist, attacked with acid: 'The only qualities for real success in journalism are rat-like cunning, a plausible manner and a little literary ability. The capacity to steal 'other people's ideas and phrases is also invaluable' – an expansion, perhaps, of Karl Krauss's dictum: 'The making of a journalist – no ideas and the ability to express them.' G.K. Chesterton's contempt was directed at the newspaper reader: 'Journalism consists largely in saying, "Lord Jones Dead", to people who never knew Lord Jones was alive.'

Journalists are often at their most pressed and effective in the short sharp prose of the telegram. There is the classic exchange between the artist, Frederic Remington, cabling to William Randolph Hearst in 1898 from Cuba:

> EVERYTHING IS QUIET. THERE IS NO TROUBLE HERE. THERE WILL BE NO WAR. I WISH TO RETURN. REMINGTON.

It is Hearst's reply which sticks in the mind:

> PLEASE REMAIN. YOU FURNISH THE PICTURES AND I'LL FURNISH THE WAR. HEARST.

And then there is the chestnut dialogue between foreign editor and far-flung reporter:

> WHY UNNEWS?
> UNNEWS GOOD NEWS.
> UNNEWS UNJOB.

Expenses can inspire acerbity too:

> SENT $400. PLEASE ACCOUNT.
> RECEIVED $400. SPENT $400. REGARDS.

Evelyn Waugh scored heavily over his editor when told to investigate the alleged death of an American nurse in Abyssinia. The message he received was REQUIRE EARLIEST NAME LIFE STORY PHOTOGRAPH AMERICAN NURSE UPBLOWN ADOWA. Waugh's reply, after checking the facts, was shorter, NURSE UNUPBLOWN. It deserves to be as famous as Cary Grant's reply to a magazine's query, HOW OLD CARY GRANT?, which was simply OLD CARY GRANT FINE HOW YOU?

As purveyors of truth, newspapers have long been a subject for debate. For the prosecution, Aneurin Bevan: 'I read the newspapers avidly – it is my one form of continuous fiction.' For the tongue-in-the-cheek defence, Rose Macaulay: 'You should always believe all you read in the newspapers, as this makes them more interesting.' Arthur Balfour, told there were two curses of civilization – Christianity and journalism – replied, 'Christianity, naturally, but why journalism?' Adlai Stevenson once considered the value of accuracy in reporting: 'Accuracy to a newspaper is what virtue is to a lady; but a newspaper can always print a retraction.' In *A Hotel in Amsterdam* John Osborne made a neat point – 'Never believe in mirrors or newspapers.'

Osborne, on himself as journalist, is even more piquant. He started work for Sir Ernest Benn and was assigned to *Gas World* and in particular to Mr Silcox:

His daughter, Primrose, acted as his secretary, fawning on him with the admiration of an ambitious wife rather than a daughter and was seldom away from his side. I was soon given the impression that every lurking eye in the building was after Primrose's body. It was clear that I was not yet a serious candidate, but Mr Silcox was on the look-out for a suitably serious working journalist son-in-law who might one day step into the Editor-in-Chief's chair at *Gas World* and display Press on the window of his baby Austin. . . . There was little enough for anyone except the Assistant Editor, preserved like a sweating kipper in his own pipe smoke, who hardly ever looked up from his proof reading all day long. . . . I became 'Round the Showrooms, by Onlooker' . . . which was supposed to be bright, snappy stuff giving information about how to evangelize the gas cause in showrooms, cinema foyers and restaurants . . . I spent almost a week wandering round the Ideal Home Exhibition, sampling healthful drinks, midday drinks, sleep-inducing drinks, fruit drinks, along with dozens of different breakfast cereals. Stuffed in the cheeks with honey, milk, malt and wheat, I watched demonstrations of cleaning, sweeping, beating, stain-removing and polishing available to the ingoing tenants of Attlee Buildings and Stafford Cripps Estate.

While still at *Gas World*, Osborne began to contemplate the move from journalism to literature. Others before him had observed the contrast between the two. 'The difference between literature and journalism is that journalism is unreadable and literature is not read', said Wilde. 'Literature', to Cyril Connolly, was 'the art of writing something that will be read twice – journalism is that which will be grasped at once.' For Dean Inge, less gloomy than usual, 'The distinction between journalism and literature is becoming blurred, but journalism gains as much as literature loses.' John Osborne embarked on his transition by subscribing to a correspondence course conducted by the British Institute of Fiction Writing:

> I received weekly lessons on thick blue paper. The syllabus was mostly concerned with disciplines like How to Choose Your Market, the Correct Size of your Margins, Spacing, Letters to Editors, Dealing with Rejection Slips, Essential Information, and so on. When it came to the Art of Fiction Writing itself this turned out to be a simple matter of observing a narrative pattern which was something like 1a), 1b), 2a), and 2c). This iron formula was inviolable and simple, based on self-evident principles of exposition, conflict, exposition of second conflict and resolution of both conflicts or variations on these.

Shy of sending in his own efforts, Osborne submitted two post-humous pieces by his father, one called 'Mouse Pie':

> which I read after his death and was obviously about me and my problem of bed-wetting. The replies of the Fiction Editor were fulsome in their praise of my promise, but he made it plain that without the expert tuition of his Institute my chafing genius would never find an outlet even in the 'class' market that I was aiming at like *Argosy* . . . I was already aiming too high to effect a sale. When I started sending in my own efforts, the response from the Head Fiction Editor soon became reproachful, impatient and eventually ill-used and sorrowful
> . . . .

So – failure – actor – playwright – grand old man. Buy the book.

We must move on from journalism to 'literature'. On from news-papers and magazines, from Trollope's *Jupiter* and Dickens's *Eatenswill Gazette* vying with The *Eaten Swill Enquirer* in insults that would put the rivalry of *The Sun* and *The Daily Star* to shame; on from the exhilarating sensationalism of America's *The National Enquirer*, in which, according to the *New York Times* humourist, Russell Baker, 'UFOs flash over the Bermuda Triangle, cancer cures are imminent, and ancient film stars at last find that love is for keeps'; on from the gossip sheet, *People* – 'It is what the world of F. Scott Fitzgerald would have been if Fitzgerald had been ghost-written by Dr Norman Vincent Peale'; on from *Playboy*, in spite of its attractions for Russell Baker: 'I sneak into the world of *Playboy* for a wallow in hedonism. In the world of *Playboy*, Ernest Hemingway wears a silk union suit in a sleeping bag at a Holiday Inn. It is a world in which Henry VIII is played by John Travolta and Oedipus tears out his eyes because the tone arm on his record changer is not properly balanced'; on from the world of *Esquire*, 'where Dante Gabriel Rossetti always seems to be jogging with Muhammad Ali while Norman Mailer is on a pub crawl with Virgil'; on from *Cosmopolitan*, a world in which, says Baker, 'women giggle when they see me and try to lure me with frozen food dinners by candlelight and with artfully constructed foundation garments. But I pay them no heed, for I know they only wish to practise their lessons in how to steal a husband on a working girl's budget'; on from all 'the cheap contractions and revised spellings of the advertising world which have made the beauty of the written word almost unrecognizable – surely any society that permits the substitution of "kwik" for "quick" and "e.z." for "easy" does not deserve Shakespeare, Eliot or Michener?'

'The only reward to be expected from the cultivation of literature is contempt if one fails and hatred if one succeeds', wrote Voltaire to Mlle Quinault, in 1728. 'There are more books upon books than upon all other subjects', said Montaigne. However, Cervantes held that 'there's no book so bad that something may not be found in it'. George Herbert preferred experience: 'Years know more than books.' Thomas Fuller galloped a step further: 'Learning hath gained most by those books which the printers have lost.' Rousseau seemed to agree: 'I hate books, for they only teach people to talk about what they do not understand.' Perhaps the most discouraging thing ever said to a writer was doled out to poor Edward Gibbon who had generously given a copy of Volume III of his *Decline and Fall* to George III's brother, the Duke of Gloucester. 'What!' exclaimed the Duke, 'Another of those damned fat, square, thick books! always scribble, scribble, scribble, eh, Mr Gibbon?' (I hope Gibbon took the book back – compare Beaverbrook's remark about Lord Blake's biography of Northcliffe: 'It weighs too much'.) Richard Porson, who considered so emphatically that Gibbon's *Decline and Fall* was the greatest literary production of the eighteenth century that he committed large passages to memory, was also heard to mutter on occasion: 'There could not be a better exercise for a schoolboy than to turn a page of it into English.'

Pope once confessed in the prologue to a play that 'Authors are judged by strange, capricious rules/the great ones are thought mad, the small ones fools.' John Gay drew attention to backbiting among writers in another couplet:

> No author ever spared a brother,
> Wits are gamecocks to one another.

Poor Wordsworth had no pretensions to wit; 'I do not think I ever was witty but *once* in my life', he confessed to a small gathering. Agog to hear the *bon mot*, his audience pressed him for it. 'I was standing some time ago at the entrance of my cottage at Rydal Mount. A man accosted me with the question, "Pray, sir, have you seen my wife pass by?" whereupon I said, "Why, my good friend, I didn't know till this moment that you had a wife!" ' When his audience realized that they had heard the punch line they burst into laughter at its pointlessness and Wordsworth in his simplicity accepted this reaction as appreciation of his wit – so both sides were happy. It does conjure up, however, a frightening picture of Wordsworth, excited by his success, forever after stopping passers-by and bending their ears with his cumbersome anti-climax.

'A successful author', warned Dr Johnson, 'is equally in danger of the diminution of his fame whether he continues or ceases to write.' This advice ought to stop some and encourage others; but it appears to have no effect on the Gross National Output of Books. Too often, of course, as Anthony Burgess says, 'The possession of a book becomes a substitute for reading it.' Pertinently, he has also said, 'There is usually something wrong with the writers the young like.'

Quentin Crisp, a late developer, holds that there are three reasons for becoming a writer: 'The first is that you need the money; the second that you have something to say that you think the world should know; the third is that you can't think what to do with the long winter evenings.' Molnar gave other justifications. He became a writer 'in the same way that a woman becomes a prostitute. First I did it to please myself, then I did it to please my friends, and finally I did it for money.' Tom Stoppard's explanation is more whimsical: 'I write fiction because it's a way of making statements I can disown. I write plays because dialogue is the most respectable way of contradicting myself.' P.G. Wodehouse was deflatory: 'Every author really wants to have letters printed in the papers. Unable to make the grade, he drops down a rung of the ladder and writes novels.' A battery of writers declare happily that inspiration comes with the contract or the cash or the commission. The candour of Cheryl Tiegs, the American model who got $70,000 for putting her name to a book she did not write entirely by herself, is refreshing. 'The problem with writing', she complained, 'is that there's not much money in it.'

The urge to shock is a common bond for many creative souls. J.R. Ackerley claimed: 'If one is not scandalous it is difficult to write at all.' Jeffrey Bernard's frequently entertaining *Spectator* column, 'Low Life', sets out to shock – or not to shock – though its title hints at lurid moments, commissioned in the hope that it may arrest attention with its boldly confessional style. Here drink is more often the bait than sex:

> Two weeks ago *The Times* carried another of those silly, melodramatic features on the subject of alcoholism. It was written by Ms Caroline Moorehead and was headed by the usual old questions which, if you could answer yes to any of them, showed that there was 'serious cause for alarm'. Well, the more I looked at these questions the less alarmed I felt. In fact, I've now come to the conclusion that I don't drink enough. Just look at this nonsense.
> Q. Do you find that you drink embarrassingly quickly and have finished your drink long before those around you?
> J.B. The speed at which I drink embarrasses others. That's to say I am frequently outfumbled. Peter Owen, for example, last

bought a round in 1971. Such men need to be reminded that one swallow does not make a summer.

Kingsley Amis's view is that 'If you can't annoy somebody there is little point in writing.' 'Impropriety is the soul of wit', was Somerset Maugham's verdict. Jules Feiffer comments, 'Writing . . . [is] mainly an attempt to out-argue one's past, to present events in such a light that battles lost in life were either won on paper or held to a draw.'

In America in the 1970s, the Supreme Court declared seven ancient Anglo-Saxon words unfit for general broadcast on radio and television. All referred to bodily wastes or sex – 'micturition', 'defecation', 'sexual intercourse', 'practitioner of fellatio', 'female reproductive canal', 'incestuous male issue', and 'female mammary glands' remained outside the pale. As Russell Baker then pointed out in the *New York Times*, 'something about the Anglo-Saxon tongue has the power to make us see red. Or, in the case of the seven unspeakable words, blue'. He speculates on whether this attitude derives from the 'civilizing' influence of the Normans who sought to suppress a 'barbarous' Saxon culture, and goes on to show the process spreading to produce a vocabulary which would make the excesses of war palatable:

> During the Vietnam war, 'bombing' was turned into 'interdiction'. Those who pointed out that it was, nevertheless, bombing, and that people were being killed, were said to be unduly emotional and urged to Latinize their thinking. Admittedly there were 'casualties', as there would be in any process of 'pacification'. People against war were Latinized into 'dissidents', with their own connivance. A 'dissident' was far less likely to disturb his neighbour than a 'war-hater' . . . General Curtis Le-May even performed the commendable feat of condensing the Latin 'nuclear' into a sharp-edged new Anglo-Saxon word, 'nuke' ('nuke 'em'). After that Le-May was persona non grata in the Government which was smart enough to realize that if people began to understand what the Government was up to, it would be in deep trouble.

Baker points out that even Government-haters make use of the device. 'It has become the fashion to "execute" helpless captives. The theory, I suppose, is that it would seem shrill if you said they

26

had been "murdered". It is a rare subject today that makes our blood run cold, but when it comes to sounds we are all very delicate.' Or, as Ken Tynan wrote: 'Any country that has sexual censorship will eventually have political censorship.'

Bernard Levin was in fine form for the *Observer* on the Longford Report on pornography:

> The mountains have laboured, and brought forth – well, not a mouse, though it amounts to very little nor an elephant, though it is extremely large and shortsighted, nor a donkey, though it makes more noise than sense, nor a flatworm, though it does not seem to be sure in which direction it is going, nor a cat, though it will not take advice, nor a tortoise, though it is slow, nor a parrot, though it repeats what it does not understand, nor a hippopotamus, though it excites mirth.
>
> What the mountains have brought forth is a Tigger, which was much given, as I recall, to pulling the tablecloth to the ground, wrapping itself up in it amid the broken crockery, rolling about the room going 'Worra-worra-worra', and finally sticking its head out and asking, 'Have I won?'

Lenny Bruce advised – 'If you can take the hot bad enema, then you cast the first stone.' Bernardo Bertolucci, film-maker, agreed: 'Pornography is not in the hands of the child who discovers masturbating, but in the hands of the adult who slaps him.' Righteous people worried Aneurin Bevan who considered that 'virtue is its own punishment'. Maurice Edelman compared censorship to an appendix: 'it is useless when inert and dangerous when active'. Clare Boothe Luce said that 'censorship, like charity, should begin at home, but, unlike charity, it should end there.' To Jonathan Miller it was 'nothing more than a legal corollary of public modesty'. Two transatlantic formula men offer their neat dismissals of censorship and pornography. To Laurence Peter, a Canadian, 'A censor is a man who knows more than he thinks you ought to'; and to an American writer, Charles Rembar, 'Pornography is in the groin of the beholder.' John Trevelyan, the British Film Censor for a long time, put it more bluntly – 'We are paid to have dirty minds.'

Obscenity oft reveals the man. Jeremy Collier was contemptuous in 1698: 'Obscenity in any company is a rustic, uncreditable talent.' Hazlitt, in 1821, was defensive: 'It is the grossness of the spectator that discovers nothing but grossness in the subject.' While George Moore, by 1888, was more tolerant: 'A taste for dirty stories may be said to be inherent in the human animal.' Mark Twain sums up: 'It is by the goodness of God that in our country we have those three unspeakably precious things: freedom of speech, freedom of conscience and the prudence never to practise either of them.'

To pass from the writers of stories, dirty or clean, to those who publish them, the starting-point is often the parody of St John XVIII, 40 – 'Now Barabbas was a publisher' – usually ascribed to Byron who is said to have had his publisher, John Murray, in mind. H.L. Mencken, however, suggests that the probable author was Thomas Campbell (1777–1844), which leaves most of us little the wiser. Mencken also reminds us of Edgar Allan Poe on publishers: 'K – the publisher, trying to be critical, talks about books pretty much as a washerwoman would about Niagara Falls or a poulterer about a phoenix.' Amanda Ross was just as forthright: 'I don't believe in publishers who wish to butter their bannocks on both sides while they'll hardly allow an author to smell treacle. I consider they are too grabby altogether and, like Methodists, they love to keep the Sabbath and everything else they can lay hands on.'

Arthur Koestler gave the thumbs-down to publishers who might be thinking of being authors themselves: 'A publisher who writes is like a cow in a milk bar.' For the defence, Michael Joseph, a publisher, argued that 'Authors are easy to get on with – if you are fond of children.' Sometimes author and publisher are kept apart by agents: 'The relationship of an agent to a publisher is that of a knife to a throat', said Marvin Josephson, an American agent. One author – Patrick Dennis – was maturely patient over a manuscript. 'It circulated for five years, through the halls of fifteen publishers, and finally ended up with the Vanguard Press which, as you can see, is rather deep into the alphabet.' Alexander Pope had much earlier versified the same experience:

> I sit with sad civility, I read
> With honest anguish and an aching head;
> And drop at last, but in unwilling ears,
> This saving counsel, 'Keep your piece nine years'.

Sir James Barrie took rather longer to express disapproval: 'Times have changed since a certain author was executed for murdering his publisher. They say that when the author was on the scaffold he said goodbye to the minister and to the reporters, and then he saw some publishers sitting in the front row below, and to them he did not say goodbye. He said instead, "I'll see you again".' 'Posterity', George Ade estimated, was 'what you write for after being turned down by publishers.'

Most discouraging of all must surely be the urge to publish slim volumes of verse. Hear Don Marquis on the matter: 'Publishing a volume of verse is like dropping a rose petal down the Grand Canyon and waiting for the echo.' It has also been one of the most tempting of literary urges. Poetry may have been 'the devil's wine' in St Augustine's time, but, without ignoring Matthew Prior in these lines:

> Sir, I admit your general rule
> That every poet is a fool:
> But you yourself may serve to show it
> That every fool is not a poet

– defining poetry is rarely an easy or witty process:

> She that with poetry is won
> Is but a desk to write upon.

Poetry can also be the 'daughter of love', 'ingenious nonsense', the 'language of the Devil', or as 'flattering a disease as consumption'. But it remains, in Dr Johnson's phrase, as hard to define as light: 'We all *know* what light is, but it is not easy to *tell* what it is.' Swift preferred poets who shielded their poems from the light: 'A copy of verses, kept in the cabinet, and only shown to a few friends, is like a virgin, much sought after and admired: but when printed and published is like the common whore, whom anybody may purchase for half a crown.' 'Prose', Coleridge insisted, 'equals words in their best order; poetry, the best words in the best order.' 'On a bad poem', Coleridge wrote:

> Your poem must eternal be,
> Dear Sir, it cannot fail;
> For 'tis incomprehensible,
> And wants both head and tale.

Oscar Wilde's verdict on the influence of poetry concurs with E.W.

Howe's remark, 'A poem is no place for an idea'. 'One should never talk', Wilde said, 'of a moral or an immoral poem – poems are either well written or badly written, that is all.' He also thought that 'all bad poetry springs from genuine feeling'. As early as 1878, Walter Pater stopped Wilde short with another observation: 'Why do you write poetry? Why do you not write prose? Prose is so much more difficult.' We should be grateful to Walter Pater. Had Wilde listened to Coleridge he might have stuck to poetry. Somerset Maugham in due course, announced that 'to write good prose is an affair of good manners. It is, unlike verse, a civil art . . . poetry is baroque'.

Perhaps genuine poets should be asked about poetry and heeded if their answers are brief enough. For surely we can do better than Rod McKuen – 'Poetry is fact given over to imagery' – and Carl Sandburg – 'Poetry is a synthesis of hyacinths and biscuits'? I like Gwyn Thomas's 'Poetry is trouble dunked in tears'. But none of them disproves Dr Johnson (above) restated by A.E. Housman: 'I could no more define poetry than a furrier can define a rat.' W.H. Auden is more accessible than most moderns who have tried to explain: 'In poetry you have a form looking for a subject and a subject looking for a form. When they come together successfully you have a poem.' However, Auden recognized the sad fact of life that 'a poet can earn much more money writing or talking about his art than he can by practising it'; and that 'poetry is the only art people haven't yet learnt to consume like soup'. Robert Graves remarked, 'There's no money in poetry but there's no poetry in money either.'

For my part I have always enjoyed Sydney Smith's 'Poetical medicine chest' – rhymed pharmaceutical advice addressed to the Hon Mrs Henry Howard:

> With store of powdered rhubarb we begin;
> (to leave out powdered rhubarb were a sin) . . .
> . . . Glauber and Epsom salts their aid combine
> Translucent streams of castor oil be thine,
> And gentle manna in thy bottles shine.
> If morbid spot of septic sore invade
> By heavensent bark the morbid spot is stayed:
> When with black bile hepatic regions swell,
> With subtle calomile the plague expel

> Anise and mint with strong Aeolian sway
> Intestine storms of flatulence allay,
> And ipecacuanha clears the way . . .

And poetry is not so stuffy that one can't have some fun at its expense. Frank Muir has collected, or invented, three appalling poetic puns –

> Which poet had his head in the gallery and his feet in the stalls? – Longfellow. Which poet wrote all his poems in the synagogue? – Rabbi Burns. What are you suffering from if you don't like poetry? – Gray's Allergy

– a reminder, perhaps, of the old music-hall joke about a regimental sergeant-major sending his lads off to an educational session: 'It's culture today, men. And the first course is a course in Keats. Keats! I'll bet most of you horrible little men don't even know what a Keat is.' (A blissful ignorance paralleled in the 1960s when Marty Wilde was taken to Angus McBean's photographic studio to have some pictures taken for the West End production *Bye Bye Birdie*. Big blow-ups of Alfred Lunt and Lynn Fontanne – husband and wife – starring in *The Visit* were proudly displayed. Everyone cooed enthusiasm for The Lunts – 'Wonderful Lunts!', 'Look at the Lunts!' until Mr Wilde's father could contain himself no longer. 'Mr McBean', he asked, 'What is a Lunt?')

No noise is quite so strident as the sound of poets squabbling. Theodore Hooke, on first looking into Shelley's *Prometheus Unbound*, wrote:

> Shelley styles his new poem 'Prometheus Unbound'
> And 'tis like to remain so while time circles round.
> For surely an age would be spent in finding
> A reader so weak as to pay for the binding.

And Thomas, Lord Erskine, passed comment on Sir Walter Scott's *Field of Waterloo*:

> On Waterloo's ensanguined plain
> Lie tens of thousands of the slain;
> But none by sabre or by shot
> Fell half so flat as Walter Scott.

But Scott, too, could show his teeth, especially in his epitaph on Patrick ('Peter') Lord Robertson:

> Here lies that peerless paper peer Lord Peter,
> Who broke the laws of God and man and metre.

King James I was happy to dismiss John Donne in prose: 'Dr Donne's verses are like the peace of God: they pass all understanding.' His state of puzzlement was perhaps unequalled until Aldous Huxley's Mr Cardan considered 'the question of the authorship of the *Iliad* . . . the author of that poem is either Homer, or, if not Homer, somebody else of the same name'. Pope's verse might have been more accessible to James I especially:

> The Right, Divine, of Kings to govern wrong.

On other poets, Pope could be equally sharp:

> . . And he whose fustian's so sublimely bad,
> It is not poetry, but prose run mad.

On over-writing:

> Words are like leaves, and where they most abound,
> Much fruit of sense beneath is rarely found.

'Read over your compositions and, when you meet a passage which you think is particularly fine, strike it out,' said Dr Johnson, on a similar tack. Oscar Wilde was more than grudging on the subject of Pope: 'There are two ways of disliking poetry. One is to dislike it, the other is to read Pope.' John Dryden's drubbing came later, at the hands of Macaulay: 'His imagination resembles the wings of an ostrich.' My own favourite among Pope's lines has nothing to do with poetry: 'The vulgar boil, the learned roast, an egg.'

One of Evelyn Waugh's best broadsides to the *Spectator* must have banged home to good effect, in 1939:

> I am replying to Mr Spender mainly because his letter forms an example of the attitude towards Mr Auden of a certain group of writers. As I said before, it is their fault, not his, that he is a public bore. He writes mediocre verse, as do a multitude of quite decent young men. No particular shame attaches to that. But a group of his friends seem to have conspired to make a

booby of him. At a guess, I should say that the literature they have produced about him is, in bulk, about ten times his own work. That is shockingly bad for a man still young, alive and, I fear, productive . . .

A little of Auden's wit is still welcome – e.g. his note on Intellectuals:

> To the man-in-the-street, who, I'm sorry to say
> Is a keen observer of life,
> The word Intellectual suggests straight away
> A man who's untrue to his wife.

From the Intellectual it is a short step to the illiterate – in Justin Richardson's quatrain:

> For years a secret shame destroyed my peace –
> I'd not read Eliot, Auden or MacNeice.
> But now I think a thought that brings me hope,
> Neither had Chaucer, Shakespeare, Milton, Pope.

Then there is Wilde on Meredith (and Browning): 'Meredith is a prose Browning – and so is Browning.'

Short, shapely, purposeful verse forms make natural clothes-horses on which wit can be hung lightly – the epitaph, for example. Take Abel Evans on Sir John Vanbrugh, architect of Blenheim Palace:

> Under this stone, Reader, survey
> Dear Sir John Vanbrugh's house of clay
> Lie heavy on him earth! for he
> Laid many heavy loads on thee.

Or Byron on a drunken carrier:

> John Adams lies here, of the parish of Southwel,
> A carrier who carried his can to his mouth well,
> He carried so much and he carried so fast,
> He could carry no more – so was carried at last;
> For the liquor he drank, being too much for one,
> He could not carry off – so he's now carrion.

Belloc did the job for himself:

> When I am dead, I hope it may be said:
> His sins were scarlet but his books were read.

Carl Sandburg's contribution is fictional:

> Papa loved mamma
> Mamma loved men
> Mamma's in the graveyard
> Papa's in the pen.

Dryden's was deeply personal:

> Here lies my wife; here let her lie!
> Now she's at rest and so am I.

G.K. Chesterton inspired at least two epitaphs. From E.V. Lucas, long assailed by his tendency to lay down the law, came:

> Poor G.K.C., his day is past –
> Now God will know the truth at last.

While anti-semitism inspired Humbert Wolfe:

> Here lies Mr Chesterton,
> Who to heaven might have gone,
> But didn't when he heard the news
> That the place was run by Jews.

David McCord has supplied a perfect 'Epitaph on a Waiter' (also, however, ascribed to George S. Kaufman)

> By and by
> God caught his eye

Even a mother's reported death can be funny:

'Regret to inform you. Hand that rocked the cradle kicked the bucket'.

Imagined last words can be as devastating as imagined epitaphs. John Hollander, an American poet, celebrated the sinking in the North Atlantic of the *Andrea Doria* – the Italian liner which inspired one of the early sick jokes – 'Two sharks meet and one says to the other, "My dear, I've discovered the most wonderful Italian restaurant. It's called the Andrea Doria".' Hollander's verses on the matter are more artful:

'Last Words'
Higgledy – Piggledy
Andrea Doria
Lines in the name of this
Glorious boat.
As I sit writing these
Non-navigational
Verses a – CRASH! BANG! BLURP!
GLUB . . . (end of quote)

This characteristic verse form, the double-dactyl was invented by Anthony Hecht and Paul Pascal. Here is another example by Hollander:

'Historical Reflections'
Higgledy-Piggledy
Benjamin Harrison
Twenty-third President,
Was, and, as such,
Served between Clevelands, and
Save for this trivial
Idiosyncracy,
Didn't do much.

We are indebted to St Paul's School – or to one of its own scholars, E.C. Bentley – for another convenient poetic form, the clerihew. Many classic clerihews have been in circulation for years but recently a long-forgotten collection of school verses came to light, including items like:

Van Eyck
Was christened Jan, not Mike.
This curious mistake
Often kept him awake.

Among the famous clerihews, these are among the ones I enjoyed most:

The Art of Biography
Is different from Geography.
Geography is about Maps,
But Biography is about Chaps.

John Stuart Mill,
By a mighty effort of will,
Overcame his natural bonhomie
And wrote Principles of Political Economy.

'I quite realized', said Columbus,
'That the earth was not a rhombus,
But I am a little annoyed
To find it an oblate spheroid.'

Sir Christopher Wren
Said, 'I am going to dine with some men.
If anybody calls
Say I am designing St Paul's.'

George the Third
Ought never to have occurred.
One can only wonder
At so grotesque a blunder.

C.A. Lejeune's Hollywood clerihew deserves a new hearing (though it's been attributed to Nicholas Bentley as well as to Anonymous):

Cecil B. de Mille
Much against his will,
Was persuaded to leave Moses
Out of the Wars of the Roses.

So does this couplet:

I always think of Sonny Tufts
As something very large from Crufts.

Not quite a clerihew, but funny and concise, was Cyril Connolly's verdict on Marx:

M is for Marx
And clashing of classes

And movement of masses
And massing of asses.

From clerihews to limericks. But where to start? One could quote from Lear easily enough but, instead, here are three reasonably recent ones by Edward Gorey, who, unlike Edward Lear, seems to have thought it a good idea to include a joke – invariably sick – in a limerick:

> Some Harvard men, stalwart and hairy,
> Drank up several bottles of sherry;
>   In the Yard around three
>   They were shrieking with glee;
> 'Come on out, we are burning a fairy?'
>
> The babe with a cry brief and dismal,
> Fell into the water baptismal;
>   Ere they gathered its plight
>   It had sunk out of sight
> For the depth of the font was abysmal.
>
> From the bathing machine came a din
> As of jollification within;
>   It was heard far and wide,
>   And the incoming tide
> Had a definite flavour of gin.

Not from Gorey, but from his most prolific competitor – 'American Anonymous' – comes:

> The heavyweight champ of Seattle,
> Defeated a bull in a battle,
>   Then with vigor and gumption
>   Assumed the bull's function
> And deflowered a whole heard of cattle.
>
>   (by Jove!)

In *The Times*, Miles Kington recently had fun with an elaborate conceit – a novel, set in the Wild West, in which famous poets fired limericks at one another, telling the story of 'King' (Edward) Lear. I cannot resist quoting it at length:

Chapter one – 'Waal, I ain't one fer admitting defeat,' said old Will Wordsworth, spitting with amazing accuracy at a daffodil nearby, 'but this little ol' limerick's got me beat.'

'Blamed if I see how it works,' said Alf Tennyson. The young man stared moodily at the tiny object. 'It ain't like an epic at all. It's so tiny there ain't nothing to it – more of a lady's weapon if you ask me.'

'Talking about my invention?' said a long, cool voice.

They gasped and swung round. There, in the middle of the Last Chance Saloon, Henley-on-Thames, deep in the heart of shootin', rowin' and puntin' country, stood a stranger. They knew him from his long moustaches and the rhyming dictionary poking from one corner of his otherwise well-cut coat. Edward Lear!

'We were just saying, Mr Lear, that your limerick is mighty hard to handle. No offence, but ten dollars says you can't get it to work.'

'A singer from out of El Paso', said Lear instantly,
Got caught up one day in a lasso.
   When he finally got loose,
   From that darn pesky noose,
He was no longer profundo basso'.

'You owe me ten bucks, gentlemen.'

After the stranger had departed, they sat and stared at each other.
'El Paso don't rhyme with lasso,' said Alf.
'Right,' said Will. 'But he still licked us.'

Two Chapters later . . . .

They were all there for the shoot-out at the OK Corral. Bob Browning, with Liz Barrett begging him not to get involved. Young Alf Tennyson, now old Alf Tennyson, Cov Patmore, Bill Thackeray, Ed Fitzgerald, 'Doc' Poe, Gerry Hopkins and Art Clough. All against the one man, 'King' Lear.

Trouble was, Lear hadn't showed up.

'Trouble is, he ain't showed up,' sneered 'Doc' Poe, whose accent did at least sound authentic.

'Oh yes, he did,' said old Alf Tennyson, pointing to the wall behind. There, written in big white paint, was the following message:

> They all came to the OK Corral,
> Fit to fight and plumb full of morale,
>   But they hadn't the brain,
>   To write a quatrain,
> Or a bar of an old Bach chorale.

Chapter Five – 'You can't rhyme "corral" with "chorale", said 'Doc' Poe, coughing.
  'I can,' said 'King' Lear.

Chapter Six – 'All right', said 'Doc' Poe, 'But I bet your talk about the Chinese limerick was so much hogwash.'
'I like your nerve, Poe,' said 'King' Lear. 'So I'll tell you. You know the Chinese do things back to front? Writin' and readin' and that?'
  'Ah've heard so,' said Poe.
  'Then listen to this,' said Lear

> 'In China, the limerick's wrong,
> A kind of back-to-front song.
>   And this is the worst,
>   The last line comes first,
> So there was a young man from Hong Kong.'

Chapter Seven – Edward Lear jumped into his bed, along with a dashing red-head. He had drunk so much whisky, he felt kinda frisky, so he . . . (That will do, thank you, Ed.)

American light verse is a growth industry. The trouble is that too many light poems today tail off from stunning opening couplets into a wasteland of words. For example, a poem by X.J. Kennedy starts:

> In a prominent bar in Seacaucus one day
> Rose a lady in skunk with a top-heavy sway . . .

and elaborates on the theme for thirty-eight more lines without improving on it. Donald Hall is infinitely more successful in a poem called 'Breasts' which consists of just one line:

> There is something between us

— than he is when writing, at length, 'To a Water Fowl', and never topping:

> There are the women whose husbands I
>   meet on aeroplanes
> Who close their briefcases and ask,
>   'What are *you* in?'
> I look in their eyes, I tell them I am in
>   poetry . . .

Other American poets *do* know when to stop — William Cole wrote a marriage couplet:

> I think of my wife, and I think of Lot
> And I think of the lucky break he got.

And 'Anonymous' sometimes has the trick — especially in this quatrain imagined as a caption run under a rugged-looking, Marlborough Man Cowboy seated upon a bale of hay:

> Carnation milk is the best in the land;
> Here I sit with my can in my hand —
> No tits to pull, no hay to pitch,
> You just punch a hole in the son-of-a-bitch.

The classic wise-cracking poets of course knew the rules. Dorothy Parker, spotting 'The Flaw in Paganism', wrote:

> Drink, and dance and laugh and lie
> Love the reeling midnight through
> For tomorrow we shall die!
> (But, alas, we never do).

not to mention her 'News Item':

> Men seldom make passes
> At girls who wear glasses.

or her 'Comment':

> Oh, life is a glorious cycle of song
> A medley of extemporanea;
> And love is a thing that can never go wrong;
> And I am Marie of Romania.

or her 'resumé':

> Razors pain you;
> Rivers are damp;
> Acids stain you;
> And drugs cause cramp.
> Guns aren't lawful;
> Nooses give;
> Gas smells awful;
> You might as well live.

Ogden Nash could keep it up or cut it short. On the short side are 'The Song of the Open Road':

> I think that I shall never see
> A billboard lovely as a tree.
> Indeed unless the billboards fall
> I'll never see a tree at all.

and 'The Turtle':

> The turtle lives 'twixt plated decks
> Which practically conceal its sex.
> I think it clever of the turtle
> In such a fix to be so fertile.

and his 'Genealogical Reflection':

> No McTavish
> Was ever lavish

not to mention his 'Reflection on Ice breaking':

> Candy
> Is dandy
> But liquor
> Is quicker.

On the long side, let me quote his 'Lines to a World-Famous Poet Who Failed to Complete a World-Famous Poem'; or, 'Come Clean, Mr Guest!':

Oft when I'm sitting without anything to read waiting for a train in a
  depot,
I torment myself with the poet's dictum that to make a house a
  home, livin' is what it takes a heap o'.
Now, I myself should very much enjoy makin' my house a home, but
  my brain keeps on a-goin' clickety-click, clickety-click, clickety-
  click,
If Peter Piper picked a peck o' heap o'livin', what kind of a peck
  o'heap o'livin' would Peter Piper pick?
Certainly a person doesn't need the brains of a Lincoln
To know that there are many kinds o'livin', just as there are many
  kinds o'dancin' or huntin' or fishin' or eatin' or drinkin'.
A philosophical poet should be specific
As well as prolific,
And I trust I am not being offensive
If I suggest that he should also be comprehensive.
You may if you like verify my next statement by sending a stamped,
  self-addressed envelope to either Dean Inge or Dean Gauss,
But meanwhile I ask you to believe that it takes a heap of other
  things besides a heap o'livin' to make a home out of a house.
To begin with, it takes a heap o'payin',
And you don't pay just the oncet, but agayin and agayin and agayin.
Buyin' a stock is called speculatin' and buyin' a house is called
  investin',
But the value of the stock or of the house fluctuates up and down,
  generally down, just as an irresponsible Destiny may destine.
Something else that your house takes a heap o', whether the builder
  come from Sicily or Erin,
Is repairin',
In addition to which, gentle reader, I am sorry to say you are little
  more than an imbecile or a cretin
If you think it doesn't take a heap o'heatin',
And unless you're spiritually allied to the little Dutch boy who went
  around inspectin' dikes lookin' for leaks to put his thumb in,
It takes a heap o'plumbin',
And if it's a house that you're hopin' to spend not just today but
  tomorrow in,
It takes a heap o'borrowin'.
In a word, Macushla,

There's a scad o'things that to make a house a home it takes not only
a heap, or a peck, but at least a bushela.

Less celebrated than Parker and Nash but nonetheless a fine,
concise, modern American poet-wit is David McCord. He has a
sharp word for people who go on and on. 'To A Certain Most
Certainly Certain Critic':

> He takes the long review of things;
> He asks and gives no quarter.
> And you can sail with him on wings
> Or read the book. It's shorter.

One of John Updike's ventures into light verse is especially memorable for the creation of his Indian author, M. Anantanarayanan:

> .. I picture him as short and tan.
> We'd meet, perhaps, in Hindustan.
> I'd say, with admirable élan,
> 'Ah, Anantanarayanan . . .'

But the discipline and compression required by modern song-
writers often sharpens the content of their verses more pleasingly
than the indulgent meanderings of the poets. American song-writers
take their lyrics so much more seriously than their English counterparts that, whatever their aspirations, they often finish up with
poetry on the page – however wry – from, say, the Stephen
Sondheim of *Company*, the razor-sharp, dead-accurate, urban wit
celebrating and dissecting a modern marriage:

> The concerts you enjoy together,
> Neighbours you annoy together
> Children you destroy together,
> . . . Keep a marriage intact

– to the equally pertinent wit of E.Y. Harburg in, for example,
the two slim volumes of verse he has published, *Rhymes for the
Irreverent*, and *At This Point in Rhyme*. For example:

> This we learn from Watergate,
> That almost any creep'll
> Be glad to help the Government
> Overthrow the people

and 'Seated One Day at the Organ',

> When our organs have been transplanted
> And the new ones made happy to lodge in us,
> Let us pray one wish be granted
> We retain our zones erogenous

and 'Tennyson, Anyone?'

> In the spring a young man's fancy lightly turns to
>   thoughts of love;
> And in the summer,
>   and in autumn,
>   and in winter,
> See above.

Job had other things on his mind. 'Oh, that mine adversary had written a book,' he said, long before the birth of Christ, and since then, as we read in Ecclesiastes, 'Of making many books there is no end; and much study is a weariness of the flesh.' 'Books are fatal', Disraeli told his readers in *Lothair*, 'they are the curse of the human race. Nine-tenths of the existing books are nonsense, and the clever books are the refutation of that nonsense. The greatest misfortune that ever befell man was the invention of printing.' Samuel Butler pulled no punches on the subject either. 'Books should be tried by judge and jury as though they were crimes and counsel should be heard on both sides.' Presumably they would be considered innocent until found guilty, unless Nietzsche was giving his snap judgment: 'Books for general reading always smell badly. The odour of the common people hangs about them' – a different and more endearing sort of stubborn élitism from 'Farve' in Nancy Mitford's novel: 'I have only read one book in my life and that is *White Fang*. It's so frightfully good I've never bothered to read another.' In a similar vein, there is Evelyn Waugh interviewed for the *Paris Review*: 'No writer before the middle of the nineteenth century wrote about the working classes other than as grotesques or as pastoral decorations. Then when they were given the vote, certain writers started to suck up to them.'

Leonard Louis Levinson, a graduate of the school of Contemporary Quippery, defines a book as 'what they make a movie out of for television'. Wilde's summary judgment on first novels was that, 'In every first novel the hero is the author as Christ or Faust.' His jaundiced view of the general decline of literature was short and simple: 'In the old days books were written by men of letters and read by the public. Nowadays books are written by the public and read by anybody.' Gwendolen in *The Importance of Being Earnest* supplied her own reading material. 'I never travel without my diary. One should always have something sensational to read on the train.' Wilde had yet another view of fiction (apart from Miss Prism's adventures with the three-volume novel): 'The good end happily, the bad unhappily. That is what fiction means.' Tangentially, in *A Woman of No Importance*, Lord Illingworth speaks of 'The Book of Life'. It 'begins with a man and a woman in a garden'. But, Mrs Allonby points out, 'It ends with Revelations.' Another character in the same play observes, 'You should study the Peerage, Gerald, it is the best thing in fiction the English have ever done.'

Moving on to non-fiction, one of the most savagely witty reviews in recent years was Auberon Waugh's attack on David Plante's 1982 book, *Difficult Women: A Memoir of Three: Jean Rhys, Sonia Orwell and Germaine Greer*. The review was imaginatively entitled, 'A Tale of Three Women and a Sensitive Plante'. It exemplifies Max Beerbohm's reflection that it is easier to write exciting prose about a subject of which the critic disapproves. Enthusiasm so often pushes a dull pen. Waugh's review is worth quoting at some length. There are hints of danger in his first paragraph:

> David Plante is an intensely sensitive young American whose earnest, introspective novels have a certain following wherever self-absorption and humourlessness are appreciated.
>
> This is his first attempt at non-fiction, a study of three 'difficult' women. The first of them, Jean Rhys, author of *Wide Sargasso Sea*, was over 80 by the time he met her: senile, incontinent, drunk, repetitive, self-pitying and boring as she had undoubtedly become, she seemed to get the measure of the earnest young American who had offered to help her with her autobiography.
>
> 'She suddenly stopped talking and looked at me for a moment in silence, blurry-eyed, then asked, "Why do you come to see me? . . . Is it curiosity?" I didn't know what to say. I said, "For some reason, I love you".'

Even by the sensitive Plante's standards, this is an extraordinary creepy reply. After reading his account of how he helped the drunken old lady off the lavatory – or rather, didn't help her – most readers will suspect that his motive was a prurient literary voyeurism.

He then moves on to Plante's second target, Sonia Orwell:

The basis of their relationship seems quite straightforward – he wanted to talk about his inner self, she wanted him to mend a shelf in her bathroom . . .

Germaine Greer is Plante's third study. Here he quotes Miss Greer on her reasons. 'I like a nice arse', she says, 'having inspected the object concerned. . .'

Oddly enough for all her language and habits – she feeds her cats on testicles – Germaine Greer emerges as an attractive, intelligent, generous and warm-hearted woman. In a rare flash of insight – Mr Plante is not really interested in anyone except himself – it is suggested that she may not have the success she deserves with men because, for her, sex is a public act, rather than a private one. Most men tend to shy away from public acts of this sort.

But even this does not quite explain why an attractive, intelligent, apparently healthy young woman like Germaine Greer should take up with someone like David Plante. Most of us could tell a mile off that the sensitive Plante was not someone to follow anything up. Perhaps a small clue is provided by Germaine's own dictum that 'sex is 90 per cent in the head'.

Anyone feeling sorry for David Plante, after reading Auberon Waugh, might care to read Gore Vidal, in turn, on Auberon Waugh in the *Spectator* in October 1982:

Mr Waugh is a parochial English writer (tautologies gush from my pen!) who has made his little name with a cheerful lowbrow column in *Private Eye* where he treats actual figures as if they were characters in fiction. This can be good fun when he puts on motley and bells, and is granted fool's licence. But when he tries to get above his cheery station in, for example, these cheerful pages, it is plain that Mr Waugh does not know much about anything. He simply has Opinions. Worse, he has managed to combine the reckless insolence of his parvenu father with the literary art of his sainted mother. The result is an on-going public failure of a sort that enchants the English quite as much as it mystifies the American observer.

For good measure in the same piece Vidal dismisses another of his critics with equally stinging invective:

Mr Julian Symons is a hack journalist half as old as time. He was one of Colley Cibber's friends . . . Permanent fringe to whatever is the current fringe, I believe Mr Symons's competence is the detective story.

Finally he launches into Ian Hamilton, another reviewer 'who now knows every widow of the late poet, Robert Lowell'. I'll spare Mr Hamilton a recitation of Vidal's attack because I am anxious to quote, or at least paraphrase, a fine piece of invective he penned when criticizing TV some years ago. I myself was the subject, but I fear that I have lost the cutting – a pity, because as a hatchet job it is hard to better. It went something like this:

Every time I think that Ned Sherrin is dead I switch on the television and see him in some dreadful, off-colour programme which brings home all too painfully the fact that he is still alive.

Vidal's targets are legion. They are as various as *Georgia*: 'Coca Cola [is] Georgia's sole gift to a nation whose first century was recently described in a book titled, eponymously, *The Alcoholic Republic* . . .' (of letters, I remember adding to myself when I first saw the book); *American literature* – 'To the end of a long life, he [Edmund Wilson] kept on making the only thing he thought worth making, sense, a quality almost entirely lacking in American literature where stupidity, if sufficiently sincere and authentic, is deeply revered and easily achieved'; *Prisons* thronged 'with people who get drunk, take dope, gamble, have sex in a way not approved by the Holy Book of a Bronze Age nomad tribe as reinterpreted by a group of world-weary Greeks in the first centuries of the last millenium'; *Thomas Love Peacock*: 'Every quarter century, like clockwork, there is a Peacock revival. The great tail feathers unfurl in all their

Pavonian splendor, and like-minded folk delight in the display; and that's the end of that for the next twenty-five years'; and, in another of his essays, on his play *Visit to a Small Planet*, his own writing predicament:

> I am not at heart a playwright. I am a novelist turned temporary adventurer; and I chose to write television, movies, and plays for much the same reason that Henry Morgan selected the Spanish Main for his peculiar – and not dissimilar – sphere of operations. The reasons for my conversion to piracy are to me poignant, and to students of our society perhaps significant. . . . By the 1950s I and my once golden peers were plunged into that dim cellar of literature characterized as 'serious', where, like the priests of some shattered god, we were left to tend our prose privately: so many exiles, growing mushrooms in the dark.

As usual, setting one prose writer on another often produces just as much spleen as the squabbles between poets that we saw earlier. Wilde – of course – had plenty to say. On Dickens: 'One must have a heart of stone to read the death of Little Nell without laughing'; on Henry James: 'Mr Henry James writes fiction as if it were a painful duty'; on George Meredith: 'Who can define him? His style is chaos illuminated by flashes of lightning. As a writer he has mastered everything except language; as a novelist he can do everything except tell a story. As an artist he is everything except articulate.'

Gertrude Stein dismissed Hemingway's output as 'not literature'. Mary McCarthy agreed; when asked on BBC TV's *Monitor* about 'Hemingway's ideas' she said, 'Oh, I don't think Hemingway was ever much troubled by an idea.' Gore Vidal asked, 'What other culture could have produced Hemingway and not seen the joke?' Zelda Fitzgerald found him 'phoney as a rubber check'. She also dismissed *The Sun Also Rises* as 'bull-fighting, bull-slinging and bull-shit'. Cyril Connolly reviewing Hemingway's posthumously published novel *Across The River And Into the Trees*, seems to have had much the same thought:

> To my sorrow, *Across the River* can be summed up in one word, lamentable.
> Despite an excellent beginning, the Colonel soon emerges as

one of the most unlikeable, drink-sodden and maundering old bores ever to have inflicted an interior monologue on those who can't answer back. His ladylove is a whimsical wax-work whose love scenes punctuate the book like a pneumatic drill on a hot afternoon, while the Colonel's fuddled war-reminiscences reveal a blind grudge against Generals, brass-hats, war correspondents and the British, but very little of the campaign. Bitter, sentimental and facetious, he mulls along from bar to bar like a mixture of Bloom and Soames Forsyte.

Somerset Maugham was delightfully mocking about Henry James, an infinitely better writer: 'Poor Henry, he's spending eternity wandering round and round a stately park and the fence is just too high for him to peep over and they're having tea just too far away for him to hear what the Countess is saying.' But so, more precisely, was that fine stylist, Philip Guedalla, in one of his essays: 'The work of Henry James has always seemed divisible by a simple dynastic arrangement into three reigns: James I, James II and James the Old Pretender.' And others have given poor old Henry – at his serpentine, wittiest best in novels like *The Spoils of Poynton* – a bad time, too – like William Faulkner who judged Henry James to be 'one of the nicest old ladies I ever met.'

The novel has been having a rough ride for some years – not helped much by twentieth-century commentators like Cocteau who have remarked that, 'The greatest masterpiece in literature is only a dictionary out of order'. ('Everybody talks too much, too many words, and gets them out of order', wrote Lilian Hellman, movingly, in *Toys in the Attic*). Philip Larkin ought to know better. His throwaway remark that 'Many (modern) novels have a beginning, a muddle and an end' is about as crass a piece of formula writing as only a good poet could commit. And how easy for a respectable critic like Edmund Wilson to parade his solemnity on the subject of Evelyn Waugh thus: 'His style has the desperate jauntiness of an orchestra fiddling away for dear life on a sinking ship.'

Recently it became clear that there was not much love lost between Anthony Burgess and Norman Mailer. Mailer's 1983 novel *Ancient Evenings* was savaged by the American press and on its English publication Burgess was asked by the *Observer* to review it. Burgess was astonished by Mailer's preoccupation with anal functions (the novel was set in Ancient Egypt) throughout the book. He concluded his review memorably:

> On the only occasion on which I met Mailer – at one of Panna Grady's literally fabulous parties (literally because the big modern sources of fable were there – Lowell, Warhol, Ginsberg *et al*) – he said to me, 'Burgess, your last book was shit.' I can see now that he was paying me a compliment.

The romantic novelist often gets it hardest in the neck. Here is Bernard Levin reviewing Barbara Cartland's novel *Love at the Helm* in *The Sunday Times*:

> Miss Cartland makes much of the fact that part of the proceeds of the book are going to the Mountbatten Memorial Trust, and indeed insists that Earl Mountbatten helped her with the writing, and had done as much for her previously, with other novels set at sea; she draws conspicuous attention to the connection on the front of the jacket (twice), in the blurb, on the back of the jacket (photographically), on the title-page, on the half-title and in an Author's Note. All that expert help, however, has still not managed to correct her apparent belief that Trafalgar came very shortly before Waterloo; perhaps she has confused English history with the London Underground system.

And Clive James was more succinct on *Princess Daisy* by Judith Krantz: 'To be a really lousy writer takes energy.' We know of course of Dorothy Parker's famous phrase that a certain book should not be tossed aside but hurled with great force. Well, Nancy Banks-Smith in the *Guardian* recently went a stage further with specific advice concerning *The Far Pavilions* by M.M. Kaye: 'one of those big, fat paperbacks, intended to while away a monsoon or two, which, if thrown with a good overarm action, will bring a water buffalo to its knees'.

Writers on themselves can be more charitable – indeed, indulgent. 'When I split an infinitive, God damn it, I split it so it stays split,' wrote Raymond Chandler in a letter to his publisher. In some, the enthusiasm eventually evaporates. By the time he got to *The Summing Up*, Somerset Maugham thought to himself, 'Thank God, I can look at a sunset now without having to think how to describe it. I meant then never to write another book.'

Rose Macaulay was entertaining but, appropriately, more ladylike, in examining her approach to writing:

I have heard of novelists who say that, while they are creating a novel, the people in it are ever with them, accompanying them on walks, for all I know on drives (though this must be distracting in traffic), to the bath, to bed itself. This must be a terrible experience; rather than allow the people in my novels to worry me like that, I should give up writing novels altogether. No; my people are retiring, elusive and apt not to come even when I require them. I do not blame them. They no doubt wish that they were the slaves of a more ardent novelist, who would permit them to live with her. To be regarded as of less importance than the etymology and development of the meanest word in the dictionary must be galling.

Dorothy Parker struck an anti-feminist blow against lady novelists. 'As artists they're rot – but as providers they're oil wells. They gush!' She aggravated the offence by saying, 'It's a terrible thing to say, but I can't think of good women writers. Of course, calling them women writers is their ruin; they begin to think of themselves that way.' Readjusting the balance, one should mention the short sharp dismissal of a man's book – the book John O'Hara's, the phrase, Malcolm Cowley's: 'Hard to lay down and easy not to pick up'.

Amateur writers of both sexes were another target hit accurately by Somerset Maugham: 'Women will write novels to while away their pregnancies; bored noblemen, axed officers, retired civil servants fly to the pen as one might fly to the bottle. There is an impression abroad that everyone has it in him to write one book; but if by this is implied a good book the impression is false.'

The inef . f . f . f . . . able Patrick Campbell, in *The Coarse of Events*, was deprecating about an artist's encounter with his public at the ordeal of a book-signing. He called the essay 'Sign the Shopping Bags Here':

. . . The manager fingered one of my own books. 'Of course' he said, 'this is a little bit slender for thirty bob'.

Two ladies in hats, looking well-heeled, had paused in the middle distance, both of them looking at me with a kind of indignant curiosity. One of them whispered something to the other, seeming to shed a brief ray of light into a singularly dark and noisome corner. At any rate, the second one nodded curtly, registering the unpleasant news. Their indignant curiosity became an unmistakable glare of outrage, but at least they were still there.

I found a smile, and presented it to them with a courteous inclination of the head. It had an instantaneous effect. Apparent terror replaced the look of outrage. They hurried away without a backward glance.

'I think,' said my publisher, standing behind me, 'it might be better if you didn't meet their eye.'

While dealing with ancillary literary activities, I can only find one quotable comment on the ghostly trade of the blurb-writer – from the regularly witty and relevant Michael Frayn, saddled with the task of introducing *The Best of Beachcomber* – one of his enthusiasms but one of my blind spots: 'There is something about a blurb-writer paying his respects to a funny book which puts one in mind of a short-sighted Lord Mayor raising his hat to a hippopotamus.'

Back in the mainstream (albeit somewhat muddy) of literature, there are thrillers – on which P.G. Wodehouse, in a charming piece which is genially witty and has no concealed claws, called 'Do Thrillers Need Heroines', is at his most whimsically helpful:

For, though beautiful, with large grey eyes and hair the colour of ripe corn, the heroine of the thriller is almost never a very intelligent girl. Indeed, it would scarcely be overstating it to say that her mentality is that of a cockroach – and not an ordinary cockroach, at that, but one which has been dropped on its head as a baby. She may have escaped death a dozen times. She may know perfectly well that the notorious Blackbird Gang is after her to secure the papers. The police may have warned her on no account to stir outside her house. But when a messenger calls at half-past two in the morning with an unsigned note saying 'Come at once', she just snatches at her hat and goes. The messenger is a one-eyed Chinaman with a pock-marked face and an evil grin, so she trusts him immediately and, having accompanied him to the closed car with steel shutters over the windows, bowls off in it to the ruined cottage in the swamp. And when the hero, at great risk and inconvenience to himself, comes to rescue her, she will have nothing to do with him because she has been told by a mulatto with half a nose that it was he who murdered her brother, Jim.

Travel inspires a disproportionately high standard of witty writing, though modern aids to travel do not always get a good press. In 'The Insolent Chariots', John Ketas takes several spirited side-swipes at the motor car:

> The automobile changed our dress, manners, social customs, vacation habits, the shape of our cities, consumer purchasing patterns, common tastes and positions in intercourse.

He goes on to argue that, 'If Detroit is right . . . there is little wrong with the American car that is not wrong with the American Public' and 'The automobile did not put the adventure of travel within reach of the common man. Instead, it first gave him the opportunity to make himself more and more common.'

In the days of the Grand Tour, travel was supposed to be an education. Not to Vanbrugh: 'The young fellows of this age profit no more by their going abroad than they do by their going to church.'

> How much a dunce that has been sent to roam
> Excels a dunce that has been kept at home?

countered William Cowper in 'The Progress of Error'. Travel – in the cause of archaeology – even squeezes a joke from the unlikely pen of Agatha Christie: 'An archaeologist is the best husband any woman can have; the older she gets the more interested he is in her.'

'In America there are two classes of travel,' wrote Robert Benchley, 'first-class and with children.' The anti-travel case was most succinctly stated by Thoreau: 'It is not worthwhile to go around the world to count the cats in Zanzibar.' This argument would have found no favour in the wittiest of travel writers, Robert Byron, who in his masterpiece, *The Road to Oxiana*, opened, like Cole Porter, in Venice:

> Here as a joy-hog, a pleasant change after that *pensione* on the Giudecca two years ago. We went to the Lido this morning,

and the Doge's Palace looked more beautiful from a speedboat than it ever did from a gondola. The bathing, on a calm day, must be the worst in Europe; water like hot saliva, cigar ends floating into one's mouth, and shoals of jellyfish. Lifar came to dinner. Bertie mentioned that all whales have syphilis.

He moves on towards Palestine, sprinkling dashes of anti-semitism and anti-holier-than-thou-ness impartially:

SS *Martha Washington*, 4 September. I found Christopher on the pier, adorned with a kempt but reluctant beard five days old.

There are 900 passengers on board. Christopher took me on a tour of the third-class quarters. Had their occupants been animals, a good Englishman would have informed the RSPCA. But the fares are cheap; and being Jews, one knows they could all pay more if they wanted. The first class is not much better. I share a cabin with a French barrister, whose bottles and fopperies leave no room for another pin. He lectured me on the English cathedrals. Durham was worth seeing. 'As for the rest, my dear sir, they are mere plumbing'.

At dinner, finding myself next an Englishman, I opened conversation by hoping he had had a fine passage.

He replied: 'Indeed we have. Goodness and mercy have followed us throughout'.

A tired woman struggled by, leading an unruly child. I said, 'I always feel so sorry for women travelling with children'.

'I can't agree with you. To me little children are as glints of sunshine'.

I saw the creature later, reading a Bible in a deckchair. This is what Protestants call a missionary.

In Persia he had trouble with the Shah's Secret Police. The Shah was the first of his family to sit on the Peacock Throne and his régime was every bit as repressive as that of his son, the last. In order to refer to him secretly, Byron and his travelling companion gave him the inspired code-name 'Marjoribanks'. The English pronunciation is idiosyncratic enough. Imagine the Secret Police working on it.

Catty comments on fellow travellers – 'Mrs Budge Bulkeley,

worth £32,000,000, has arrived here accompanied by some lesser millionairesses. They are in great misery because the caviare is running out' — are mixed with wonderfully sustained, lyrical descriptions of the country and the architecture Byron had travelled to admire:

> The beauty of Isfahan steals on the mind unawares. You drive about under avenues of white tree trunks and canopies of Shining Twigs; past domes of turquoise and spring yellow in a sky of liquid violet blue: along the river patched with twisting shoals, catching that blue in its muddy silver, and lined with feathery groves where the sap calls: across bridges of pale toffee brick, tier on tier of arches breaking into piled pavilions, overlooked by lilac mountains, by the Kuh-i-sufi shaped like a Punch's hump and by other ranges receding to a line of snowy surf. And before you know how, Isfahan has become indelible, has insinuated its image into that gallery of places which everyone privately treasures.

Who would not wish to visit Byron's Isfahan? But perhaps, not to stay in his digs:

> I went to swim at the YMCA opposite the hotel. This necessitated paying two shillings, the waiving of a medical examination, changing among a lot of hairy dwarves who smelt of garlic, and finally having a hot shower accompanied by an acrimonious argument because I refused to scour my body with a cake of insecticide soap. I then reached the bath, swam a few yards in and out of a game of water-football conducted by the Physical Director, and emerged so perfumed with antiseptic that I had to rush back and have a bath before going out to dinner.

Although Charles Lamb, in his own words, was quite happy to 'give away' biography and autobiography, these forms of words remain favourites with many people. 'Autobiography', said Lord Altrincham, 'is now as common as adultery and hardly less reprehensible.' Much earlier, Franklin P. Adams might have agreed: 'An autobiography usually reveals nothing bad about its writer except his memory.' Wilde, inevitably, had something pertinent to say about biography: 'Every great man nowadays has his disciples and it is always Judas who writes the biography.' 'A well-written life,' in Carlyle's view, 'is almost as rare as a well-spent one.' George Moore held that 'Biographies should be a man's conversation not his deeds.' He feared, perhaps, the fate that President Grover Cleveland foresaw for himself: 'There are now three projects on foot to serve me up and help people to breast or dark meat, with or without stuffing.' J. B. Priestley was uncharacteristically daunted by biographies: 'I have never read the life of any important person without discovering that he knew more and could do more than I could ever hope to know or do in half a dozen lifetimes.'

One of the best of biographers, Philip Guedalla, is apologetic: 'Biography, like big game hunting, is one of the recognised forms of sport, and it is as unfair as only sport can be.' On autobiography Guedalla held that it is 'an unrivalled vehicle for telling the truth about other people'. Quentin Crisp sees autobiography as 'an obituary in serial form with the last instalment missing'. Writing in the *New York Times* in 1977, Donal Henahan was sceptical: 'Next to the writer of real estate advertisements, the autobiographer is the most suspect of prose artists.' An autobiography at the end of a period of high office can represent a crock of gold as alluring as a place on the board of a bank. As an American publisher, Roger Jellinek, observed: 'The purpose of the Presidential Office is not power, or leadership of the Western World, but reminiscence, best-selling reminiscence.' Marshal Pétain believed that 'To write one's memoirs is to speak ill of everybody except oneself.' Evelyn Waugh viewed the task without enthusiasm – perhaps too much of his life had already surfaced as fiction: 'Only when one has lost all curiosity about the future has one reached the age to write an autobiography.'

Which all goes to underline Mark Twain's observation that 'Wit is the sudden marriage of ideas which before their union were not perceived to have any relation' – but Joseph Addison, writing in the *Spectator* in 1711, shook his head sadly:

Among all kinds of writing, there is none in which authors are more apt to miscarry than in works of humour, as there is none in which they are more ambitious to excel.

2
SHOWBIZ

'They shot too many pictures and not enough actors'
– Walter Winchell

Frequently, in the theatre, the strains of a production work like a pressure cooker – tempers rise, temperaments clash, and the desire to score a point or settle a score becomes irresistible. A classic encounter – perhaps apocryphal, but I hope not – occured when Mike Nichols directed Walter Matthau in Neil Simon's comedy *The Odd Couple*. As their disagreement became more acrimonious the insults flew more wildly until Nichols put a period to the row with a crushing riposte. There was an awkward pause before Matthau, accepting defeat, said quietly, to break the mood, 'Hey, Mike, can I have my prick back?' Nichols simply snapped an imperious finger and thumb and called, 'Props!'

Although Dorothy Nevill once said that 'the real art of conversation is not only to say the right thing in the right place, but to leave unsaid the wrong thing at the tempting moment', theatrical wit often depends on *not* leaving unsaid the wrong thing at the tempting moment. Many years ago, the fine character actress, Irene Browne, was greatly irritated by the success of the enchanting juvenile girl during a pre-London tour of Noel Coward's musical *After The Ball* – based on Wilde's *Lady Windermere's Fan*. At every town the young actress, Patricia Cree, was greeted with ecstatic notices. Miss Browne's impatience swelled and finally she saw her opportunity. At Bristol, Miss Cree was late for an entrance. To keep the stage waiting is a cardinal sin. Eventually, Miss Cree arrived and played her scene and they both made their exits. Miss Browne bore down on her looking furious. Vanessa Lee, the leading lady, intervened: 'Oh, don't hit her, Irene; poor little thing – she's thin as a match!' 'Exactly,' snapped Miss Browne. 'She should be struck and thrown away!'

Repartee, it is often said, is what one thinks up on the way home. When Victor Mature was rejected by a smart Californian golf club on the grounds that actors were not allowed to be members, he had time to think up his reply: 'I'm *not* an actor', he wrote back, 'and I enclose my press cuttings to prove it'. In showbiz, however, the adrenalin often produces repartee on the spur of the moment. Robert Mitchum, in reply to an interviewer who had asked what he looked for in a script, said promptly, 'Days off!' Coward was a past-master at repartee, prodigally capable of the genuinely fresh retort. In his production of one of his own masterpieces, *Hay Fever*, at the National Theatre, Edith Evans played Judith Bliss, the leading role. Strictly speaking, she was too old but, like the elderly châtelaine of some great house, she did an impeccable job of showing the audience all over the bravura part she was playing. Coward's rhythms, however, need precise playing and Dame Edith was often unsure of her lines in rehearsal. Some she could not get right – particularly the sure laugh as she describes the view: 'On a clear day you can see Marlow.' It always came out as, 'On a very clear day you can see Marlow.' 'No, no!' Coward finally snapped. 'On a clear day you can see Marlow, Edith. On a *very* clear day you can see Beaumont and Fletcher!'

Noel Coward was not always in sympathy with modern drama, and dismissed David Storey's fine play, *The Changing Room*, on account of its male nude scene: 'I didn't pay three pounds fifty just to see half a dozen acorns and a chipolata' (a formula reminiscent of all those jokes which surrounded those who went to the first production of *Hair*, on the lines – 'just to see which members of the cast were Jewish'.)

When Laurence Olivier was made a Master of Letters, to add to his other honours, Coward was unimpressed. 'Four letters, no doubt,' he observed. His doctor, Patrick Woodcock, once confessed that he had occasional lapses of memory – 'lacunae' he called them. Ever afterwards, Coward always greeted him in the same way, 'Ah! Here comes the Lily of Lacunae.' He was the master of the one-word reply, especially to newspaper reports. 'Mr Coward, have you anything to say to *The Star*?' – 'Twinkle!' 'To *The Sun*?' – 'Shine!' To *The Times*?' – 'Change!' (He didn't always win. Meeting Edna Ferber in the Algonquin in her trouser suit he tried, 'My God, Edna, you look almost like a man', laying himself wide open. 'So do you', she snapped.) Often the bite of the wit was slight but his precise timing and carefully enunciated syllables, allied with the sense of expectation induced in the listener, gave his witticisms more punch than if they had come from another's lips. Hear even the most ordinary Coward phrase in his own tones in your mind's ear and they bounce back into favour:

'Mr Coward, can you say something for Australia?'
'Kangaroo'.

'What are your views on marriage?'
'Rather garbled'.

'On Hollywood?'
'I'm not too keen on Hollywood. I'd rather have a nice cup of cocoa.'

'Mr Coward, I always say you act much better than you write.'
'How odd, I'm always saying the same about you.'

On being told that his accountant had blown his brains out:
'I'm amazed he was such a good shot.'

'We expected a better play, Mr Coward' (after *Sirocco* which was booed).
'I expected better manners.'

On hearing of Clifton Webb's grief over the death of his mother, Mabel: 'Well over 90 . . . and gaga . . . it must be tough to be orphaned at 72.'

On being unable to stop Webb's floods of tears over a long distance phone call: 'Clifton, if you don't stop crying, I shall reverse the charges.'

'Will you call me, Noel?' said a tiresome actress.
'I certainly will – many things.'

'I knew my lines backwards last night.'
'That's the way you're saying them this morning.'

'If you go on like that Noel, I shall throw something.'
'Why not start with my cues?'

'Why did she become an actress?'
'She didn't.'

Coward often used telegrams – a literary form which suited his staccato style. To Gertrude Lawrence on getting her first straight role he wired: LEGITIMATE AT LAST WONT MOTHER BE PLEASED. And on her marriage: DEAR MRS A. HOORAY! HOORAY! AT LAST YOU ARE DEFLOWERED ON THIS AS EVERY OTHER DAY. I LOVE YOU. NOEL COWARD. From Rome he once cabled his secretary: AM BACK FROM ISTANBUL WHERE I WAS KNOWN AS ENGLISH DELIGHT. I like particularly his cosy sigh of pleasure towards the end of his life when he was tucked up at home and 'not on the road with a Broadway musical' (which recalls, too, John Schlesinger's remark that 'If Hitler were alive today he'd be on tour with an American musical').

In Coward's diaries there is an account of his sharing a flat briefly with Marlene Dietrich. 'She was in a tremendously *haus frau* mood and washed everything in sight, including my hairbrush (which was quite clean) and gave me a wonderful new sleeping pill suppository, which I rammed up my bottom and slept like a top'.

John Osborne has recalled an incident when Tony Richardson called him to Nottingham to see a tour of Coward's translation of Feydeau's *Look After Lulu*. 'You've got to come up. Noel's determined to be witty. All the time.' Coward's style was different from Feydeau's – Feydeau was happy to let the jokes arise from his impeccable farcical clockwork. Coward, as adaptor, was determined to put his signature on the piece, sublimely confident that his autograph could only improve its value. In short, his personality ill-accorded with Feydeau's – as, for that matter, it did with Osborne's. When they had dinner together some years later, Osborne remembered that:

> His second or third question was, 'How queer are you?' A
> baffled depression overcame me. I felt that both of us deserved
> better than this. 'How queer are you?' The fatuous game was
> afoot and I played it feebly. 'Oh, about 30 per cent'. 'Really?'
> he rapped back. 'I'm 95'.

But Osborne recognizes Coward's achievements, largely the result of Coward's determination that 'Work is much more fun than fun'. 'There'll never be another. There never was', Osborne wrote, reviewing Noel Coward's *Diaries*. 'He was a genius like Max Miller . . . author of about the three best comedies in the English language who also wrote five of the finest lyrics to be read rather than spoken.' And it is in this context that Osborne introduces his measured criticism. 'He affected to despise most of the best writers in the world. See him on Proust, Greene, Dickens, Pinter ("a sort of cockney Ivy Compton Burnett"), *The Three Sisters* ("always a rather tiresome play"), *King Lear* ("far, far too long"), (try the *whole* of *Design for Living* for length), Strauss, Verdi, Shakespeare – all far, far too long. Most of all he vented himself on Oscar Wilde. Noel would never have given away the world for a witty answer.'

However, Coward's perceptive insights were invariably expressed in a concise phrase. Harold Nicholson once looked 'like a summer pudding' and the Fonda family 'lay on the evening like a damp mackintosh'. Kenneth Tynan's epitaph on his career is perhaps the wittiest and most affectionate: 'Forty years ago he was Slightly in Peter Pan, and you might say he has been wholly in Peter Pan ever since.'

Tyrone Guthrie was nearly as famous as Coward for his come-backs to actors. At Stratford, Gwen Frangcon-Davies played Catherine of Aragon for him in *Henry VIII*. At a rehearsal she came to the front of the stage, somewhat vexed. She felt the crowd were not giving her public a clear view of her. 'I think I am being masked', she said distinctly. The silence lasted a few seconds and then Guthrie's voice from the back of the stalls murmured simply, 'Lower the prices for the Wednesday matinée.' And, directed by Tyrone Guthrie in *All's Well*, Edith Evans heard him tell a young actress to 'camp it up a bit'. 'What does it mean, Tony, "camp"?' she asked. 'Don't ask silly questions, dear,' said Guthrie. 'You invented it.'

Emlyn Williams is another versatile theatrical conjuror; whether as actor, director or writer he maintains his reputation for a stinging tongue. 'Ah, Victor', Williams said to Victor Spinetti once, 'still struggling to keep your head below water?' In a variation of an old joke – or presiding over its birth? – he heard of the arrest of a distinguished actor in a public lavatory. There was concern about how the affair might be hushed up. He mentioned the name of a leading theatre public relations officer not known for her publicity coups: 'Why don't you try telling Vivienne Byerely?' he suggested. He was bored to death at dinner one night by Marlene Dietrich's catalogue of tragedy: 'Such a week . . . first my darling Edith Piaf's funeral . . . the crowds mob me, in spite of my three black veils . . .

then my darling Jean Cocteau's funeral . . . six veils, but again they mob me . . . When I get home I ask myself what will it be like at *my* funeral?' The silky, slightly sibilant Emlyn Williams's voice crept in, 'Why don't you try dying at sea, Marlene?'

Among actresses the ripple of wit runs from Mrs Patrick Campbell to Coral Browne. There are, of course, the quips which sound manufactured: Zsa Zsa Gabor on her fifth husband, George Sanders – 'He taught me housekeeping; when I divorce I keep the house'; Bette Davis's view of a passing starlet: 'There goes the good time that was had by all', and the crack on the marriage of a famous American musical comedy star and an unprepossessing film actor: 'I'll have the pick of the litter'; and the honestly crafted Joan Rivers shaft: 'Elizabeth Taylor is wearing Orson Welles designer jeans.' But they pale beside the genuine article, for example, the vision of Katherine Hepburn, swathed in shawls and shovelling snow away from her East Side town house in New York. A passer-by examined the spectacle closely: 'You're Joan Crawford, aren't you?' she asked. Miss Hepburn kept right on sweeping: 'Not any more,' she croaked. (There is a similar story about A.J.P. Taylor selling a house. A couple looked it over, sensing that they knew the vendor's face. By the end of their inspection they had identified it. 'Are you A.J.P. Taylor?' inquired the wife. Taylor smiled modestly. 'Well,' he said, 'somebody has to be.') Miss Hepburn, who was once dismissed as 'Katherine of Arrogance', said, later in life, 'If you survive long enough you're revered like an old building.' She also remarked, 'I don't care what is written about me so long as it isn't true', so if the story of her snowbound encounter is inaccurate, perhaps she will forgive me.

Then there is the always-attributable Tallulah Bankhead. 'Are you really Tallulah Bankhead?' she was asked. 'What's left of me, dahling,' came the reply. Her views of herself were often honest and critical: 'As pure as the driven slush'; 'cocaine isn't habit-forming – I should know – I've been using it for years'; 'the only thing I regret about my life is the length of it. If I had to live my life again I'd make all the same mistakes – only sooner'; 'I have only two temperamental outbursts a year – each lasts six months'; on a play with pretension, 'There is less to this than meets the eye'; on Shirley Temple, 'They used to shoot her through gauze. You should shoot me through linoleum'; and on life, 'I read Shakespeare and the Bible and I can shoot dice. That's what I call a liberal education.'

Remembering Tallulah, whom I met only once, I prefer a vignette from the 'thirties, picturing the scene as she and Miss Estelle Winwood (who recently turned a hundred) are swaying on rocking chairs outside New York. There's a hot summer noon overhead as they sip their second or third cocktail. Over the radio comes the news of the arrest of Bruno Hauptman, the killer of the Lindbergh baby. Miss Winwood opens one large sleepy eye and looks across to her gently swaying partner: 'Well, Tallulah,' she drawls, 'we're *well* out of that.' Fred Keating summed up Tallulah's usual conversation style: 'I've just spent an hour talking to Tallulah for a few minutes.'

Top of the class of formula female wits comes Mae West, with a string of fine lines like – 'It's not the men in my life, it's the life in my men'; 'Goodness, what beautiful diamonds!' 'Goodness had nothing to do with it'; 'I used to be Snow White, but I drifted'; 'The best way to hold a man is in your arms'; 'Love conquers all things – except poverty and toothache' (echoes there of Sophie Tucker's robust realism: 'I've been poor and I've been rich – rich is better'); 'Whenever I'm caught between two evils, I take the one I've never tried'; 'A man has one hundred dollars and you leave him with two. That's subtraction'; 'A hard man is good to find'; 'When I'm good I'm very good but when I'm bad I'm better'; on becoming a life-jacket: 'I've been in *Who's Who* and I know what's what, but this is the first time I've been in a dictionary'; 'I've been things and seen places'; and on being told a man was six feet and seven inches: 'Let's forget the six feet and talk about the seven inches.'

I like her impromptu exchange with Alison Skipworth who suspected rightly that Miss West was stealing a scene from her: 'I'll have you know I'm an actress,' said Miss Skipworth. 'It's alright, dearie,' replied Mae, 'I'll keep your secret.' And I can't help admiring Gilbert Harding's reply to Miss West's American manager who impertinently suggested, 'Can't you sound a bit more sexy when you interview her?' – or words to that effect. Whatever the effect it was less than that of Harding's comeback: 'If, sir, I possessed the power of conveying unlimited sexual attraction through the potency of my voice, I would not be reduced to accepting a miserable pittance from the BBC for interviewing a faded female in a damp basement.'

Publicists for Marilyn Monroe modified the West formula. 'Did you have anything on?' Monroe was asked about her nude calendar. 'Oh yes, I had the radio on.' And 'What do you wear in bed?' – 'Chanel No. 5.' 'Sex is part of nature and I go along with nature.' 'Censors worry when a girl has a cleavage. They ought to worry when she doesn't.' 'A sex symbol is a thing. I hate being a thing.' In truth, Miss Monroe was more witted against than witty. 'Egghead weds Hourglass', a newspaper headlined her marriage to Arthur Miller. And Nunnally Johnson, the screenwriter and director, summed her up as ' . . . a natural phenomenon like Niagara Falls or the Grand Canyon. You can't talk to it. It can't talk to you. All you can do is stand back and be awed by it.'

Edith Evans was no slouch herself at rather more whimsical repartee. Entering Fortnum and Mason during the Second World War she bought a fruit, a pineapple perhaps, for the exorbitant price of seventeen shillings and sixpence. The assistant proffered the two-and-sixpence change. Dame Edith declined it. 'Keep the change,' she said, 'I trod on a grape on the way in.' I once saw her stare in blank incomprehension at a face that was waiting anxiously for recognition. Unable to bear the awkward moment any longer, the lady introduced herself. 'Lady Clark', said the wife of the Lord of Civilization. Dame Edith pounced. She looked at me in pained surprise, 'Why is she telling me her name?' she inquired. 'I know perfectly well who she is.' At Stratford she was said to have introduced a curious gobbling noise into the middle of one of her big speeches as Volumnia in *Coriolanus*. Day after day the other actors waited for it to go away. It didn't. Finally the director felt that he must take her aside. He asked her in what obscure folio she had found the puzzling word. Realizing that her game was up she broke into a sad smile. 'Oh dear, you noticed. And I hoped it was going to become as famous as "A handbag!" '

Mrs Patrick Campbell was an actress of flashes of brilliance and a wilful spirit which did not always allow her to use the former to best advantage. By 1942 James Agate could write of her, 'This was an actress who, for twenty years, had the world at her feet. She kicked it away and the ball rolled out of her reach.' Her correspondence with Shaw ripples with spontaneous wit. She told Shaw (a virgin vegetarian), 'One day you'll eat beefsteak and no woman in London will be safe.' 'When you were quite a little boy,' she admonished him on another occasion, 'somebody ought to have said "hush" just once.'

(She must have known the consequences of baiting Shaw. He got his own back in print when he reviewed her in Sardon's *Fedora*: 'It is greatly to Mrs Patrick Campbell's credit that, bad as the play was, her acting was worse . . .') Her impromptu shafts were usually cruelly to the point. About a visiting actress, she said: 'She is a great lady of the American stage. Her voice is so beautiful that you won't understand a word she says.' Reproved by a very young Noel Coward for sleeping through his performance, she turned up for the next in white gloves and ostentatiously clapped everything he did. Later, when he was at the height of his fame, she invaded a crowded dressing room in which he was holding court after a successful cabaret performance. 'Don't you love it,' she enquired cooingly of the band of devotees, 'when he does his little hummings at the piano?' 'Many people say that I have an ugly mind,' she once protested. 'It isn't true. I say ugly things, which is different.'

My favourite Mrs Campbell story records her meeting with the playwright Henry Arthur Jones, who, with Pinero, did something to provide British audiences with stately re-interpretations of Ibsenite dilemmas. (Agate puts it neatly, after declaring himself reluctant to be convinced by his argument; 'Pinero, having taken the trouble to learn Ibsen's language, was heard to speak it indifferently'.) However, Jones also massacred English with a pronounced Cockney inflection and a wayward way with an 'H'. Called to Mrs Campbell's home near the Gloucester Road to read his new play aloud to her, as was the custom in those days, he ploughed through some three hours while Mrs Campbell listened, stretched out on a *chaise longue*. As Jones closed the book the actress yawned: 'Very long, Mr Jones,' she said ungraciously, 'even without the H's.'

She was perceptive on Tallulah Bankhead's acting: 'Watching Tallulah on stage is like watching somebody skating on thin ice. Everyone wants to be there when it breaks.' And she was a genuine original. How much more resonant is her view of marriage than Mae West's. Miss West's formula is trim: 'Marriage is a great institution, but I'm not ready for an institution yet.' Mrs Pat's ('They *will* call me Mrs Pat,' she said, 'I can't stand it. The "Pat" is the last straw that breaks the Campbell's back') is famously luxuriant: 'Marriage is the deep, deep peace of the double bed after the hurly burly of the *chaise longue*.' On extra-marital subjects Mrs Campbell is equally famous for her tolerance of homosexuals: 'As

long as they don't do it in the streets and frighten the horses.' Her
witty rudeness was a byword in her heyday and with courage she
kept it up when she was a near-destitute, virtually unemployable old
lady, scattering buckshot across those who came to her aid. As
Alexander Woollcott wrote, 'She was a sinking ship firing on her
rescuers.' She went to see *Hamlet* and afterwards sailed into the
actress who played Gertrude. 'Why do you sit on the bed?' she
inquired. 'Only housemaids sit on the bed.' When she played
Mélisande to Sarah Bernhardt's Pelléas at the old Coronet at
Notting Hill, she planted a live goldfish in a stage fountain. The play
did not find favour. 'Both ladies', wrote one critic, 'are old enough
to know better.'

Two other theatrical ladies who clashed were the great English
comedienne, Irene Vanbrugh, and Ruth Draper, the American
monologist. Seeing Miss Vanbrugh's brilliant white kid gloves – was
she jealous or an early preservationist? – Miss Draper said rudely:

'Skin of a beast!'

'Why, what do you wear?' asked Miss Vanbrugh.

'Silk, of course,' Miss Draper sniffed.

'Entrails of a worm,' muttered Miss Vanbrugh.

Lilian Braithwaite, a near-contemporary actress, took a friend to
a Novello matinée towards the end of her life. As a particularly
broad tune sang out the friend tut-tutted. 'Naughty Ivor,' she
whispered, 'that's an old Welsh hymn.' 'More than you can say for
its composer, dear,' Miss Braithwaite hissed back.

To leap to a contemporary legend – Coral Browne, she of the
vivid turn of phrase and wicked wit, as well as great eloquence and
beauty. She once dismissed one unelectric actor as 'like acting with
210 pounds of condemned veal'. Just as vivid is her phrase for an
over-busy actor: '. . . like a rat up a rope'. She is said to have referred
to an early admirer, Firth Shepherd, a successful impresario, in
glowing terms: 'Firth is my shepherd, I shall not want.' Going to
Russia in *King Lear*, she asked if there was not a part for her first
husband. 'No,' said the management, 'nothing suitable'. 'Give me
the script,' she said, rifling through it until she found the scene she
was looking for. 'There you are,' she said, smiling wickedly and
pointing at the perfect part, 'A camp near Dover.' On another
occasion, a middle-aging man unwisely brought a much younger,
more handsome youth across to her table in a restaurant and

introduced him. 'He just arrived from South Africa this morning,' he said, by way of explanation. 'Oh yes,' replied Miss Browne briskly, 'got the trip wires out at Victoria Station again, have we?'

Between marriages Miss Browne arrived at the Old Vic one day for rehearsals of a new Shakespeare production. Her fancy hit upon a young actor, a new member of the company, not noted as a ladies' man. She made enquiries and was told that she was unlikely to be lucky there. Fired by a challenge she bet a pound that she would bring it off. Next morning when she got to rehearsal the informant rushed up to her to see if he had won his wager. Miss Browne did not look entirely happy. 'I owe you seven and six,' she admitted. On a spring and winter romance between a pert young actress and a Grand Old Man of the theatre she was just as down-to-earth. 'I could never understand what Sir X saw in Miss Y', she remarked, 'until I saw her at the Caprice eating corn-on-the-cob'.

Beatrice Lillie's acting was always a distillation of witty clowning. Of her title by marriage – Lady Peel – she used to say, 'I'm a lady in my own wrong'; and at one time she had a habit of answering the telephone, 'C'est Lady Peel qui parle.' Apocrypha recalls that she was once billed as Lady Peel, not as Beatrice Lillie, when appearing in a solo concert somewhere in the mid-West. A misconception ran round the audience that this unknown, impoverished aristocrat was trying to work her passage back to the old country. As each wilder piece of comic invention succeeded each earlier act of immaculate clowning the polite crowd managed to keep their faces straight in sympathy while the baffled star strove in vain to make them laugh. Keeping a straight face while watching Beatrice Lillie must have been a cruel test. She was more successful at Buckingham Palace when a waiter spilled soup on her new dress. 'Never darken my DIOR again!' she cried. Asked if she had performed during the First World War, she countered, 'At the end of the First World War I was knee-high to a hiccup!' To a pigeon who flew into her New York apartment she said simply, 'Any messages?' And paying off a boringly talkative Irish taxi-driver in New York she said, 'Something for you, driver – buy yourself a sense of humour.' She delivered an unanswerable rebuke to the wife of a Chicago meat-packing tycoon, Mrs Armour, who had complained to her crimper that if she'd known so many theatricals would be in the salon, she would never have come. Miss Lillie ignored Mrs Armour and told the manageress in cut-glass tones, 'You may tell the butcher's wife that Lady Peel has finished.' Another snob looked hard at her pearls one night: 'Are they real?' she asked. 'Of course.' The woman grabbed them and tried to bite them. 'They're not,' she claimed, 'they're cultured.' 'How would you know?' Miss Lillie smiled, 'with false teeth.'

It is unfair to give the impression that only old *actresses* are quotable. Old actors do not do so badly. John Gielgud – more famous for gaffes – was once asked to improvise along with a whole company of actors directed by Peter Brook. When told to say something terrifying he walked to the front of the stage and said simply, 'We open in two weeks'. Sir Herbert Beerbohm Tree gave and took, more than most, in his time. He was on the memorable end of two of W.S. Gilbert's shafts. After one energetic performance, Gilbert regarded Tree's sweaty efforts with 'Your skin has been acting at any rate', and after his Hamlet, he was congratulated in a second exercise in Tree-felling. It was, Gilbert said, 'Funny without being the least bit vulgar.' Tree's famous rejection letter to an aspiring author, is his own most notorious creation:

> My Dear Sir,
> I have read your play.
> Oh, my dear Sir!
> Yours faithfully,
> H. Beerbohm Tree.

I have always wondered how Tree replied in another one-sided correspondence. This time we have only the applicant's letter. Tree was casting for a production of *Macbeth* and had the idea of using black witches – 'secret black and midnight hags'. The message was beaten out on the tom-toms of London theatre gossip and candidates duly appeared. One letter went straight to the point.

> Dear Sir,
> I hear you are looking for dark people.
> I would like to see you.
> Signed – SARDANAPULUS.
> P.S. I can lift a grand piano with my teeth.

Tree sprinkled quips around. Today his verdict on Israel Zangwill, the fine Jewish actor, might smack of anti-semitism: 'His face shining like Moses, his teeth, like the Ten Commandments, all broken.' To a fellow-member of the Garrick Club who complained, that when he joined, all the members were gentlemen, Tree said simply, 'I wonder why they left?' On fans he said, 'The only man who wasn't spoilt by being lionized was Daniel'; A.B. Walkley was 'A whipper-snapper of criticism who quoted dead languages to hide his ignorance of life'; on interior decoration, 'The national sport of England is obstacle racing. People fill their rooms with useless and cumbersome furniture, and spend the rest of their lives in trying to dodge it'; on an actress better known in bed than on stage, 'She kissed (sic) her way into society. I don't like her. But don't mis-understand me: my dislike is purely platonic.' To an actress whose vowel sounds were over-careful he remarked, 'Oh my God! Remember you are in Egypt. The *skay* is only seen in Kensington.' As for an old bore of his acquaintance, 'even the grave yawns for him.'

Tree's whimsies are even more endearing. For instance, he met a man in the street buckling under the weight of the monumental grandfather clock he was carrying. 'My poor fellow,' Tree sympa-thized, 'why not carry a watch?' In a post office, he practised an eccentricity of Ralph Richardsonian proportions. He enquired if they sold stamps. The girl admitted that they did. 'Then show me some', Tree asked. Presented with a sheet he pointed to one in the middle. 'I'll have that one, please', he said politely.

Once he was billed in big letters outside a theatre. 'When I pass my name in such large letters,' he said, 'I blush, but at the same time instinctively raise my hat.' His proudest achievement, however, was his creation of Her Majesty's Theatre. He hailed a taxi to go there one day. The driver asked for the destination. 'Do you think,' Tree inquired, 'that I am going to mention the name of my beautiful theatre inside a common cab?' Nowadays, at the top of Her Majesty's Theatre, there is an impressive set of offices and a lavish rehearsal space. It is suggested that this was Tree's domain, where legends celebrate his voracious and indiscriminate sexual habits. When I take auditions here I like to think that it is the scene of my favourite Tree legend. If it is true, it goes like this. Esmé Percy, then a decorative young member of Tree's company, was invited up to the Manager's suite for dinner after a performance. The Manager had been impressed, perhaps even excited by Percy's delicate features. An elaborate table awaited them: something cold to start, something warm in a chafing dish, champagne in a bucket, wine complacently reaching room temperature. As Manager and young man sat down to dinner à deux, the door was flung open. There stood Lady Tree, taking in the situation at a glance. 'Enjoy your supper, Mr Percy,' she is supposed to have said, 'the port is on the chim-a-ney piece, and it's *still* adultery!'

Poor Laurence Olivier (or rich Laurence Olivier – have it which way you will) is always being saddled with remarks which don't sound as though he made them – if only because his usual public pronouncements are couched in never-ending strings of multi-syllabled words which do not quite add up to a sentence. His little public jokes come out neatly crafted and slightly tired. For example, 'We used to have actresses trying to become stars; now we have stars trying to become actresses'; and on the Bacon-and-Shakespeare debate, 'What self-respecting actor would be prepared to be a member of the Royal Bacon Company.' (The definitive funny words on *that* controversy were written by Brahms and Simon in their book *No Bed for Bacon*. Shakespeare is trying to make a start on *Love's Labour Won*. First Burbage interrupts him. ' "I've been thinking," he said, "I'd like to play a Dane – young, intellectual – I see him pale, vacillating, but above everything sad and prone to soliloquy." "I know," said Shakespeare, "introspective". The curtains parted. Bacon had come back. He pulled out a sheaf of papers from his pocket and laid them on the desk. "By the way, Will," he said. "I almost forgot. When you've got a moment to spare, you might polish up this essay . . ." ')

In spite of Max Beerbohm's reservation – 'When I dislike what I see on stage, I can be vastly amusing, but when I write about something I like, I am appallingly dull' – it is possible to be a witty critic without bitching, but it does defy the laws of gravity. Kenneth Tynan wrote of Greta Garbo, 'What, when drunk, one sees in other women, one sees in Garbo sober,' which is both witty and positive. However, the critic as eunuch, parasite or pariah is a more familiar role. 'Critics are like eunuchs in a harem; they know how it's done, they've seen it done every day, but they're unable to do it themselves', said Brendan Behan. 'Criticism is a study by which men grow important and formidable at very small expense', wrote

Samuel Johnson. 'You might not mind so much if your sister married one of them, and two or three asked in after dinner would not for a certainty spoil the party, but taken as a group the drama critics of New York are so much suet pudding', said Heywood Broun, the Broadway wit and critic. In fact, most drama critics are agreeable people sometimes driven to desperate acts by the behaviour they are paid to witness. The argument would not, however, have convinced Richard Le Gallienne; 'A critic is a man created to praise greater men than himself, but he is never able to find them.' A quiet resignation is in order. As Immanuel Kant wrote, 'If a man is often the subject of conversation, he soon becomes the subject of criticism.' Defensively, Whitney Balliet argues, 'A critic is a bundle of biases held loosely together by a sense of taste' (though perhaps that should read 'a *good* critic . . .'). For the prosecution, the actor, Eli Wallach, says that, 'Having the critics praise you is like having the hangman say you've got a pretty neck.' And the composer, Erik Satie, commented, 'Last year I gave several lectures on "Intelligence and the Appreciation of Music Among Animals". Today I am going to speak to you about "Intelligence and the Appreciation of Music Among Critics". The subject is similar.' Pained acceptance comes from Peter Ustinov: 'Critics search for ages for the wrong word which, to give them credit, they eventually find.' It is hard to be sure which is the easier target – the artist on his occasional outings or the critic trapped in his duty to report regularly, accurately and entertainingly. Not witty, but about as far as you can go in favour of critics, is Walt Whitman: 'Criticism, carried to the height worthy of it, is a majestic office, perhaps an art, perhaps even a church.' (Write to Walt Whitman, not to me.)

Diana Rigg has collected a deal of criticism in her valuable book, *No Turn Unstoned*, which includes Dorothy Parker's famous review of Katherine Hepburn's performance in *The Lake* in 1933 at the Martin Beck Theatre in New York, graveyard of a thousand flops and occasional home of a long run: 'Watch Katherine Hepburn run the gamut of emotion . . . from A to B.' But I have always been more struck by Dorothy Parker's comparison between Miss Hepburn and the splendid character actress who supported her in the same production. Ms Parker pointed out that Miss Hepburn always put a certain distance between herself and her distinguished colleague, 'lest she catch acting from her'. Another favourite Parker piece is her review of *America's Sweetheart*. It was a Rodgers, Hart and Fields show, but chief among Ms Parker's victims was Jeanne Aubert, a French actress, 'whose husband, if you can believe the papers, recently pleaded through the French courts that he be allowed to restrain his wife from appearing on the stage. Professional or not, the man is a dramatic critic.' But perhaps the best of critical musical chestnuts is by another American, Percy Hammond: 'I have knocked everything but the knees of the chorus girls, and nature has anticipated me there.'

Artists who have spent years writing or months planning or weeks rehearsing or days lighting a play are understandably put out when they are dismissed in a word – and it takes a good joke to justify such flippancy. So many people have been credited with saying or writing at the end of *I am a Camera* – 'Me no Leica' – that there seems little point in apportioning the blame. Several pens have made a stab at paraphrasing Mrs Campbell's 'Once I was a *tour de force*, now I'm forced to tour'. A similar disease infects critics faced with musicals. Far too many go out 'Singing/whistling/humming the scenery'; if I read it again I shall be taken out screaming their by-line. 'Going in humming the tunes' is no better and is just as frequently borrowed. Yet there is much to be said for putting the hopeful artist and potential audience out of their misery. When Tynan called *Flower Drum Song* 'The World of Woozy Song' we knew what he meant, and some smiled – not me; but when Robert Garland reviewed an *Uncle Vanya* – 'If you were to ask me what *Uncle Vanya* is about, I would say about as much as I can take' – those of us who love the play accordingly judged Mr Garland more sharply than Dr Chekhov. Those of us who did not see the performance would wonder how accurate George Jean Nathan was in saying that 'Ralph Richardson's Uncle Vanya is just his Falstaff with a hangover', because we might have expected Richardson to be as well and variously cast in the one part as in the other.

The limited patience of Robert Benchley is partly responsible for this school of writing. He wrote dramatic criticism in America over a long period of time and frayed at the edges. 'People laugh at this every night, which explains why democracy can never be a success'; 'Just about as low as good clean fun can get'; 'The kind of comedy you eat peanuts at'. About one drama he penned, 'See Hebrews 13.8'. The relevant passage in the Bible to which he refers reads –

'Jesus Christ, the same yesterday and today and forever.' A fair verdict on many plays, even if arrived at obscurely.

And there were others, less inspired, who saw *The Shoemaker's Holiday* as 'a load of cobblers', and said of *No Love, No Leave* – 'No comment'. But am I falling into the reviewers' trap of quoting a joke with disapproval hoping it will still get a laugh? Another example? 'The plot was designed in a light vein that somehow became varicose', said David Lardner. I much prefer Ring Lardner's devastating assassination of the Hollywood wit, Irvin Cobb: 'Mr Cobb took me into his library and showed me his books, of which he had a complete set.' (I like the item in the 'Best of Cobb' in which he says that a sure sign of recession in the movie industry is when a major studio starts laying off relatives.) James Agee practised a relentless dismissal of the movies. On *Tycoon*: 'Several tons of dynamite are set off in this picture – none of it under the right people,' and on *You Were Meant For Me*: 'That's what you think.' An anonymous reviewer was neater when reporting on De Mille's *Samson and Delilah* – the capsule review ran, 'A Movie for de Millions.'

A precursor of the ·Benchley tradition was Eliot Field of the *Denver Post* with his famous line, 'Mr Clarke played the King all evening as though under constant fear that someone else was about to play the Ace.' Dorothy Parker soon mastered the style: '*House Beautiful* is play lousy'; and of a performer, 'Guido Natso is natso guido.' George S. Kaufman – conversationalist not critic in this case – said to Howard Dietz about the Dietz and Schwartz musical, *Beat the Devil*: 'I understand your play is full of single entendre.' He also labelled an unfortunate appearance by Gertrude Lawrence in a straight play, 'A bad play saved by a bad performance.' Stanley Kauffman, who infrequently set the breakfast table on a roar, finished off an American production of *The Taming of the Shrew* with admirable despatch: 'If a director doesn't really want to do the *Shrew*, this is a pretty good way not to do it.' The quip blunt is more frequent than the quip subtle. Another head-on specialist, Douglas Watt of the *New York Daily News*, savaged Jane Alexander in *Goodbye Fidel* in 1980 writing, 'She's about as Latin as a boiled New England dinner' – which could be a compliment to Miss Alexander's qualities in their own right as well as a slam at her miscasting. However, there was no doubt about what John Mason Brown meant when he wrote of one of Tallulah Bankhead's excursions into Shakespeare, 'Tallulah Bankhead barged down the Nile last night as Cleopatra and sank.' Or what F.P. Adams meant when he dismissed Helen Hayes's performance as Shaw's Cleopatra as 'fallen archness'.

Josephine Hull, a marvellous comedienne, had the right advice for actresses who are ambitious to play Shakespeare: 'Playing Shakespeare is very tiring. You never get to sit down, unless you're a King.' Perhaps life with the Shakespeares is even harder for Russians. Charles Morgan pounced on Eugenie Leontovich in 1936 playing Cleopatra, for Komisarjevsky, opposite Donald Wolfit. Shakespeare wrote:

> O, withered is the garland of the war,
> The soldier's pole is fall'n: young boys and girls
> Are level now with men.

What Morgan heard was:

> O weederdee degarlando devar
> Desolderspo lees falln: yong boisengwls
> Alefelnow wimen.

Agate called his review 'Anton and Cleopatrova; a Trajedy by Komispeare' and had a go at pseudo-Komispeare translating:

> When you sued staying
> Then was the time for words

to:

> Wen you suet staying
> Den was the time for wurst.

It is clearly neither easy nor advisable for charming émigrés to play Shakespeare on their home ground.

The simile method of dramatic criticism is the most tempting to the critic. I always shudder as I approach the outskirts of a simile – it is easy to recognize the signs: 'Like a . . .', 'With all the . . . of . . .', 'Reminds me of . . .', 'Resembled that of . . . ', 'Came to resemble a . . .', 'Gives the impression of . . .' It may be the critic's trap again but I shall have to produce some examples, of which it is fair to add, the victims themselves are proud:

74

'Richard Briers played Hamlet like a demented typewriter' – W.A. Darlington.

'Miss (Maureen) Stapleton played the part as though she had not yet signed her contract with the producer' – George Jean Nathan.

'Miss (Nancy) Walker reminds me of nothing so much as a Bundle-for-Britain with ears' – Hedda Hopper.

'As for Miss (Jane) White, her every look, gesture and move is that of a fish wife suffering in equal measure from neurasthenia and megalomania' – John Simon.

'James Earl Jones (a tribune in *Coriolanus*) sounded like a one-stringed double bass with a faintly Calypso accent, and rolled about like a huge barrel set in motion by a homunculus within' – Simon again.

Diana Rigg bravely bares the scars of Simon's description of her own nude triumph in *Abelard and Heloise*: 'Diana Rigg is built like a brick mausoleum with insufficient flying buttresses'.

Frances de la Tour nobly contributed to Miss Rigg's anthology a notice by Michael Billington which described her as looking 'astonishingly like James Coburn's twin sister'.

Anthony Hopkins in *Macbeth* 'gives the impression that he is a rotarian pork butcher about to tell the stalls a dirty story' – Felix Barker.

Caryl Brahms used to tell a story of Robert Helpmann bearing down on her after a bad notice and saying, 'Caryl, *I* never read my notices, but my *mother*, who is *sensitive* to *criticism* . . . !' Paul Scofield, as Othello, had to suffer at least two bad similes – if he reads his notices. First *The Field* appropriately saw Scofield 'come with the stiff swagger of a peacock and an equally awkward accent which makes him sound less like a Moor and more like a man wrestling with a new set of National Health teeth.' Then Peter Jenkins in the *Spectator* felt that 'his black man's form of speech . . . reminded me of Hutch . . . his idea of a black man's movement consisted of a kind of Firbankian prancing which, in moments of deep anguish, came to resemble an orangutan choreographed by Sir Frederick Ashton', which somehow manages to be rude to the innocent Sir Fred as well as the blameless orangutan.

Brooks Atkinson, another American critic who showed the sweat when he worked hard at being witty, reviewed Farley Granger in a musical version of *Pride and Prejudice*: 'Farley Granger played Mr Darcy with all the flexibility of a telegraph pole.' Bernard Levin, a champagne wit most of the time compared to Atkinson's stale beer, slipped to a neighbouring simile to describe Denis Quilley's performance in *High Spirits*: 'All the charm and animation of the leg of a billiard table.' But, by God, it *is* a dull part, in spite of the high regard in which its author held it.

How pleasant when a critic works that much harder and employs more art and craft in sliding in a stunning phrase – or has the courage of his observations and goes for a direct hit. Henry James, for example, on Salvini's *Othello*: 'Salvini's rendering of the part is the portrait of an African by an Italian.' Another American, J. Ranken Towse, said of the popular Clara Morris playing Lady Macbeth, 'Her audacity was largely in excess of her equipment.' Shaw was clinically helpful in bestowing advice on a young actress, Miss Hope Booth: 'I must somewhat tardily acknowledge an invitation to witness a performance at the Royalty Theatre by Miss Hope Booth, a young lady who cannot sing, dance or speak, but whose appearance suggests that she might profitably spend three or four years in learning these arts, which are useful on the stage.' George Jean Nathan wrote of Vincent Price as Abraham Lincoln in 1942: 'The Price Lincoln, had Booth not taken the job himself, would have been shot on the spot by every dramatic critic in Ford's theatre on that fateful night.' (Playing Lincoln is plainly a thankless task and makes an inviting target. George S. Kaufman saw Raymond Massey in the movie and wrote: 'Massey won't be satisfied until he's assassinated'.)

Dorothy Parker failed to stifle Rudolph Besier's *The Barretts of Wimpole Street* at birth in the *New Yorker* in 1931, in spite of writing, 'Now that you've got me right down to it, the only thing I didn't like about *The Barretts of Wimpole Street* was the play.' Ms Parker's casual buttonholing of the reader is as effective as her direct assaults. In a solid demolition job on A.A. (Whimsey-the-Pooh) Milne's *Give Me Yesterday*, I like this aside: ' "Ah!" I said to myself, for I love a responsive audience, "so it's one of those plays".' Alan Brien in the *Spectator* managed a nice combination of the 'to simile or not to simile schools' in reviewing Michael Hordern's 1959 *Macbeth*: 'Half his time on the stage he cringes like an Armenian carpet seller in an ankle-length black dressing gown of fuzzy candlewick while his ruched gold-cloth sleeves sag like concertinas around the tips of his fingers . . . this Thane of Cawdor would be unnerved by Banquo's valet, never mind Banquo's ghost.' A hundred years earlier, critics were no kinder. G.H. Lewes (on a night away from George Eliot or did she put the thought into his head?) saw off the infinitely respectable Edmund Kean's *Macbeth*: 'He makes Macbeth ignoble, with perhaps a tendency towards Methodism.'

I cherish the memory of a luncheon with the late Phyllis Neilson Terry, who played Lady Macbeth to Donald Wolfit's Scottish king. I had read that James Agate considered her the best Lady he had ever seen and mentioned the notice. 'Ah yes,' she said, 'that was with Donald . . . I don't know if you are aware that Donald had a reputation for being a very selfish actor. On the first night after the murder he hissed at me, "Don't touch me". I was playing his wife, I had put my hand on his shoulder to give him support in his moment of need – if I couldn't do that what could I do? If I couldn't touch him then all I could do was listen and that was really very silly of Donald, because when I listen . . .' – she was a large, beautiful woman and she raised one long elegant arm to her ear and stretched the other to the side at its full length. The pose was striking as she said, '. . . when I listen, *everybody* looks at me.' Miss Neilson Terry was not only a noticeable, but a witty, listener.

In recent years, Peter O'Toole's *Macbeth* has excited most comment – and most of it hostile. Robert Cushman in the *Observer* wrote that 'his performance suggests that he is taking some kind of personal revenge on the play', and Michael Billington quoted an unusual Shakespearean critic on the play, 'It was P.G. Wodehouse who memorably said that the "Tomorrow and Tomorrow and Tomorrow" speech has a lot of spin on it but, as delivered by Mr O'Toole, it is hit for six like a full toss.' Billington's dogged perseverance with Wodehouse's metaphor suggests that, by incredibly agile footwork, O'Toole scored a triumph – a view at variance with the opinions of most commentators on the production, and with the rest of his report. 'He delivers every line with a monotonous tenor bark as if addressing an audience of deaf Eskimos' (simile time again). Irving Wardle in *The Times* thought that 'his manner is that of a man in an intricate, danger-fraught situation, not that of someone who owns the place.' I never saw this now-famous version of the play. I missed the first night having been bidden to attend on Dame Edna Everage down the road, and to go and see Peter's performance after the notices seemed like voyeurism. And one should choose those moments.

James Thurber emerges as another unlikely Shakespearean scholar in his view of *The Macbeth Murder Mystery*:

I opened the copy of the play, which I had with me and turned to Act II, Scene 2. 'Here', I said, 'you will see where Lady Macbeth says, "I laid their daggers ready. He could not miss 'em. Had he not resembled my father as he slept, I had done it". Do you see?' 'No,' said the American woman, bluntly, 'I don't.' 'But it's simple!' I exclaimed. 'I wonder I didn't see it years ago. The reason Duncan resembled Lady Macbeth's father as he slept is that it actually was her father!' 'Good God!' breathed my companion softly. 'Lady Macbeth's father killed the King', I said, 'and, hearing someone coming, thrust the body under the bed and crawled into the bed himself'. 'But,' said the lady, 'you can't have a murderer who only appears in the story once. You can't have that.' 'I know that,' I said, and I turned to Act II, Scene 4. 'It says here, "Enter Ross with an old Man". Now, that old man is never identified and it is my contention that he was old Mr Macbeth,* whose ambition it was to make his daughter Queen. There you have your motive.' 'But even then,' cried the American lady, 'he's still a minor character!' 'Not,' I said, gleefully, 'when you realize that he was also one of the weird sisters in disguise!' 'You mean one of the three witches?' 'Precisely,' I said. 'Listen to this speech of the old man's. "On Tuesday last, a falcon towering in her pride of place, was by a mousing owl hawk'd and kill'd." Who does that sound like?' 'It sounds like the way the three witches talk', said my companion, reluctantly. 'Precisely!' I said again.

While we are on Thurber and the theatre, there is his seminal piece on dubious re-titling – from *The Case for Comedy*. The

---

* Should it not have been Mr Macbeth-in-law?

technique has been used a dozen times since, especially in re-titling or re-inflecting songs: e.g. *What Is This Thing Called, Love?*, '*Someday*, my Prince *Will Come.*' Thurber stuck to plays. 'Once, last summer, when the robin woke me with his Gershwin tune, I lay there re-titling certain plays to fit the temper and trend of the present day, and came up with these: "Abie's Irish Neurosis", "I Dismember Mama", "They Slew What They Wanted", "Toys in the Psychomatic", "The Glands Menagerie", "Destroy Writes Again", "The Manic Who Came to Dinner", and a title calculated to pop you out of bed and into a cold tub, "Oklahomosexual".'

But, once again, an earlier age could be more violent. Herbert Farjeon considered a *Julius Caesar* produced in the Herbert Beerbohm Tree tradition at His Majesty's in 1932: 'plenty of lictors and vestal virgins'. (Tree was once overheard supervising some brazen American extras due to appear with him in *Henry VIII* in New York with the words, 'Ladies, just a little more virginity, if you don't mind'.) Farjeon continues, 'The company (of stars) is rather like a football team consisting entirely of full-backs. The lines of blank verse succeed each other like bowls bowling down a bowling alley. The actors seem mesmerized by their own voices. The nimble flame of Shakespeare is extinguished by the hooves of elephants. Here once again is the awful Shakespeare we ought to like . . . As for the crowd, it is massive and vociferous and suggestive in some of its effects of a sort of Chu-Chin-Caesar.' Farjeon heard a 'super who shouted "shut-up" during Antony's funeral speech' . . . it was a jolly moment, even jollier, I thought, than the moment when Casca and Cassius sheltered from the streaming rain under a real lamp in what looked like the entrance to a real old Roman nightclub.' That pushy extra reminds me of the actress in the film *Tom Jones* who, besought by Tony Richardson to improvise more period realism into the insults the crowd were hurling at Diane Cilento's scarlet woman, was heard distinctly through an unfortunate moment of silence during the screening of rushes the next morning, to be shouting with conviction, 'Gerraght, you eighteenth-century cunt!'

Not only small-part actors are entitled to acclaim. They also serve who only sit and prompt; and sometimes they get notices. In this case the anonymous star (1930 vintage) is being congratulated by Max Beerbohm:

While Signora Duse walked through her part (Hedda Gabler), the prompter threw himself into it with a will. A more raucous whisper I never heard than that which preceded the Signora's every sentence. It was like the continuous tearing of very thick silk. I think it worried everyone in the theatre, except the Signora herself, who listened placidly to the prompter's every reading, and, as soon as he had finished, reproduced it in her own way. This process made the matinée a rather long one. By a very simple expedient the extra time might have been turned to good account. How much pleasure would have been gained, and how much hypocrisy saved, if there had been an interpreter on the OP side, to shout in English what the prompter was whispering in Italian.

To return to critics on principal strutters and fretters – Michael Billington reviewed the miscasting of Kenneth Williams (admirable comedian), 'of the flared nostrils, funny voices and camp outrage', as 'a respectable, lecherous suburbanite' in a play (a disaster) by Georges Feydeau. The play was entitled *Signed and Sealed*. (Feydeau's titles have almost always been translated with wild, self-important independence by English scribes. I think this particular whim was by Christopher Hampton – no great farceur. Caryl Brahms and I once translated the same playwright's – Feydeau, not Hampton – *La Main Passe*, which makes some allusions to card playing and to thwarted love. We called it *Lucky at Cards*, only to find that Peter Coe, who was engaged to direct it, renamed it *A Fish Out of Water*, for no better reason than he 'thought it sounded more like a title'.) As one Rhetta Hughes said, 'There are two kinds of directors in the theatre. Those who think they are God and those who know they are.') Anyway, to get back to Billington on the casting of the superb Kenneth Williams which made nonsense: 'There is no point in seeing a man reduced to hysterical panic if hysterical panic is his forte.'

I don't think anyone would object to the notion that the most celebrated critical wits of the last hundred years have been Beerbohm, Shaw, Agate and Tynan. They need reading at length: we have only limited room.

There is Beerbohm's genial cricket metaphor for Benson's company giving *Henry V* at the Lyceum:

Mr F.R. Benson is an Oxford man, and he is in the habit of recruiting his company from his university ... Alertness, agility, grace, physical strength – all these attributes are obvious in the mimes who were, last week, playing *Henry the Fifth* at the Lyceum. Every member of the cast seemed in tip-top condition – thoroughly 'fit'. Subordinates and principals all worked well together. The fielding was excellent, and so was the batting. Speech after speech was sent spinning across the boundary, and one was constantly inclined to shout 'Well played, sir! Well played indeed!' As a branch of university cricket, the whole performance was, indeed, beyond praise. But, as a form of acting, it was not impressive.

There is Shaw's fine passage from 1897:

I never see Miss Ada Rehan act without burning to present Mr Augustin Daly (her impresario) with a delightful villa in St Helena, and a commission from an influential committee of his admirers to produce, at his leisure, a complete set of Shakespeare's plays, entirely re-written, reformed, rearranged, and brought up to the advanced requirements of the year 1850. He was in full force at the Islington Theatre on Monday evening last with his version of *As You Like It* just as I don't like it.

The prose marches on majestically with a vivid description of the anomalies, excesses and infelicities Mr Daly set down in Arden; for example – 'the Orlando, with the harmony of his brown boots and tunic torn asunder by a piercing discord of dark volcanic green, a walking tribute to Mr Daly's taste in tights'. It stops off to reiterate that Shaw would not like Daly assassinated – St Helena would do – and goes on to congratulate the manager on his early success with Irish-American, Yanko-German comedies, which 'secured him a position in London which was never questioned until it became apparent that he was throwing away Miss Rehan's genius.' Shaw soon begins to sound like early Bernard Levin on early Vanessa Redgrave ...

I cannot judge from Miss Rehan's enchanting Rosalind whether she is a great Shakespearean actress or not; there is even a sense in which I cannot tell, whether she can act at all or not. So far, I have never seen her create a character. She has always practised the same adorable arts on me, by whatever name the play-bill has called her – Nancy Brasher (ugh!), Viola or Rosalind. I have never complained; the drama with all its heroines levelled up to a universal Ada Rehan has seemed no dreary prospect to me. In Shakespeare (what Mr Daly leaves of him) she was and is irresistible; at Islington on Monday she made me cry faster than Mr Daly could make me swear. But the critic in me is bound to insist that Ada Rehan has as yet created nothing but Ada Rehan. She will probably never excel that masterpiece; but why should she not impose a character study or two on it! It is because nobody in England knows the answer to that question, that nobody in England as yet knows whether Ada Rehan is a creative artist or a mere virtuosa.

In today's theatre, over-lighting is becoming as distracting a feature of under-nourished theatrical productions as over-designing used to be. However, it is a surprise to find, as long ago as 1887, Henry James wittily drawing his readers' attention to its effect on Irving's rendering of Goethe's *Faust*:

We care nothing for the spurting flames which play so large a part, nor for the importunate lighting which is perpetually projected on somebody or something . . . the said lighting effect is always descending on someone or other, apropos of everything and nothing; it is disturbing and vulgarising, and has nothing to do with the author's meaning. That blue vapours should attend on the steps of Mephistopheles is a very poor substitute for his giving us a moral shudder . . .

Leaving the lighting James then goes for Irving's jugular . . .

That deep note is entirely absent from Mr Irving's rendering of him, though the actor, of course, at moments displays to the eye a remarkably sinister figure. He strikes us, however, as superficial – a terrible fault for an arch-fiend.

James Agate always reads better on performances than on plays. But he was writing in a period when – apart from a clutch of great comedies and the usual generous helping of Irish genius – the native drama was less exciting than it had been since the first half of the nineteenth century. Performances offered a richer challenge. It is, perhaps, unfair to quote Agate on scenery; but Agate-fanciers must plough through the portentous titles of the compilations of his criticism – *Thus to Revisit, Immoment Toys, Brief Chronicles* – to read him at his best; and since Henry James has cautioned lighters – sorry, lighting designers – here is Agate on scenic artists. In 1923 he went to see Robert Atkins in *Richard III* at the Old Vic:

> The scenery was admirable throughout, by which I mean that it was almost non-existent. A few bits of cardboard covered with brown paper made up a battlement; some bigger bits, aided by good lighting, did for Richard's tent; the whole so imaginatively composed that it never got in the actor's way or stood between us and the play. I doubt whether this mounting cost a five pound note; I am certain that no production has ever given me greater pleasure, though their graces of York and Ely need not have had quite such dirty hands.

'In the course of a theatrical season, the critic's proud spirit is gradually subdued,' Max Beerbohm apologized – though he and Shaw and Tynan show few signs of this wasting disease which certainly attacked Agate. But here is Agate's verdict on Edith Evans's Rosalind – a performance much disputed since she gave it. Fifty-seven years on, he seems wittily and eloquently to sum up the arguments pro and con: 'It may be that for some ten minutes or so what you might call the pictorial aspect of Miss Edith Evans's Rosalind does not quite satisfy. But you soon forget the bubbling seas of Renaissance wit on which this gracious artist launches you, and which she herself rides like some fair frigate out of a Book of Romance. She does it all so buoyantly, carelessly, understandingly and rightly. There is just the proper note of mischief and the exact love-lorn nuance.'

Another Rosalind – Margaret Leighton – takes us directly to Kenneth Tynan, unrivalled among the critics of his generation. Of Miss Leighton he wrote, 'This Rosalind was a gay and giddy creature – loads of fun, game for any jape, rather like a popular head girl – but a tiring companion, I felt, after a long day.' How right, as so often, he was.

One of Tynan's watching briefs on Edith Evans was her Countess in *All's Well*. If Dame Edith was technically too old for Rosalind she could not be too old for this particular role. It was a magical performance described by Tynan as in 'her characteristic later manner – tranquillized benevolence cascading from a great height.' (He spoils it, though, by adding, 'like royalty opening a bazaar' – the phrase misses the inventive wit and sparkle with which Dame Edith could invest a phrase. I would back her to beat any royal on 'I hereby declare this bazaar open'.)

But here is Tynan in more overt criticism of the formidable Sonia Dresdel (in *Doctor Jo*, by Joan Morgan in 1956) in her attempts to convey benevolence and self-sacrifice: 'Her affectionate scenes with a young nephew are especially sinister, it being apparent that, given the smallest textual encouragement, Miss Dresdel could and would bite her little friend's arm off at the elbow. It is to the Eumenides and not the humanities that this intimidating actress should confine herself.'

Tynan's image of Robert Helpmann's 'favourite facial expression' (here exhibited in *Hamlet*) – 'that appalled look out of the corner of his eye, as who should say, "My God, there's an owl on my shoulder" ' – is indelible, and his description of Charles Laughton's unfunny Bottom is similarly accurate: 'He certainly takes the audience into his confidence, but the process seems to exclude from his confidence everyone else in the cast . . . (he) behaves throughout in a manner that has nothing to do with acting, although it perfectly hits off the demeanour of a rapscallion uncle dressed up to entertain the children at a Christmas party.' (Caryl Brahms found a similar avuncular quality in Laughton's Lear in the same unfortunate season: an 'autumnal uncle . . . diminishing himself by a bravely rendered "You should see me dance the polka" on the drawing-room carpet without enough breath to keep his coat tails flying.')

Dame Sybil Thorndike, who was always insisting that she overdid things and needed to be 'cut down' must have sympathized with Tynan's view of her 'Jocasta':

The prima donna tragedienne (an oracular Sybil), with plump arms and a bellowing contralto, given to sudden hawk-like sweeps up and down the stage, she played with that traditional blazing intensity, which, so far from illuminating the personality, strangles it into a sort of red-hot anonymity. She treated every line as if it were the crucial line of the play: it was all so ponderously weighted that when the big hurdles approached, the horse couldn't jump.

Tynan is vivid on Orson Welles's voice: 'bottled thunder, so deeply encasked that one thinks' (prophetically, this was only 1955) 'of those liquor advertisements which boast that not a drop is sold till it's seven years old.' Ian Dallas gave Tynan a marvellous joke with which to decorate a first-night disaster in Welles's production of *Moby Dick*. Olivier's *Hamlet* had just come out labelled as 'the tragedy of a man who could not make up his mind'. Welles wore an extravagant false nose as Ahab and it nearly fell off on the first night. Tynan neatly used Dallas's joke, '*Moby Dick* nearly became the tragedy of a man who could not make up his nose.' But Ken found a wonderful conceit of his own when confronted by *Blitz* and Sean Kenny's sets:

> They swoop down on the actors and snatch them aloft; four motor-driven towers prowl the stage, converging menacingly on any performer who threatens to hog the limelight; and whenever the human element looks like gaining control, they collapse on it in a mass of flaming timber. In short, they let the cast know who is boss. They are magnificent and they are war; who (they tacitly inquire) needs Lionel Bart? I have a fearful premonition of the next show Mr Kenny designs. As soon as the curtain rises, the sets will advance in a phalanx on the audience and summarily expel it from the theatre. After that, the next step is clear: Mr Kenny will invent sets that applaud.

And here is Tynan on *Timon of Athens* at the Old Vic – from his second collection of criticism, *Curtains*:

> The best that can be said of Michael Benthall's production of *Timon of Athens* is that its cuts and transpositions are clever. The rest is aimless improvisation. Leslie Hurry's settings are as coarse as his costumes, a dissonance of sequins, Pepsi-Cola purple, and desiccated mud. And to those who imagined the play to be a study of benevolence warped by ingratitude, Mr Benthall administers a succinct slap: it is, by his curious lights, the story of a scoutmaster betrayed by his troop. To the role of the scoutmaster Sir Ralph Richardson brings his familiar attributes: a vagrant eye, gestures so eccentric that their true significance could be revealed only by extensive trepanning, and a mode of speech that democratically regards all syllables as equal. I select, for instance, Sir Ralph's thanks to the

Amazons for enlivening his feast. 'You have added,' he said distinctly, 'worth, and toot, and lustre.' It took a trip to the text to reveal that 'and toot' meant 'unto't'. Yet there was in his performance, for all its vagueness, a certain energy, and it was a relief to hear Timon's later tirades spoken with irony instead of fury. The stone-throwing scene with Apemantus was the best thing of the night.

Perversely, the wittiest British critic of the 1980s writes about a tinier medium, television. Russell Davies, at his most parochial, has unerringly dissected the BBC:

> The BBC has always given the impression of having a Head for every conceivable commodity it uses or dispenses. Head of Light Entertainment, Head of Gramophones, Head of Paper-clips (South-West Region), the Controller of Radio, for all I know, carries the sub-title Head of Steam. Somewhere in the kitchens, I daresay, the Head of Celery goes crisply about his work.

That last sentence is, perhaps, my favourite of all those quoted in this book. And Davies saw off the BBC television production of *King Lear* just as sharply as Shaw or Tynan would have done in the theatre:

> In fact the longer the drama went on, with Frank Middlemass's chubby old Fool chuntering off, and Penelope Wilton giving Regan curious overtones of Penelope Keith, the more I felt that this is what it would be like if *Lear* was ever put on, in a staggering burst of professionalism, by the Bank of England Repertory Company.

Davies is quite capable of being serious about serious subjects but he brings a fine mock-seriousness to trivia. Two more examples – he does not need to be heavy about Light Entertainment:

> Let us give thanks, for we have passed beyond the grim sentinels that stand at the gate of the winter: The Royal Variety Performance (BBC1) and Miss World 1982 (ITV). There may come a time when broadcasting is so fragmented that we are grateful again for these moss-covered monoliths of the tele-

vision year, looming over November like the Cenotaph; but that time is not yet.

The Variety event is at least conscious of its possible failings. It tried a new theme this year: Old Material. Male singers of dangerously pensionable age made much of the evening rough on the ear, and the high spots were provided by an ersatz Crazy Gang, Jimmy James's son recreating his dad's old act, and Frankie Howerd producing the monologue whose structural parts we all know by heart. Undoubtedly the well-known phrase or saying ought to read 'Familiarity Breathes Content'.

And Davies can coax fresh mileage out of the tired tyres of soap-opera, in this case, by an indulgent but intoxicating orgy of word abuse:

> *Dynasty* is the one about the indescribably rich oil tycoon with a new wife called Krystle. As in krystle shanderlear. Pivot of the programme, she is a well-built girl. There is a certain visual emphasis on Krystle's brystles. Were they to pass you in the street, you would whystle. Facially, Krystle's expression is vacant, lystless, suggesting Krystle has sat on a thystle and can't get off (which is indeed the story of her married life to come). But I suspect she is no softie. Beneath that yielding flesh there is moral fibre – well, grystle. At the moment, she is still finding her way about, learning how to be horrid to the servants, how to distinguish between her gay stepson and nympho step-daughter, how to walk around the set as though she were not modelling a costume, and so on. But the husband is already a well-formed creation, as evil as the Sex Pystles and smooth as Sacha Dystle. This is what people want on a Saturday night, as any American tele-dramatystle tell you. Someone you can hate yourself for loving to love to hate.

More recently Davies laid into *The Winds of War* in general and Robert Mitchum in particular:

> As for Mitchum, the time has come when we must start taking seriously his own estimate of his acting. 'Paint eyeballs on my eyelids and I'll sleepwalk through any picture' he tells us in the *TV Times*. This is about right. Nowadays Mitchum doesn't so much act as point his suit at people.

Already we have seen . . .

Mitchum lugging his great coffin of a body to a Hitler rally, where from a box he has watched Schmistory being made. And we have seen him turn to his companion and say, in tones that should have pierced the very wallets of the TV network executives, 'I can't believe they're buying this tripe'.

But once again Davies can bring wit into the service of praise as well as blame. The same week he watched Angus Wilson's *The Old Men at the Zoo*:

any story that begins with a cancerous giraffe stamping on the genitals of its keeper must surely be marked high for cliché-avoidance.

Davies's only rivals for the title of Wittiest TV Critic were Clive James in the *Observer* (though he has now thrown in the regular sponge), Richard Ingrams in his occasional backwoods grunts in the *Spectator*, and Nancy Banks-Smith in the *Guardian*. First, in this extract, James is reviewing *Love from A to Z* with Charles Aznavour and Liza Minelli:

Liza can't settle for being admired for her artistry. She wants to be loved for herself. Charles, to do him the credit he's got coming as the composer of the odd passable song in the relentlessly up-and-down-the-scale French tradition, is less innocent. In fact he's so worn by experience he's got bags under his head. He knows the importance of at least feigning to find his material more interesting than his own wonderful personality – a key trick for prolonged survival, which Liza will have to learn, or go to the wall. The show was recorded at the Rainbow. It was pretty nearly as bad as anything I have seen in my life, and deepened the mystery of why it is that it is always the BBC, and not ITV, which brings us these orgies of self-promotion by dud stars: package deals which consist of nothing but a wrap-up.

Then Ingrams has a good time stifling yet another chat-show at birth:

The greatly over-rated composer Andrew Lloyd Webber had been invited to host a 'chat show' on BBC2. With open-neck shirt and a wet Cheshire cat grin, Lloyd Webber seemed ill at ease as he had every right to be. I find Mr Lloyd Webber's phenomenal success one of the great mysteries of modern times. I have listened to many of his tunes and never once heard one that I wanted to hear again. On this occasion he sat rather gawkily at the end of a grand piano, being showered with compliments by a group of musicians including the opera singer Placido Domingo: 'You are for me the Puccini of our day'. Webber replied by complimenting the guests on their own very wonderful achievements: 'You are gorgeous,' he told the unappealing American pop star Suzi Quatro, 'there's only one word for it'. The pianist John Lill repeated his astonishing claim that he is in close personal touch with Beethoven who gives him a few tips before performances.

Nancy Banks-Smith probably holds the record for pungency over a long period: recently she was moved to view a long, solemn programme on Extra Sensory Perception:

You won't remember this, Monica, having your own teeth and all but many years ago The Good Lord Grade appointed and ordained that there should be a series called The Champions. In this the three protagonists developed Strange Powers after meeting some old poop standing in his dressing gown in the snow claiming to be a lama. One of them could see further than anyone else, one could hear further than anyone else and Alexandra Bastedo had a bigger bust than anybody else. They went around doing good or making money for The Good Lord Grade which was, of course, the same thing.

I always say life imitates art, don't you Monica? What do we find in Horizon: The Case of ESP (BBC 2) but three protagonists, Pat Price, Hella Hamid and Duane Elgin, with powers of clairvoyance which 'take them to the limit of human ability.' (I quote from the yellowing publicity for The Champions). The resemblance was the more striking as Price, 'A bluff, no-nonsense police commissioner', has died and was played by an actor with electronic background music whenever his guesses got warm.

Under the improbably-named team of Puthoff and Targ they have been working on Scanate, the Stanford Research

Institute's classified project for psychic spying. Price was a sad loss as, according to Hella Hamid, he could read documents inside safes. As they were presumably in Russian one wonders if much was gained from this.

Russia is particularly interested in psychokinesis, the power to move matter (shot of a plaster bust staring astounded at an egg rising from its cup) and may intend to demoralise the west with airborne eggs. Lariss Vilanskaya, who worked on Russian psychic research, described one gripping experiment in which Lamenski in Moscow strangled Nikolai in Leningrad 'Until he was on the edge of an unconscious state.' Americans are worried, unnecessarily one feels, that trained Russian psychics may be able to influence the mind of President Reagan. One trusts that Duane Elgin, the last of the psychic spies, is still making with the mystic powers on behalf of democracy.

Somewhat huffed at scepticism – 'There is no way to deal with people who don't want to know' – Russell Targ peeled off from the programme to found Delphi, which aims to make psychic power profitable by predicting, for instance, the volatile price of silver. This is minimally less repulsive than Morpheus which employs psychic detectives and will, for 5,000 dollars, solve a murder.

Let me advise you, Monica, do not in America buy silver shares from anyone called Gypsy Rose or eat at any restaurant called Moms.

And when the great Australian saga, *The Thorn Birds*, finally hit British television screens in January 1984 it stirred her to even greater flights of fancy. 'Dallas with kangaroos' she called her piece:

'I missed you at evensong' said God. 'Yes, I'm sorry about that. I was watching The Thorn Birds for my work.' 'Who's in it?' said God. 'Funny you should ask that. You have a bit part.' 'Stroll on' said God. 'What was I doing?' 'You were failing to fill Richard Chamberlain.' 'You'd better,' said God after a short pause, 'begin at the beginning.'

'Well. It is a turbulent, epic saga of forbidden love, ambition, desire, wealth, power, passion and adventure that spans half a century and two continents.' 'Oh, one of those.' 'Yes. The hero is Father de Croissant played by Richard Chamberlain.' 'Is he,' asked God, 'handsome, brilliant, ambitious, magnetic and outspoken?' 'How did you know?' 'I'm omniscient,' said God modestly.

'He is lusted after rather a lot.' 'He would be,' said God. 'There is powerful, malicious Barbara Stanwyck, one of the oldest and richest women in Australia, who dresses almost exclusively in d'oyleys, and her indomitable, strong-willed niece, Rachel Ward.' 'Not,' said God, 'the British beauty who is regarded as one of Hollywood's hottest new imports?' 'None other' I said. 'She fills the space that You can't fill. I don't know if You've heard of Heineken? There is also a beauty queen in a purple swim suit who simpers at Father de Mollusc and says "Give me something to confess on Sunday." I don't know who she was.' 'I do,' said God grimly.

'You might,' I mused, 'call it Dallas with kangaroos. There is a poor little chap called Stooey who spends his life being chased by wild boar and billy goats. It seems very hard.' 'Better on balance than being chased by women,' said God. 'He stood a sporting chance.'

'I suppose,' I said uneasily, 'the scene you might take exception to is the one where Father de Cassock strips off on the verandah and Barbara Stanwyck kneads his neck and polishes his pectorals and says he is the most beautiful man she has ever seen.' 'Is he the most beautiful man Barbara Stanwyck has ever seen?' 'Oh come on, she was married to Robert Taylor. She wants Richard Chamberlain to be a cardinal because he would look magnificent in red. He's on the front cover of Radio Times so you can judge for youself.' 'We've not been getting Radio Times lately.' 'Well, I'd say he looks rather eerily embalmed.' 'We are none of us as young as we were' said God reprovingly.

'Frank seems to be in love with his mother and Maggie's in love with Father de Hassock but it's all right really because at moments of uncontrollable passion . . .' 'At the seaside?' suggested God. 'Yes, generally at the seaside, there is always a full orchestra present, plinking and plonking and bowing and blasting and generally keeping an eye on things.'

'Is it,' asked God after a thoughtful pause, 'set in India?' 'No.' 'Well,' he said, 'that's something.'

The Thorn Birds proved addictive for Nancy Banks-Smith. She returned for another deep draught of the drug at the end of the series, brilliantly sustaining the wit throughout the entire passage:

A rare redbreast bird has arrived at Slimbridge which Sir Peter Scott, who doesn't watch a lot of television and is totally out of touch, has identified as the Bulgarian Goose. This was obviously the exceptionally rare and probably insane Thorn Bird which, according to Richard Chamberlain, impales its breast on a thorn and dies singing while the whole world stills to listen and God in his heaven smiles.

Why God in his heaven smiles is a matter for conjecture unless He has already seen the script, but it is a fact that the whole world stills (or as we would say stops) to listen to The Thorn Birds (BBC1). At 9.10 last night you could have felt the earth give a sudden lurch to the left as everybody got up and walked to the kitchen to put the kettle on.

After the penultimate episode the Central Electricity Generating Board reported an increase of 2,200 megawatts more than after the royal wedding. Evidently the Archbishop of Canterbury should have had a more starring role, worn a sensitive look and, possibly, jodphurs like Cardinal de Bricassart. The last episode of this turbulent saga of love, ambition and desire (Radio Times) was – you must bear with me while I compose myself – extremely emotional.

Richard Chamberlain has been pipped at the post as Pope having failed, I assume, the mental arithmetic. Due to an inability to count to nine on his fingers, he does not realize that he is the father of Meggie's son, Dane. Dane, a striking instance of heredity, is, like his father, a priest and much pursued by women ('Cute.' 'I wonder how we can meet him?') As he is a good chap but only a so-so swimmer, the last we see of him is a pair of soles disappearing under the sea.

Well, I can't begin to tell you. It is as though the torrid heat of the story had set off a sprinkler system. Meggie, all set and cold like a blancmange, says 'Dane was your son!' And Richard Chamberlain breaks down. Meggie's mum, who has worn a series of depressing hats with great stoicism for half a century, finally breaks down too and so does Meggie and her daughter Justine. 'Meggie, it's not too late!' 'Oh Mom, oh Jussie, I've made you pay so dearly!' 'Oh Mom, I did love Dane!' 'Oh Jussie, I do love you.' Justine is a great tragic actress who has played Phaedre to a rather cool critical reception, but Richard Chamberlain is the star so he gets to sob the most.

Meanwhile back at the ranch, Richard Chamberlain who has just returned from burying Dane, dies himself among a tremendous upsurge of roses and the theme song from the series and sheep-buying in the background and Justine taking off in an aeroplane, flying fearless into the future and another lot of dreadful notices for her Cordelia. In the circumstances it was hardly worth Richard Chamberlain coming back from the cemetery at all. Just made a lot more work for everybody.

Emmys have been scattered on The Thorn Birds like bird-seed but, in my opinion, nothing like enough. I would like to present my own award the Bulgarian Goose:

To Barbara Stanwyck's agent, who kept her name up there in the credits 50 years after she was supposed to die. A striking proof of life after death.

To Judy, the maid at the Ranch, who when Drogheda was ringed with bushfires was abruptly ordered to 'Make stew for a hundred.'

To the dialogue coach who worked so selflessly on the cast that they seemed to get more Irish as time went on, as if they were practising. Though their insistence on calling the Ranch Drawheeda would purse the lips of Irish purists, the ideal being a more throat clearing sort of sound.

To Father Terence Sweeny, the religious consultant to the series, for spiritual guidance. The Catholic Information Service keeping, unlike God, a perfectly straight face said it was delighted at the sudden interest in the priesthood.

To the Central Electricity Generating Board without which none of this would have been possible.

The appeal of some Far Eastern 'entertainment' in the shape of the television treatment of another novel, *The Far Pavilions*, shown at virtually the same time as *The Thorn Birds*, was just as beckoning to Nancy Banks-Smith:

The first essential of a burra-sahib in The Far Pavilions is to have a double-barrelled name. This makes the introductions almost as long as the processions. 'Ashton Hilary Pelham-Martyn,' says our hero. 'Walter Richard Pollock-Hamilton,' replies the man who is to become his great chum. 'I shall call you,' says our hero and not, as it proved, without reason, 'Wally.'

This is where George Garthorne, another chum, fell so tragically short. He was the only chap in India without a hyphen. Overwhelmed by this, he shoots himself. With, inadequate to the end, a single-barrelled gun.

A crew of 111, including a government censor and not counting the man who bought the buns for the elephants, laboured more than four months and spent £6 million, give or take a bun, making this. If in doubt the director organises a procession, and the love scenes, with Ben Cross and Amy Irving revolving like chickens on a spit, are of course in slow motion.

The pace is funereal – in fact the last episode is a funeral – whereas all you can do with this sort of stuff is play it fast. It is like sawing a lady in half. If you do it slowly the agony is frightful.

When, as an actor or director or writer, you're on the receiving end, I suppose it's not surprising that there is an irresistible urge to answer back. Very occasionally the artist will give as good as he gets. Take John Osborne replying to Michael Billington in the *Guardian*. Whether it's wit or invective, it's not dull:

Sir,

Michael Billington cannot have read the plays of George Bernard Shaw since his Oxford days. To call him 'the greatest British dramatist since Shakespeare' is close to having a critical brainstorm, as well as perpetuating an exam-crazy classroom myth. Having recently seen *Saint Joan* in London and *Caesar and Cleopatra* in Sydney, it is clearer to me than ever that Shaw is the most fraudulent, inept writer of Victorian melodramas ever to gull a timid critic or fool a dull public. He writes like a Pakistani who had learned English when he was twelve years old in order to become a chartered accountant . . . But 'the greatest British dramatist since Shakespeare'? Ben Travers could have had GBS before breakfast in Australia watching the Test.

By the time I was 25 I had been in (admittedly bad, but no matter) productions of: *Arms and the Man, Candida, You Never Can Tell, Devil's Disciple, Caesar and Cleopatra, Saint Joan, Major Barbara* and, perhaps worst of all, Chekhov-for-philistines, *Heartbreak House.*

Try learning them, Mr Billington; they are posturing wind and rubbish. In fact, just the sort of play you would expect a critic to write. The difference is simply: he did it.

> Yours faithfully,
> John Osborne

On to Hollywood now. It is a contradiction easily understood, that a temple of the philistines produced a bible of wit. Or one can see it as a pressure cooker in which so many writers, bought expensively from the delicatessen of the Algonquin and shipped from the supermarket of Broadway, blew their tops in the vocabulary which spiced their work. Hollywood has survived a barrage of criticism and learnt little from it:

'Behind the phoney tinsel of Hollywood lies the real tinsel.' – Oscar Levant.

'Hollywood: They knew only one word of more than one syllable there, and that is "fillum".' – Louis Sherwin.

'A place where the inmates are in charge of the asylum' – ascribed to Laurence Stallings.

'She says that she has been so long among the false fronts and *papier-mâché* mansions on the set that nowadays she finds herself sneaking a look at her husband to see if he goes all the way round or is just a profile' – P.G. Wodehouse quoting an actress who had returned to Broadway after a year in Hollywood.

'All Americans born between 1890 and 1945 wanted to be movie stars.' – Gore Vidal.

'Hollywood is a sewer – with service from the Ritz Carlton.' – Wilson Mizner.

'The only place you can wake up in the morning and hear the birds coughing in the trees.' – Joe Frisco.

'The most beautiful slave-quarters in the world.' – Moss Hart.

'The biggest train set a boy ever had.' – Orson Welles.

'Bounded on the north, south, east and west by agents.' – William Fadiman.

The screenwriter, Nunnally Johnson, was concerned (well, not *very* concerned) about the image of Hollywood: 'Hollywood is every public man's pigeon. There is no editorial writer so dull that he can't straighten out the movies at least three or four times a year. There is no preacher who can't get at least three rousing sermons annually out of Hollywood. There is not even a congressman so benighted that he can't speak with confidence on what ought to be done about that business out there.' Harry Kurnitz, another witty scriptwriter, lunched at the new American drugstore in Paris and described it as 'lunch Hollywood-style – a hot dog and vintage wine'. He liked large cars, preferably Rolls Royces. One Paris visit was nearly scuppered when his large car broke down. When he eventually arrived in Paris, Kurnitz was asked what he thought of the Volkswagen which had rescued him. 'I've been in bigger women', he snapped.

The classic movie statements will fall on many ears like old confidences:

The unidentified wit who celebrated Louis B. Mayer's promotion of his daughter's husband (David O. Selznick) with 'The Son-in-Law also Rises'.

Warren Beatty's 'Movies are fun, but they're not a cure for cancer.'

Ogden Nash's couplet,
> Uncle Carl Laemmle
> Had a very large family.

George Bernard Shaw's, 'The trouble with you, Mr Goldwyn, is that you are only interested in art – and I am only interested in money.'

(A moratorium on more Goldwynisms – oh well, then, just one: A Goldwyn set-up for a Thurber pay-off. Goldwyn screened *The Secret Life of Walter Mitty* for the author of its source. After a few comments by Thurber, Goldwyn apologized. 'I'm sorry you thought it was too blood and thirsty.' 'Not only did I think so,' said Thurber, 'I was horr and struck.')

Bud Schulberg, on Louis B. Mayer – 'Csar of all the rushes.'

Arthur Caesar on Darryl Zanuck – 'From Poland to polo in one generation.

William Faulkner to Irving Thalberg – 'Ah don't believe ah know which pictures are yours. Do you make the Mickey Mouse brand?'

From the Columbia boss, Harry Cohn – 'If my fanny squirms, it's bad. If my fanny doesn't squirm, it's good. It's as simple as that.' (Herman Mankiewicz on the fanny test – 'I didn't know the whole world was wired to Harry Cohn's ass.')

Billy Wilder on Spyros Skouras, Head of Fox Studios – 'The only Greek Tragedy I know.'

Harry Kurnitz on Billy Wilder – 'Let's face it, Billy Wilder at work is two people – Mr Hyde and Mr Hyde.'

'Scratch an actor and you'll find an actress' – Dorothy Parker.

'Actors are cattle' – or, he later insisted, 'Actors should be *treated* like cattle' – Alfred Hitchcock.

'I started at the top and worked down' – Orson Welles.

'There but for the grace of God, goes God' – Herman Mankiewicz on Orson Welles (echoing Churchill on Sir Stafford Cripps).

Wilson Mizner – ushered in to Jack Warner's office on commencing an engagement to write scripts, dropped an L.A. telephone book on the boss's desk – 'This might have been good for a picture,' he said, 'but there are too many characters in it!'

'When you steal from one author,' Mizner said on another occasion, 'it's plagiarism: if you steal from a lot it's research.'

Joe Pasternak on former bathing beauty Esther Williams – 'Wet, she was a star – dry she ain't.'

Jack L. Warner on hearing that Ronald Reagan was seeking the nomination for Governor of California – 'No, No! Jimmy Stewart for Governor – Reagan for Best Friend.'

Before moving on to the acknowledged Hollywood wits – or at least those who were witty and had a nodding acquaintance with, or hatred of, Hollywood – let me sprinkle some Hollywood quips which may or may not have come from the minds of those whose lips we are told spoke them. Script, life, observation or interpretation? For instance, did Anne Baxter say of anyone, 'I knew her when she didn't know where her next husband was coming from?' Did Mary Tyler Moore say, 'Diets are for those who are thick and tired of it'? Or Marlon Brando, 'An actor's a guy who, if you ain't talking about him ain't listening'? Or Jack Carson, 'A fan club is a group of people who tell an actor he's not alone in the way he feels about himself'? Was it Jerry Lewis or his writers who invented 'When I was a kid I said to my father one afternoon, "Daddy, will you take me to the zoo?" He answered, "If the zoo wants you let them come and get you".'? Did Bob Hope really conceive, 'Middle age is when your age starts to show around your middle', and 'My old movies have been on so many channels lately, I can flip the dial and watch the hair line recede'?

Dorothy Parker, however, *is* genuine. As so often, she has the last word on tinsel-town. She could see its advantages in the thirties: 'It's alright. You make a little money and get caught up on your debts. We're up to 1912 now.' She also celebrated it in verse:

> Oh, come my love and join with me
>   The oldest infant industry
> Come seek the bourne of palm and pearl
>   The lovely land of boy-meets-girl.
> Come grace this lotus laden shore,
>   The isle of Do-What's-Done-Before.
> Come curb the new and watch the old win,
> Out where the streets are paved with Goldwyn.

'Hollywood money isn't money,' she said. 'It's congealed snow. Melts in your hand, and there you are.' On a writer whom she considered overvalued she remarked, 'He's a writer for the ages – for the ages of four to eight.' One Hollywood night her tiresome escort muttered of another guest, 'I can't bear fools.' 'That's queer,' said Ms Parker, 'your mother could.' Another time, fighting back, she exploded, 'Whenever I meet one of those Brit-ishers I feel as if I have a papoose on my back.'

Parker's witty dismissals were not always prepared and liberally basted with midnight oil – as the wire to Robert Sherwood's wife, congratulating her on the arrival of a much worried-over baby, might have been: 'Dear Mary, we all knew you had it in you.' Judging by the available evidence, her favourite straight person was Clare Boothe Luce, who once stood back for her saying, 'Age before beauty', to be countered by, 'Pearls before swine.' Later, when Ms Parker was told that Miss Luce was always kind to her inferiors, she inquired innocently, 'Where does she find them?'

She attempted to conceal a beguiling vulnerability when she married Alan Campbell: 'People who haven't talked to each other in years are on speaking terms again today – including the bride and groom.' To a fellow-suffering wife, her advice was – 'Don't worry, if you keep him long enough he'll come back in style.' She was more sharp than she was reassuring, but so are most wits: 'That woman speaks eighteen languages and can't say No in any of them.'

I treasure her put-down to an American actor who had come back from London and lost some of those hard American consonants – like 'skedule' for schedule' – and other betraying mannerisms. She must, I think, have been head-first into her cups when she said to him, 'If you don't mind my saying so, I think you're full of skit.'

She saw off Basil Rathbone as, 'Two profiles pasted together', and a political witch-hunt with, 'The only "ism" Hollywood be-lieves in is plagiarism.' A bar-room bore who pushed the pro-McCarthy line she despatched by saying to him, 'With the crown of thorns I wear, why should I be bothered by a prick like you?'

More universally: 'And I'll say of Verlaine too: he was always chasing Rimbauds.' And more nonsensically, 'There I was trapped. Trapped like a trap in a trap.' 'Scratch a lover, find a foe' has the ring of truth of yesteryear; but, 'If all those sweet young things present were laid end to end, I wouldn't be at all surprised,' is eternal as well as beautifully constructed with the sting and the twist in exactly the right place. She was perhaps too keen on the double-entendre that 'lay' offers up. When she was looking for a new apartment the old recipe served: 'All I need is room enough to lay a hat and a few friends.' She inspired one of Tallulah Bankhead's confessionals by asking her to a particularly wild party: 'The more I behave like Whistler's Mother the night before, the more I look like her the morning after.' She called Miss Bankhead 'Whistler's Mother' ever afterwards.

In another famous phrase, she commented on a party, 'Enjoyed it! One more drink and I'd have been under the host.' More soberly, she could generalize on successful American writers: 'It is our national joy to mistake for the first rate, the fecund rate.' To the assembled American Horticultural Society she announced, 'You can lead a whore to culture but you can't make her think' – a remark originally coined as an Algonquin competition. She wrote her own epitaph: 'Excuse my dust. This is on me.'

Robert Benchley, whom we have already seen in his role as drama critic, was another New York transplant to Hollywood who never quite 'took', unless it was the mickey. Asked why he never sunned himself in the great Californian outdoors, he said, 'What? And get hit by a meteor?' 'Would you get us a taxi?' he once asked a uniformed man outside the Brown Derby restaurant. Indignantly the man protested that he was a Rear Admiral in the United States Navy. 'Alright,' said Benchley, 'get us a battleship.'

Of his own work he was deprecatory. 'It took me fifteen years to discover that I had no talent for writing, but I couldn't give it up because by that time I was too famous'; and, 'He hasn't got much to say, but at least he doesn't try to say anything else.' Of his sedentary writing habits he remarked, 'I do most of my work sitting down. That's where I shine.'

On amateur jokesters: 'In Milwaukee last month a man died laughing over one of his own jokes. That's what makes it so tough for us outsiders. We have to fight home competition.' And, when he shared a spectacularly small office with Dorothy Parker, he dismissed it saying, 'One cubic foot less of space and it would have constituted adultery.' 'Tell us your phobias,' he once comforted a drunken friend, 'and we will tell you what you are afraid of.' And once, in desperation, he suggested, 'Let's get out of these wet clothes and into a dry martini' (a remark often attributed to Alexander Woollcott).

Two Mankiewiczs embellish the Hollywood legend: Joseph, particularly, in his screenplays, his brother Herman in scripts and in conversation crammed with effrontery. Joseph L. Mankiewicz reported an exchange one night at the Brown Derby when Rufus Le Maire, an executive for Paramount, came past the table he was sharing with Wilson Mizner. Le Maire had arrived from a premiere and was decked out in an Inverness cape. Taking in the spectacle, Mizner whispered to Mankiewicz, 'That, my boy, sets the Jews back six hundred years.' Brother Herman was faced with a query about mythical beasts at a Screenwriters' Guild Meeting in Hollywood – low-paid, 75 dollar-a-week writers. 'Tell me,' said his questioner, 'do you know any 75 dollar-a-week writers?' 'Yes,' said Mankiewicz, 'I know lots of them, but they're all making 1500 dollars a week.'

Herman is perhaps the most endearing, would-be defeated, Hollywood-transplanted wit. He counselled a friend about one movie which he himself probably wrote. 'Do you have any idea how bad that picture is? I'll tell you. Stay away from the neighbourhood where it's playing – don't even go near that street! It might rain – you could get caught in the downpour, and to keep dry you'd have to go inside the theatre.' He blows up a similar balloon of whimsy only to puncture it in this valentine: 'Barbara Stanwyck is my favourite. My God, I could just sit and dream of being married to her, having a little cottage out in the hills, vines around the door. I'd come home from the office, tired, weary, and I'd be met by Barbara, walking through the door holding an apple pie that she had cooked herself – and wearing no drawers.'

One of his best lines is disputed (aficionados claim it for Howard Dietz at a dinner in New York). Herman Mankiewicz is reported to have said it at a dinner given by Arthur Hornblow Jnr in Hollywood. For the story it is important only that the host had social pretensions and that the society was naive. The wit (whichever) was sick at this chic dinner party. 'Don't worry,' Mankiewicz said to his host, 'the white wine came up with the fish!'

Alexander Woollcott, too, had a love-hate relationship with Hollywood. When offered 1000 dollars a week to write for films he said, 'When I take up streetwalking, the street will be Broadway, not

Hollywood Boulevard!' Woollcott's friends were ready to sharpen their tongues on his pudgy, pushy person. Edna Ferber called him a 'New Jersey Nero who mistakes his pinafore for a toga.' The editor of the *New Yorker* called him 'a fat duchess with the emotions of a fish.' (Woollcott countered by saying, 'I think your slogan, "Liberty or Death" is splendid and whichever one you decide on will be all right with me.') Heywood Broun called him 'The Smartest of Alecs' and George S. Kaufman said he was 'improbable'. Woollcott himself called Dorothy Parker 'a mixture of Little Nell and Lady Macbeth'. And, to a barely recognized friend at a college reunion, he managed, 'I can't remember your name, but don't tell me.' On the George S. Kaufmans' fifth wedding anniversary he sent them a telegram: I HAVE BEEN LOOKING AROUND FOR AN APPRO-PRIATE WOODEN GIFT AND AM PLEASED HEREBY TO PRESENT YOU WITH ELSIE FERGUSON'S PERFORMANCE IN HER PLAY. He too wrote his own epitaph: 'I shall probably talk myself to death: those who live by the word shall perish by the word.'

Among Hollywood performers, let us go for Groucho Marx, though as with all actors the line between creation and interpret-ation is blurred. The more potent the interpreter the more beholden the writer of the crack. It is easier to parody a personality than create a character. We can surely allow Groucho, on taking off Greta Garbo's hat to check to whom he was talking: 'Excuse me, I just thought you were a fellow I once knew in Pittsburg.' Of his brother, Chico, he said, 'There were three things that Chico was always on – a phone, a horse or a broad.' His 'I don't care to belong to any club that will accept me as a member' will be stolen and played with forever. Towards the end, with less risk of plagiarism, he could say, 'I've been around so long I knew Doris Day before she was a virgin.' Of another woman, perhaps less pleasing, he said, 'I never forget a face, but I'll make an exception in your case.' After one performance he said, 'I didn't like the play, but then I saw it under adverse conditions – the curtain was up.' In a moment, perhaps, of doubt, or at least self-deprecation, he said, 'My mother loved children – she'd have given anything if I'd been one.' Asked if his real name was Groucho, he replied, 'No, I'm breaking it in for a friend.' To a priest who thanked him for all the pleasure he'd given the world, he replied, ungraciously, 'And I want to thank you for all the enjoyment you've taken out of the world.'

When we cross the blurred line from life to movie scripts, Groucho's manner is the same: 'I don't have a photograph, but you can have my footprints. They're upstairs in my socks'; 'In my day a college widow stood for something – she stood for plenty'; 'Do you think I could buy back my introduction to you?' And, perhaps to complement the chapter heading in his autobiography which reads 'Come back next Thursday with a specimen of your money', there is the line from *Monkey Business* – 'I've worked myself up from nothing to a state of extreme poverty.' (Recently there are Dick Vosburgh's superb pastiche lines on the Marx brothers in his *A Night in the Ukraine* – and one I cherish which he wrote for a TV special: Man: 'Can I have a table near the floor?' Groucho: 'Certainly, I'll have the waiter saw the legs off.' Or, even more evocatively, 'Since days of yore – and any day of yore is a day of my.')

W.C. Fields was another whose life and screen persona were blended into an astringent, comic cocktail which had an acquired but endearing taste. 'I must have a drink for breakfast.' 'I exercise strong self-control. I never drink anything stronger than gin before breakfast.' 'What contemptible scoundrel stole the cork out of my lunch?' and 'I got Mark Hellinger so drunk last night that it took three bell boys to put me to bed.' He could also be pressed into giving advice. 'If at first you don't succeed, try, try again. Then quit. No use being a damn fool about it.'

Where Fields was only an occasional Algonquin visitor, playwright and journalist George S. Kaufman was one of its leading lights. The phrase Kaufman used in order to indicate that he was about to 'beat, pummel, satirize and laugh (something) off the face of the earth' was, 'Pay a little respect to . . .' – wonderfully oblique. A ribbon salesman and budding journalist when he was eighteen, Kaufman launched into a theatrical career and sent the first of the telegrams for which, among other things, he was to become famous – this one, in the middle of a disastrous week with a stock company in Troy, New York, was to his father. It read, LAST SUPPER AND ORIGINAL CAST WOULDN'T DRAW IN THIS HOUSE. Soon he was tempted into print by the President of the United States: 'Mr Wilson's mind, as has been the custom, will be closed all day Sunday.' Of the US Senate he wrote: 'Office hours are from 12 to 1 with an hour off for lunch.' Earlier, as a kid, his mother had told him his aunt was coming to visit. 'It wouldn't hurt us to be nice, would it?' she asked. 'That,' he said precociously, 'depends on your threshold of pain.' As drama editor of the *New York Times*, his pen was lethal: 'There was laughter in the back of the theatre,' he once wrote, 'leading to the belief that someone was telling jokes back there.'

As a member of the Algonquin Round Table, Kaufman often sat quietest for longest and then spoke shortest to greatest effect. In the Depression he professed sympathy for his friend, Harold Vanderbilt: 'Poor Harold, he can live on his income alright, but he can no longer live on the income from his income.' When he announced his intention of killing himself at eighty, a shocked table asked how: 'With kindness', he countered.

Confronted once by the producer, Jed Harris, who had the disarming habit of occasionally working in the nude, he conducted the interview without comment until he left the room, when he turned and said, 'Jed, your fly is open.' To convince a collaborator, Marc Connelly, that a funny line would not work in the context they had set it, he allowed the line to be delivered to silence three or four times and then said to him, 'There's only one thing we can do, Marc, we've got to call the audience tomorrow morning for a ten o'clock rehearsal.' When he wrote for the Marx Brothers, he was irritated by their ad-libbing. Watching them one day, he asked his guest to excuse him and walked nearer the stage. When he came back, he explained, 'I thought I heard one of the original lines of the show.'

To a playwright who was afraid to tell his cast of the cuts he had made in a show, he advised, 'Tell them the author giveth and the author taketh away.' He shared a flop with Woollcott and referred to 'mixed notices – they were good and rotten'. But he also knew the potency of an acknowledged hit comedy: 'The audience comes in after the first few weeks and laughs at the programme.' With *Of Thee I Sing* he won the first Pulitzer Prize for a musical. He shared it with the lyric writer, Ira Gershwin, and his collaborator, Morrie Ryskind – scandalously, George Gershwin, the composer, was denied the honour. The $1,000 prize was divided $333.33 Ira Gershwin, $333.33 Ryskind, $333.34 Kaufman. 'I got the extra penny,' said Kaufman, 'because I was the eldest.'

Wit had started as a defence mechanism for Kaufman. As he had to earn a living it became his way to pre-eminence in his profession.

Like many another wit, any stray joke going the rounds claimed him as its father. When the late, and now notorious, Alfred Bloomingdale, then the department store heir, was backing a flop musical, Kaufman is reputed to have said, 'If I were you, I'd close the show and keep the store open nights' (though Kaufman's biographer tracks down the source of this quip as the writer-producer Cy Howard).

A pun which has earned a new lease of life, with the advent of 'punk' as a new word, is his little parable, 'A man had two daughters, Lizzie and Tillie, and Lizzie is alright, but you have no idea how punctilious.' Asked to read a book which he got in manuscript form he was shocked by the spelling. He wrote to the author, 'I'm not very good at it myself, but the first rule about spelling used to be that there is only one Z in is.' To a dinner invitation which arrived only at 8.30 pm, phrased, 'What are you doing for dinner tonight?' he answered, 'Digesting it'. He listened patiently to Ruth Gordon describing an avant-garde part she was rehearsing. 'There's no scenery at all. In the first scene, I'm on the left side of the stage and the audience has to imagine I'm in a crowded restaurant. In Scene two, I run over to the right side of the stage and the audience has to imagine I'm home in my own drawing room.' 'And the second night,' he said, 'you'll have to imagine there's an audience out front.'

When he was spotted in the lobby of a theatre where *Strike Up The Band* was playing before its Broadway opening, a backer mistook him for the composer. 'Mr Gershwin,' he yelled, 'how could you let a thing like this happen?' 'My score is perfect,' he countered, 'the whole trouble is with Kaufman's book.' He out-boasted a millionaire who professed to be 'born into this world without a single penny'. 'When I was born I owed twelve dollars', said Kaufman. His verdict on his hypochondria was practical: 'The kind of doctor I want is one who, when he's not examining me, is home studying medicine.' When Leonora Corbett referred to a wretched performance she had just given in a Broadway play as *fantastic*, he said to his co-author, Nunnally Johnson, 'You've heard of people living in a fool's paradise? Well, Leonora has a duplex there.' After a disastrous preview in Philadelphia, he went to supper at 3.00 am. 'I want something,' he told the waiter, 'that will keep me awake thinking it was the food I ate and not the show I saw.'

Moss Hart, one of his great collaborators, was also one of the targets with whom he dealt more affectionately. He delighted to watch Hart, a younger achiever, revel in spending money. When it was on an elaborate landscape estate in Bucks County, the compliment had its twist: 'This is what God could have done if He'd had the money.' Later he said, 'I like to be near you, Moss. It comes under the heading of gelt by association.' He advised another friend to turn down a purchase. 'Pay no attention to this. Moss can take you to Cartier's and get you the same thing for three times the money.' Hart pondered a commission to write the screenplay of Laura Z. Hobson's novel, *Gentleman's Agreement*. He asked Kaufman if he liked the book: 'I don't have to pay three dollars fifty to find out what it feels like to be a Jew.'

His habit of waiting in patient silence while minting his comment was given ample scope when he became a director. Directing Jane Cowl, an American actress, who also sat and wrote, he returned late in the run to find that she had been embellishing her role. Another telegram was sent: DEAR MISS COWL. YOUR PERFORMANCE IS BETTER THAN EVER. DELIGHTED I CANNOT SAY AS MUCH FOR YOUR LINES. To a pushy actress who unwisely inquired in rehearsal, 'How can I do this with all these interruptions?' he replied, 'Don't you know what those interruptions are? Other actors reading their lines.' A stage-doorkeeper once failed to recognize him and barred his way. Kaufman insisted, so he asked, 'I beg your pardon, sir, are you with the show?' 'Let's put it this way,' said Kaufman, 'I'm not against it.' A box-office manager in Boston gave him bad news: the advance was about eighty dollars. Boston was heavy in a heatwave. Wearily, Kaufman replied, 'Kid, I've been in this business thirty years and this is the first time the temperature has been higher than the advance.'

The Kaufman stories are legion – even without those which celebrate his sexual prowess – so I must stop, albeit on a sad note. David Merrick, the Broadway producer, had always wanted to do a show with him. Finally he had his chance – Peter Ustinov's *Romanov and Juliet*. The tour was bedevilled by a search for an adequate replacement for the juvenile lead. Kaufman, by now too old and too tired to help with the writing or directing he had been engaged to mastermind, made a last stand putting in, in the words of his biographer, Howard Teichman, 'a fervent impassioned plea to stop ruining the morale of the company by changing actresses nightly . . . he still knew right from catastrophe.' Merrick, though he saw that his idol's contribution was minimal, refused to replace Kaufman. 'I would rather have a flop than fire George Kaufman at this stage of his life and career.' Ustinov, to his credit, agreed, and the play ran a year.

3

MUSIC

'Heard melodies are sweet: but those unheard are sweeter'
– John Keats

Music holds so many mysteries for the uninitiated that it fosters the pretentious and overheats the philistine. Both pontificate. But war is carried on not only between the musical and the unmusical; there is civil war inside the art itself. Musical invective, some of it witty, some of it repetitious, is a weapon used by one generation on the next, by the classical musician against the jazz man, by the jazz man against the popular music fanatic, by him against the rock'n'roller, then by the rock'n'roller against punk music, and so on. Meanwhile, conductors mock singers, composers lash conductors and the dignity of one instrument is dismissed in favour of the claims of another. Critics and practitioners snipe across the boundaries of their traditional battlefields.

My most concentrated course in the subject came when, at Arthur Lowe's prompting, Caryl Brahms and I wrote a play about Sir Thomas Beecham – the Disraeli, Wilde, Shaw or Mencken of music, so often and so widely is he quoted – in whose mouth innumerable neat quips have been placed by retellers anxious to clothe a suspect sentiment with more authority and the promise of laughter. As we talked to Sir Thomas's old colleagues and adversaries, the same quips were lovingly dusted down, and as the show went into rehearsal more were offered by post and telephone. I had first made the acquaintance of Sir Thomas as a result of reading Neville Cardus's *Memoir* (1961) in which, early on, he tackled the apocryphal aspect of Beecham's wit:

> Several stories about Sir Thomas, though not true in fact, are true in character. One or two (at least) I invented and put into circulation myself. . . . Long after his seventieth birthday . . . he accused me of making up, and foisting on him, a question supposedly put by him to a singer in his opera company. . . . He asked Sir Thomas for advice – 'About my son, he'll be

leaving Oxford next year. I've spent a lot of money on him and he doesn't know what sort of a job to take up.' Beecham stroked his chin.

'Aren't you going to make a singer of him?'

'Oh no, Sir Thomas.'

'But, why?'

'Well, he hasn't got a voice, not really.'

'Ah,' said Sir Thomas in dulcet tones, 'Ah, I see – a family failing'.

That joins the brood of 'offspring' foisted on Beecham like 'Try anything once except incest and folk-dancing', traced to Sir Arnold Bax's *Farewell my Youth* published in 1943. It is probably also only a matter of time before Beecham is awarded W.S. Gilbert's reply to a musically illiterate woman who asked if Bach was still composing – 'No, madam, decomposing', came the answer.

Then Neville Cardus supplied an elegant and witty commentary on the conductor so that Beecham's chestnuts slid easily onto the page. For example, they met for the first time at the Salzburg Festival in 1931:

> ... His blue eyes took in at one swift scrutiny a whole scene in the Europa foyer ... and at once he picked me out of the human traffic. He took me by the shoulder leading me to an elegant cocktail bar. When he asked me to choose an aperitif, I suggested sherry. To tell the truth I was not at this time in my career greatly experienced in cocktails or wine, or in hotels called Europa and the like. 'No, my dear fellow, not sherry,' said Sir Thomas, 'very liverish, sherry – for a musical critic. Try a White Lady.'

Cardus went on to analyse Beecham's humour:

> He was a comedian. Or, as this is a term which the English associate with red-nosed buffoonery, I had better describe him as an artist in comedy. But he was not a wit in the epigrammatic way of Oscar Wilde – with whose sayings Beecham's are often compared. Sir Thomas indulged not so much in wit as in waggery. He was not 18th century of manner in the least. He belonged entirely to the 19th century when wit became broadened with nature into waggery, and when the aristocrat became more closely related to an English bourgeois geniality.

Beecham's background was a Lancastrian family 'enriched by the manufacture of pills', and one of his early excursions into studied humour was a commission from his father to produce a version of a Christmas carol which would promote the family product. Young Thomas came up with,

> Hark! the herald angels sing!
> Beecham's pills are just the thing.
> Two for a woman, one for a child . . .
> Peace on earth and mercy mild!

'These sentiments', he explained later, 'especially the ellipsis, seemed to me admirably to express the rapture which is occasioned by a good, effortless release.'

To a musical ignoramus like me, Beecham was a spirited introduction to the literature of music. Music itself is so elusive a target that it plays hell with the easy formulae of definitions. 'Music', said Dr Johnson to Boswell on their way round the Hebrides, 'is a method of employing the mind without the labour of thinking at all' – which makes it much the same as washing up. 'A musicologist', Beecham liked to say, 'is a person who can read music but can't hear it.' When it is pinned down to practitioners, however – conductors, orchestras, sopranos, instrumentalists are all targets that have been sighted and assailed – music is invariably a battle between artist and philistine. 'Good music isn't nearly as bad as it sounds', said Harry Selzer. Oscar Wilde argued for the defence (he will be heard for the other side later): 'Music is the condition to which all other arts are constantly aspiring', he told a New York audience in 1882. He at least had Confucius on his side – 'Music produces a kind of pleasure which human nature cannot do without.' (The Eastern connection reminds me of Donald Wolfit vetoing the choice of an actress for a musical play – 'Not a happy idea', he said, 'she has a curious, oriental disposition to sing in the minor key.' The business of putting the persuasive case *for* music was done as lightly, romantically, personally and wittily by Duke Ellington as by anyone:

> I am almost a hermit, but there is a difference, for I have a mistress. Lovers have come and gone but my mistress stays. She is beautiful and gentle. She waits on me hand and foot. She is a swinger. She has grace. To hear her speak you don't believe your ears. She is ten thousand years old. She is as modern as

tomorrow. A brand-new woman every day . . . Living with her is a labyrinth of ramifications. I look forward to her every gesture. Music is my mistress and she plays second fiddle to no one.

George Herbert said the only sound thing *against* music: 'Music helps not the toothache.' Others have gone to greater lengths but said less. Baudelaire, for instance, struck a glancing blow at Wagner: 'I love Wagner, but the music I prefer is that of a cat hung up by its tail outside a window and trying to stick to the panes of glass with its claws.' The good news–bad news formula was coined in a musical context at least as long ago as 1732 by Samuel Fuller in *Guoncologia* – 'Give the piper a penny to play and two pence to leave.' Perhaps that's not as damning as Jimmy Durante's comment: 'I hate music', he said, 'especially when it's played'; nor is it as cogently philistine as Charles Lamb's repeated assaults, in the early nineteenth century, first in a letter to Mrs William Hazlitt –

> Some cry up Haydn, some Mozart –
> Just as the whim bites, for my part
> I care not a farthing candle
> For either of them, or for Handel . . .

– and then in his essay 'Chapter on Ears': 'A carpenter's hammer, in a warm summer noon, will fret me into more than midsummer madness. But those unconnected, unset sounds are nothing to the measured malice of music.'

Beecham's contempt was directed towards the inferior, the unadventurous, the pretentious and the foreign: 'Why do we in England engage at our concerts so many third-rate continental conductors when we have so many second-rate ones of our own?' He knew his own worth of course: 'I am not the greatest conductor in this country. On the other hand, I'm better than any damned foreigner.' As far as English music was concerned, Beecham was determined to make it better: 'British music is in a state of perpetual promise. It might almost be said to be one long promissory note.' He knew his public, too: 'The English may not like music, but they absolutely love the noise it makes.' He had two golden rules for an orchestra: 'Start together and finish together. The public doesn't give a damn what goes on in between.' Max Beerbohm chases the same hare in *Zuleika Dobson*: 'I don't', Zuleika says, 'know anything about music, really. But I know what I like.'

Sometimes the philistine is a sensitive, self-deprecating musician: 'Mine was the kind of piece', said Oscar Levant, 'in which nobody knew what was going on, including the composer, the conductor, and the critics. Consequently I got pretty good notices.' Voltaire, in the eighteenth century, was aware of the pretension that often goes with music: 'The most high have a decided taste for vocal music provided it be lugubrious and gloomy enough.' I myself was interrupted in the middle of a recent radio show by an announcement of the sinking of a warship during the Falklands campaign. There was nothing to report beyond the disaster but instead of coming back to our discussion the BBC chose to play 'lugubrious and gloomy' music which we could hear lapping around the room. 'I recognize that tune', said Anthony Quinton, who was one of the frustrated conversationalists, 'that's Prokofiev's "You Can't Win 'Em All!" ' Dr Johnson, on musical snobbery, remarked, 'Of all the ladies that sparkle at a musical performance a very small number has any quick sensibility of harmonious sounds. But everyone that goes has the pleasure of being supposed to be pleased with a refined amusement and of hoping to be numbered among the votaresses of harmony.' The good doctor's claims for music itself were modest: 'Of all the noises I think music the least disagreeable.'

Oscar Wilde also saw music in terms of its social possibilities and pitfalls: 'If one hears bad music it is one's duty to drown it by one's conversation' (*Picture of Dorian Gray*); 'If one plays good music people don't listen and if one plays bad music people don't talk' (*Importance of Being Earnest*); 'Musical people are so absurdly unreasonable. They always want one to be perfectly dumb when one is longing to be absolutely deaf' (*An Ideal Husband*). Frank Zappa, of more recent repute, tackled musical appreciation more directly: 'Most people wouldn't know music if it came up and bit them on the ass.' Or, as Ulysses S. Grant put it, 'I only know two tunes. One of them is "Yankee Doodle" and the other isn't.'

Opera raises the passions quicker than anything. 'No opera plot can be sensible, for in sensible situations people do not sing', said W.H. Auden. Beaumarchais's maxim, 'That which is not worth saying is sung', and Voltaire's, 'What is too silly to be said can be sung', preceded Auden. 'Opera in English', said H.L. Mencken, 'is, in the main, just about as sensible as baseball in Italian.' Noel

Coward insisted, 'People are wrong when they say that opera is not what it used to be. It *is* what it used to be. That is what is wrong with it.' 'Opera is when a guy gets stabbed in the back and instead of bleeding, he sings', said Ed Gardner, on 'Duffy's Tavern', an American radio show. 'Going to the opera, like getting drunk, is a sin that carries its own punishment with it – and that is a very serious one', said Hannah More as long ago as 1775. 'One goes to see a tragedy to be moved, to the opera one goes either for want of any other interest or to facilitate digestion', said Voltaire, again. And finally the humourist Cleveland Amory, back in this century, reckons that 'The opera is like a wife with a foreign title – expensive to support, hard to understand, and therefore a supreme social challenge.'

Expensive to support, certainly. There are arguments on both sides of the Atlantic about the costs of staging opera. In 1983 the Metropolitan Opera in New York celebrated its centenary with what Peter Conrad, in *The Observer*, called 'an orgy of concupiscent and conspicuous consumption – the kind of occasion New York adores, opulent and excessive':

When the curtain parted on a gaudy de Mille-like pagan temple, where the Met ballet was to cavort in the bacchanal from 'Samson et Dalila,' a gasp of pleasure and of recognition fluttered through the audience like the rustle of fresh money: this brazen edifice for the worship of material values was an idealised version of the Met these people cherished, and – no doubt – of the Louis XIV condominiums where they lived.

In a world no longer affluent, opera is the last resort of the high style and the grand manner; even, it seems, of haute couture. The singers came bedecked like Christmas trees. Régine Crespin's Carmen wore a harlequin's outfit; Marilyn Horne augmented her biceps with epaulettes of midnight blue; between Joan Sutherland's shoulder blades perched an elephantine lime-green butterfly.

Jessye Norman – affectionately known backstage as 'Jessy-enormous' – appeared to be wearing an entire orchestra. A double bass the size of a full-grown oak tree inclined across her bosom, while around her hem there clustered enough quavers and crotchets to make a Wagner opera. When she turned

113

round for her magisterial exit, another world was disclosed on her back, peopled by the giant faces of musical divinities. Cowboy chic, too, qualified as a courtly uniform: James McCracken played the delirious Otello in a Texan string tie, fastened at his throat by a brooch.

Particular operas have come in for witty criticism on many occasions. Is it its length, solemnity or its immediately identifiable and faintly funny title which makes Wagner's *Parsifal* a favourite target? '*Parsifal* is the kind of opera', said David Randolph, 'that starts at six o'clock. After it has been going three hours, you look at your watch and it says 6.20.' Mark Twain was snappier: 'The first act of the three occupied two hours. I enjoyed that in spite of the singing.' Rossini was less charitable: 'One can't judge *Lohengrin* after a first hearing and I certainly don't intend hearing it a second time.' 'Wagner', he concluded, 'has some wonderful moments but awful half-hours.' (Gounod's *La Redemptión* had a similar effect on Shaw: 'If man will only take the precaution to go in long enough after it commences and to come out long before it is over you will not find it wearisome.')

Noel Coward, leaving *Camelot*, found it 'like *Parsifal*, without the jokes'. Beecham was once caught making a practical approach to Wagner. Neville Cardus recalls a production of *Siegfried* in the 1930s at Covent Garden:

> For two acts . . . a musical delight, finished in detail and balanced to a glowing serenity. Then, in the third act, Beecham went berserk. Again I chastised him in print . . . Next day, he explained, 'You critics are inhumane. I chanced to look at my watch, laid on my desk before me, and we were still not halfway through Act III. It was getting on for eleven o'clock. In the audience were many poor souls who had to go home to such remote habitations as Putney, Streatham and Swiss Cottage. And the public houses would close at eleven, and my orchestra, slaving away since six o'clock, were thirsty. So I just let Wagner rip.'

Beecham believed:

> Nearly all the questionable works of the great musical geniuses have been prompted by religion. Wagner's *Parsifal*, the

Requiem of Brahms, and Elgar's *Gerontius*, described by my friend George Moore as 'holy water in a German beer barrel'. Each is, I think, my most potent aversion. Too much counterpoint. Protestant counterpoint. What dreadful crimes have been committed in the name of religion.

Shaw suggested that 'Orchestras only need to be sworn at, and a German is consequently at an advantage with them, as English profanity, except in America, has not gone beyond the limited terminology of perdition.' Well, explosions between singers, players and conductors are not as frequent as clashes between leaders of parties in the House of Commons, but they are often more fun. However, lashing an orchestra tends to be one-sided, though soloists can answer back. 'You are there and I am here; but where is Beethoven?' Artur Schnabel once enquired of a conductor. But a player in one of Barbirolli's orchestras paid a parking fine pleading, 'I prefer to face the wrath of the police than the wrath of Sir John Barbirolli.' Stokowski boasted, 'I am more than a martinet – I am martinetissimo!' According to Kostelanetz, a conductor has an advantage – 'not seeing the audience'. To one player Beecham said, 'We cannot expect you to be with us all the time, but perhaps you could be good enough to keep in touch now and again'; to another, 'Cor anglais, kindly give me some indication of your presence at four bars after letter G.' When an oboist called on to give an A came up with a wide vibrato, Beecham looked around the orchestra and said simply, 'Gentlemen, take your pick.' With Jean Pougnet, the violinist, he appeared with an orchestra so overawed that the opening bars of their rehearsal were disastrous. Beecham persevered and they got better. 'Don't look now', he said, leaning towards Pougnet, 'but I believe we're being followed'. Again, 'Gentlemen in the clarinet department, how can you resist such an impassioned appeal from the second violins? Give them an answer, I beg you.'

Beecham's grapeshot splattered both singers and orchestra impartially. He stopped a rehearsal of *La Bohème* because the tenor was inaudible. He lay on the bed upon which Mimi was also dying, and yelled 'Mr Nash, I can't hear you. Sing up!'

'How do you expect me to sing my best in this position, Sir Thomas?' said Nash.

'In that position, my dear fellow', replied Beecham, 'I have given some of my best performances'.

Diaghilev's Russian dancers had no language in which to protest when Beecham upped the tempo on their first London appearance. 'I made the little buggers hop', he smiled. When an Australian soprano had trouble with the score of the *Messiah*, she pleaded that she would be all right for the performance. She had been working hard on the score for months, taking it to bed with her every night. 'In that case', he reassured her, 'we shall have an immaculate conception.' A lady cellist in a roughish orchestra was making heavy weather. 'Madam', Beecham pleaded, in one of his most famous remarks, 'you have between your legs an instrument capable of giving pleasure to thousands – and all you can do is scratch it!'

However, from the hero of Dame Ethel Smyth's opera *The Wreckers*, which he rehearsed for its first performance in 1909, Beecham had to cope with some of his own medicine. The tenor stopped. 'What's the matter, Mr Coates?' asked Sir Thomas. 'I was just wondering', said Coates, 'is this the place where I'm supposed to be drowned by the waves or the orchestra?'

The naked in-fighting between men of one profession invariably comes as a surprise to those of another. They tend to think that the temperaments of their colleagues are unique. Actors are thus amazed by the viciousness of clerics, doctors taken aback by the bitchiness of academics, novelists impressed by the passion with which chefs put away other chefs' triumphs as poison. Conductors have composers, singers and players as supporting targets; but most especially they, too, have each other. Take Beecham on Von Karajan: 'a sort of musical Malcolm Sargent'; on Toscanini: 'a glorified Italian bandmaster': 'Much is made of the fact that he always conducts without a score . . . Toscanini is so short-sighted that he wouldn't be able to use a score . . . but though it is generally known that Toscanini invariably conducts from memory, and though it is generally known that he is half-blind, nobody apparently is aware that also he is tone deaf. . .'; on Barbirolli: 'He has done splendid work with the Hallé since they brought him back from New York . . . a good, strong, north of England orchestra, masculine and vigorous . . . Barbirolli . . . has transformed it into the finest chamber orchestra in the country'; on Sir Adrian Boult: 'He came to see me this morning – positively reeking of Horlicks'; on Malcolm Sargent: 'Malcolm is an extremely accomplished musician and an incredibly accomplished conductor. I appointed him my deputy . . .

take my advice, if ever you appoint a deputy, appoint one whom you can trust technically; but his calibre must be such that the public will always be glad to see *you* back again.'

On hearing that Mr Sargent had become Sir Malcolm, Beecham retorted, 'I didn't know he'd been knighted. I knew he'd been doctored.' Beecham is said once to have heard that Sargent had been in Tokyo. 'Malcolm in Tokyo? What was he doing?'

'Conducting', came the reply.

'I see. A flash in Japan'.

The same Japanese tour continued and a news report claimed that a gun had gone off in the audience one night when Sir Malcolm was conducting. 'I had no idea that the Japanese were so musical', mused Beecham.

Edgard Varèse, the composer, once made a distinction between European and American conductors: 'In Europe when a rich woman has an affair with a conductor they have a baby. In America she endows an orchestra for him.' But Beecham was more sweeping: 'All the arts in America are a gigantic racket run by unscrupulous men for unhealthy women.'

In the course of diligent research for our play about Beecham, I asked Leonard Bernstein if he had any suitable stories. 'Not really', he said, 'we shared a dressing room once, sharing a ballet pro- gramme at the Met. He was extremely kind to me . . . but that's not really what you want, is it?' No in-fighting there, clearly. However, Oscar Levant, once described as 'a lap dog with rabies', was less kind to Bernstein: 'He uses music as an accompaniment to his conducting.' And he added, 'I think a lot of Bernstein – but not as much as he does.' After one of Bernstein's popular musical lectures, Levant volunteered, 'Leonard Bernstein has been disclosing musical secrets that have been known for over four hundred years.'

Composers are similarly rough on other composers. Ravel was hard on Saint-Saens: 'I'm told Saint-Saens has informed a delighted public that since the war started he has composed music for the stage, melodies, an elegy and a piece for the trombone. If he had been making shell-cases instead it might have been better for music.' Erik Satie was hard on Ravel: 'M. Ravel refuses the Legion d'Honneur but all his music accepts it.'

André Previn tells a story of a young composer who came to Brahms and asked if he might play for the master a funeral march which he had composed in memory of Beethoven. Permission was granted and the young man played away. When he had done he asked Brahms for his verdict. 'I'll tell you', said Brahms, candidly, 'I'd be much happier if you were dead and Beethoven had written the march.' (Previn's re-vamped source appears to be Oscar Levant who said much the same in similar circumstances when George Gershwin died in 1938 and Previn was about ten years old.) 'I occasionally play works by contemporary composers', Jascha Heifetz once admitted, 'and for two reasons. First to discourage the composer from writing any more and secondly to remind myself how much I appreciate Beethoven.' Ansermet once addressed an orchestra sternly: 'Just play the notes as they are rotten.'

Beecham, of course, had plenty to say about other composers. On Vaughan Williams: 'I very much like some of Vaughan Williams, for example his *Fantasia on a Theme of Thomas Tallis*. Unfortunately, in his compositions published subsequently he omitted to take the precaution of including a theme by Thomas Tallis.' On a symphony of Bruckner's in which the composer fails sometimes to organize and develop an idea: 'In the first movement I took note of a dozen pregnancies and half a dozen miscarriages.' On a symphony which Elgar declined to allow him to cut: 'Elgar's A flat symphony is a large work . . . the musical equivalent of St Pancras station, Neo-Gothic don't you know!' On Benjamin Britten, asking Cardus about his *Rape of Lucrece*:

> He uses a twelve-piece orchestra in *The Rape*, doesn't he? When I was a young bachelor in London, I would sometimes wander in the purlieus of the Tottenham Court Road on summer evenings, inspecting the windows of the furniture shops, hoping to get some insight into the way the poor live. And I would see cardboard signs advertising a six-piece, or a twelve-piece suite, at such and such a price. All obtainable on the hire system. And today, God help us, we have lived to hear an opera with a twelve-piece orchestra – obtainable on the hire system of an Arts Council!

Mozart was the only composer who escaped Beecham's sallies – just as he was the only composer he would never 'misconduct': 'The only thing that is really important, in playing, in conducting – yes, even in misconducting – is this. Whatever you do, do it with conviction.' Shaw was equally humble towards Mozart. 'There is no shadow of death anywhere in Mozart's music', he wrote:

> Even his own funeral was a failure. It was dispersed by a shower of rain, and to this day nobody knows where he was buried or whether he was buried at all or not. My own belief is that he was not. Depend upon it, they had no sooner put up their umbrellas and bolted for the nearest shelter than he got up, shook off his bones into the common grave of the people and soared off into universality.

Mozart contributed a suitably blunt epitaph of his own: 'I write music as a sow piddles.'

As for Beethoven, laymen can, of course, join in with John Ruskin: 'Beethoven always sounds like the upsetting of bags – with here and there a dropped hammer.' Beecham had strong views on the third movement of Beethoven's Seventh Symphony: 'What can you do with it? It's like a lot of yaks jumping about!' Beethoven himself once said to a fellow-composer, 'I like your opera, I think I will set it to music.'

Insulting singers is not only a conductor's prerogative. Literary figures such as Coleridge could write:

> Swans sing before they die – 'twere no bad thing,
> Should certain persons die before they sing.

While Ambrose Bierce was even less kind:

> The actor apes a man – at least in shape,
> The opera performer apes the ape.

But the spectacle of Toscanini placing two indulgent hands on a singer's breasts – Milanov's, I believe – and then raising them gently to her brow and muttering sadly, 'If only these were these,' is as evocative as that of an exasperated Beecham inquiring tetchily, 'How would you like it tonight, Madam, too fast or too slow?' Toscanini was once presented with flowers – only once. Rejecting them he said simply, 'They are for prima donnas or corpses. I am neither.'

There's no doubt, though, that composers' criticisms of singers come more directly from the heart. Sopranos in particular have suffered. 'If', said Berlioz scathingly, 'she can strike a low G or F like a death rattle and a high F like the shriek of a little dog when you step on its tail, the house will resound with acclamations.' So large were sopranos in earlier days that one wag called them Venuses de Kilo. The frailty of the ageing soprano was lampooned in the 1950s by an intimate revue number following a disastrous performance by the lady who was making a comeback in a Noel Coward musical:

> Sweet voice that used to be
> Still cracking on Top C.

Of another soprano, Coward himself said, 'Her voice was precisely like a stringed instrument that one imagined to have fallen into disuse when the viola came along to replace it.' George Ade recollected 'a town-and-country soprano of a kind often used for augmenting grief at a funeral'. Beecham once told *Newsweek* that 'most sopranos sound as if they live on seaweed'.

Anonymity cloaks the source of two judgments, one on tenors – 'There are three sexes; men, women and tenors' – the other on contraltos – 'A contralto is a low women who sings'. Hans von Bulow (the first husband of Cosima Liszt) judged a tenor to be 'not a man but a disease'. Tenors were defined by Harold Schonberg, the American critic, as 'usually short, stout men (except when they are Wagnerian tenors in which case they are large, stout men) made up predominantly of lungs, rope-sized vocal chords, large-fronted sinuses, thick necks, thick heads, tantrums and *amour propre*. It is certain that they are a race apart, a race which tends to act reflexively rather than with due process of thought.'

Byron, turning to specific cases in *Don Juan*, found:

> The tenor's voice is spoilt in affectation,
> And for the bass, the beast can only bellow;
> In fact, he had no singing education,
> An ignorant, noteless, timeless, tuneless fellow.

The prima donna fared little better at his hands:

> . . though a little old,
> And haggard with a dissipated life,
> And subject, when the house is thin, by cold,
> Has some good notes.

Singer-resistance has been fashionable since 35 BC at least. 'All singers have this fault', wrote the poet Horace, 'if asked to sing among their friends, they are never so inclined, if unasked they never leave off.' 'When in doubt, sing loud', confided Robert Merrill to the *Saturday Evening Post*, a remark which would have struck a chord in the composer, Frank Loesser, who believed firmly that loud was good. Let us, however, abandon the human voice on a genial note, quoting Gilbert's *Bab Ballad* in which –

> They began to sing
> That extremely lovely thing
> 'Scherzando!' ma no troppo, ppp.

As the voice of the singer dies away the instruments of the orchestra strike up. There are differing definitions, first, of the piano:

> The piano is a harp in a box – Leigh Hunt.

> Five and thirty black slaves
> Half a hundred white
> All their duty but to sing
> For that Queen's delight.
> – Sir William Watson.

Old piano players never die – they only fake away – Anon

Beecham had it in for the harpsichord: 'The harpsichord sounds like two skeletons copulating on a corrugated iron roof – in a thunderstorm.' After his second wife had rehearsed a piece at Croydon, Beecham saw two stage-hands arrive to move the piano off-stage. 'Don't bother', he said, 'after that performance it will probably slink off!' 'Please do not shoot the pianist,' Oscar Wilde (not Mark Twain) observed on a notice in an American saloon – 'he's doing his best.' More measured is J.K. Stephen's 'Parody of Walt Whitman':

The clear cool notes of the cuckoo, which has ousted the
    legitimate nest holder,
The whistle of the railway guard, dispatching the train to the
    inevitable collision,
The maiden's monosyllabic reply to a polysyllabic proposal,

The fundamental note of the last trump, which is
    presumably D natural;
All these are sounds to rejoice in, yes to let your very ribs
    re-echo with,
But better than all is the absolutely last chord
Of the apparently inexhaustible pianoforte player.

Shaw was impatient with Paderewski's fortissimos. He called
them 'brutal contests between piano and pianist to settle the question of the survival of the fittest'. Emerson's approach was sociological: ' 'Tis wonderful how soon a piano gets into a log hut on the
frontier', he wrote, having no doubt heard many pianos which lived
up to Ambrose Bierce's definition – 'A parlor utensil for subduing
the impenitent visitor. It is operated by depressing the keys of the
machine and the spirits of the audience.'
Bierce thought no better of the flute: 'A variously perforated
hollow stick intended for the punishment of sin, the minister of
retribution being commonly a young man with straw-coloured eyes
and lean hair'; nor of the fiddle: 'An instrument to tickle human ears
by the friction of a horse's tail on the entrails of a cat' – a sentiment
rhymed by G.T.Lanigan:

> A squeak's heard in the orchestra
> The leader draws across
> The intestines of the agile cat
> The tail of the noble hoss.

However, according to Peter de Vries, 'The tuba is certainly the
most intestinal of instruments – the very lower bowel of music.' But
Isaiah had already prophesied: 'My bowels shall sound like a harp.'
As with the violin, Anon records that:

> The world is a difficult place indeed
> And people are hard to suit
> And the man who plays on the violin
> Is a bore to the man with the flute.

Schoenberg was once told that a new concerto would have to await
the arrival of a six-fingered violinist before it could be performed.
'Very well, I can wait', he replied. Dr Johnson had occasion to
comment on a violinist's efforts to play: 'Difficult, do you call it, Sir?
I wish it were impossible.' A Jack Benny violin concert was reviewed

in no uncertain terms: 'Jack Benny played Mendelssohn last night. Mendelssohn lost.'

I rather enjoy the delicate mystery of Sheldon Harnick's lines from *Fiddler on the Roof*:

> A fiddler on the roof
> A most unlikely sight
> It might not mean a thing
> And then again it might.

There's no mystery, however, in this anonymous limerick:

> A tutor who tooted a flute
> Tried to teach two young tutors to toot,
> Said the two to the tutor
> Is it harder to toot, or
> To tutor two tutors to toot

— or in this anonymous verdict on the oboe: 'An ill wind that nobody blows good.'

Put all the instruments together and you have the promise of a concert. There is something splendidly civilized about contemplating a visit to a concert. A bare hall, no décor, hard chairs, no compromises – except perhaps the programme. But according to Coleridge, it was not always so:

> Not cold, not stern, my soul! Yet I detest
> These scented rooms, where to a gaudy throng,
> Heaves the proud harlot her distended breast
> In intricacies of laborious song . . .

Eighty-six years later, Gilbert had a more benevolent point of view in *The Mikado*:

> A series of masses and fugues and 'ops'
> By Bach, interwoven
> With Spohr and Beethoven
> At classical Monday Pops.

The musicians' attitude is less romantic. 'Applause is a receipt, not a bill', said Artur Schnabel, declining to play encores. 'If nobody wants to go to your concert, nothing will stop them', mourned Isaac Stern. And the composer, Ned Rorem, sums up for sceptics: 'To the social-minded, a concert is what surrounds an intermission.' Henry Miller dismissed it as 'a polite form of self-torture'.

As for festivals, in Beecham's words, they 'are for the purpose of attracting trade to the town. What that has to do with music, I don't know.' Sydney Smith attended the York Musical Festival, held regularly in the 1820s (in the 1950s Caryl Brahms wrote a radio play about a mini-Aldeburgh, neatly entitled *Nymphs and Shepherds Go Away*), and in 1823 he wrote, 'Nothing can be more disgusting than an oratorio. How absurd to see 500 people fiddling like madmen about Israelites in the Red Sea.' And two years later he wrote:

> The music went off very well . . . I did not go once. Music for such a length of time (unless under sentence of jury) I will not submit to. What pleasure is there in pleasure if quantity is not attended to as well as quality. I know nothing more agreeable than a dinner at Holland House; but it must not begin at ten in the morning and last until six.

His last broadside is dated 1828:

> The Festival seems to be at a discount. Mr Dickson is said to have written to Catalani to know if her voice was really as good as it used to be. No answer, perhaps no Catalani. Two or three of their other female singers are (it is said) in the family way, and expect to be confined about the musical week; nevertheless, they will come, though their medical advisers are rather apprehensive of the effects of grand choruses, but I hope all will go off quietly.

But he must have modified his views by 1844, for when he wrote in that year to the Countess of Carlisle he said: 'If I were to begin life again I would devote it to music. It is the only cheap and unpunished rapture upon earth.' Oratorio – the form Smith was subjected to – was a subject on which Ernest Newman, author and critic, had idiosyncratic views: 'If I had the power, I would insist on all oratorios being sung in the costume of the period – with a possible exception in the case of *The Creation*.'

Sydney Smith's involvement with '500 people fiddling like madmen about Israelites in the Red Sea' takes us perilously close to the musical amateur. 'Hell', wrote Shaw in *Man and Superman*, 'is full of musical amateurs. Music is the brandy of the damned.' An Italian proverb prays, 'God save me from a bad neighbour and a beginner on the fiddle.' And George Ade deftly sketches the problem of the listener in an acutely domestic context when he recorded that 'The music teacher came twice a week to bridge the awful gap between Dorothy and Chopin.' Artur Schnabel once interviewed a student who asked if he could become his pupil. Schnabel tested him and agreed.

'How much are your lessons?' asked the pupil.

'Five guineas each,' replied Schnabel.

'I'm afraid I couldn't afford that.'

'I also give lessons at three guineas, but I don't recommend them.'

Musical amateurs frequently get what is coming to them. Edward Lear wrote to Lady Strachey in 1859 in no uncertain terms about the noise below him:

> A vile, beastly, rotten-headed, fool-begotten, brazen-throated, pernicious, piggish, screaming, tearing, roaring, perplexing, splitmecrackle, crashmecriggle, insane ass of a woman is prac-tising howling below-stairs with a brute of a singing master so horribly that my head is nearly off.

The critic of the *West Wilts Herald* was slightly less caustic when he commented in 1893 on a duet by two young lady amateurs: 'It is a pity that the composer did not leave directions as to how flat he really did want it sung.'

If the talent of the musical amateur is reviled, the moral turpitude of the professional causes just as much comment. Wayward, un-reliable and immoral, wandering minstrels, things of shreds and patches – they were a rough lot. This attitude has come down to the twentieth century in the much-quoted, never-identified saw, 'never marry a musician'. Antisthenes felt the same in 400 BC: 'He must be a poor sort of man for otherwise he would not be so good a piper.' Hindus have always believed that three things take crooked ways, 'Cats, boats, and musicians'. In 1749 Lord Chesterfield advised his son:

> If you love music, hear it; go to operas, concerts and pay fiddles to play to you: but I insist on your neither piping nor fiddling yourself. It puts a gentleman in a very frivolous contemptible light. A taste for sculpture and painting is in my mind as

becoming as a taste for fiddling and piping is unbecoming in a man of fashion. The former is connected with history and poetry, the latter with nothing that I know of but bad company.

Archduke Ferdinand's mother felt much the same when she heard of her son's inclination to employ Mozart:

> You ask my opinion about taking the young Salzburg musician into your service. I do not know where you can place him, since I feel that you do not require a composer, or other useless people. . . . It gives one's service a bad name when such types run around like beggars; besides, he has a large family.

On one occasion Toscanini was dressing down his orchestra. He knew what would hurt them most: 'After I die I shall return to earth as door-keeper to a bordello; but I won't let one of you in.' Woody Guthrie probably felt the same about music as Toscanini – but not about bordellos: 'You can't write a good song about a whorehouse unless you've been in one.' Are the morals of modern musicians any better? Recently a distinguished orchestrator and conductor of popular music – a man – changed sex, much to the surprise of his friends and colleagues. When she returned to work after her operation, her first commission was a mammoth score for a spectacular film. As she faced her orchestra, sensibly skirted, to conduct the first band-call, there was an air of tension. She gave a few formal, precise instructions. Then she asked if there were any questions. A ribald trumpeter shattered the nervous atmosphere. 'I suppose', he inquired, raising his hand, 'I suppose a fuck's out of the question?'

  Generally women in music do not have an enviable reputation. 'All the daughters of music shall be brought low. . .' said Ecclesiastes. Another Eastern proverb counsels wisdom before the event: 'Consort not with a female musician, lest thou be taken in by her snares.' A lesser authority, *Time* magazine, pronounced, 'Men compose symphonies. Women compose babies.' Beecham had no liking for them in his orchestras. 'A pretty woman will distract the other musicians', he said, 'and an ugly one will distract me.' 'There's no music when a woman is in the concert', wrote Dekker in *The Honest Whore*. 'Women and music should never be dated', said Goldsmith, more kindly, in *She Stoops to Conquer*. Johnny Mercer's lyric goes:

> .. when the sweet talkin's done
> A woman's a two-face,
> A worrisome thing who'll leave ya t'sing
> The Blues in the Night.

But Jules Goncourt, the French diarist, was an enthusiastic defender: 'What I love best about music is the women who listen to it.'

Popular music ('popular because people like it', said Irving Berlin) again divides loyalties. I warm to musicians who are fond of their own music – even if they pretend not to be. 'I don't like my music', said Frederick Loewe, with his tongue in his witty, Viennese cheek, 'but what is that against the opinion of millions of others?' Liberace might have been playing Loewe's tune when he minted his memorable phrase, 'What you said hurt me very much. I cried all the way to the bank.' Prominent among complaints about modern popular music is the age-old accusation of noise. 'I realize with a gasp . . .' says John Simon (writing about Streisand's film *A Star is Born* for *New York* magazine in 1977), '. . . that this progressively more belligerent caterwauling can sell anything . . . concerts, records, movies, and I feel as if our entire society were ready to flush itself down in something even worse than a collective death-wish – a collective will to live in ugliness and self-debasement.' Frank Zappa hit back: 'Most rock journalism is people who can't write interviewing people who can't talk for people who can't read.'

Wit rarely shines out from the pages of rock and pop criticism; but recently Richard Williams, in *The Times*, beautifully sustained a mocking metaphor to herald the return of the gyrating pop-star Tom Jones to delight his faithful following at the Albert Hall. Williams's piece was headed 'The Cojones Boy'.

> In midnight blue matador jacket, ivory silk dress shirt slashed to reveal a gold crucifix, dark trousers sprayed on to his withers, and neat high-heeled boots, he presented himself as the archetypal Hollywood Mexican: the Cojones Boy, come to reclaim his old estancia from the marauding Manilow Gang.
>
> Ecstatic at the sight of their hero, who had been lured away and detained so long in a foreign land, the grateful peasants rushed forward in supplication, presenting him with embraces and keepsakes: flowers, handkerchiefs and a small native vegetable known as the leek, bound with red and green

ribbons. Some of the younger women, who could afford no special gift, revived an antique custom and laid their scanty nether garments at his feet.

It was as silly as that, and as unconvincing. Last night Tom Jones returned to London with a show whose script might have been lifted entire, in all its flat contrivance, from his television series of many years ago.

Then Richard Williams turned his fire on the hapless Richard Clayderman, a popular pianist: 'He is to piano playing as David Soul is to acting; he makes Jacques Loussier sound like Bach; he reminds us how cheap potent music can be.'

But in fact a new vitality and lively vocabulary have been admitted by the anarchic impact of jazz and pop and rock and punk. Patti Smith defined her attitude to her performances: 'When I'm performing I don't even think about whether I'm a girl or a boy or even what planet I'm from. My whole concept of performing is like screwing without touching.' 'Rock 'n' Roll', wrote Peter York in *Style Wars*, is 'the hamburger which ate the world.' At the Royal Variety Performance in 1963 John Lennon encouraged the audience: 'Those in the cheaper seats clap. The rest of you rattle your jewellery.'

The Beatles' first press conference in America established them, Lennon in particular, as ready wits:

'Are you a part of social rebellion against the older generation?'
'It's a dirty lie.'

'What about the movement in Detroit to stamp out The Beatles?'
'We have a campaign to stamp out Detroit.'

'What do you think of Beethoven?'
'I love him,' said Ringo, 'especially his poems.'

'Do you have a leading lady for your film?'
'We're trying for the Queen,' said George Harrison, 'she sells.'

Three rock musicians testify to the modernity of the art: 'To me music's not something you sit down and write. It's something you feel like a punch in the ear' – Pat Collier. 'It's . . . well, I know it's better than working at Fords' – Ian Drury. 'I don't know anything about music . . . in my line you don't have to' – Elvis Presley. Disc jockeys – D.G. Bridson's 'wriggling ponces of the spoken word' – tend to confer undue importance on the artists they peddle. Bob Dylan's modest corrective is neat – 'I'm just the postman. I deliver the songs.' Lieber and Stoller in their vivid, witty vignettes of inner-city life in East Coast America also avoid the pretentious:

> Three cool cats
> Standin' on the corner wish they had a car
> Dividin' up a nickel candy bar,
> Talkin' all about how cool they are,
> These three cool cats . . .
>
> Three corner romeos making a play
> One's black.
> One's white.
> One's café-au-lait.
> And they can't seem to get out of each other's way.

or:

> You ain't nothin' but a hound dog
> Quit snoopin' round my door
> You can wag your tail but I ain't gonna feed you no more.

Ray Davies of The Kinks, Paul Simon, Bernie Taupin (with Elton John), and countless other modern lyricists prove that it is still possible to walk on, walk on, wittily and amusingly, through the storm of noise. The Beatles, however, remain the outstanding phenomenon, their rise to incredible fame best charted by Bernard Levin in *The Pendulum Years*:

Among these last (disciples of the Maharishi) were The Beatles MBE, four pleasant young men who had grown up in a hard school, convinced that their problems would be solved when, and perhaps only when, they had a million pounds. Many believe as much but it is given to few to test the belief: to the Beatles, however, it was given: heaped up, pressed down and running over. Not merely one million pounds, but several, came their way: to their dismay, they found that their problems were still not solved.

129

Could it be true, after all, that money did not bring happiness? . . . They had, these four young Beatles, set the fashion for a generation, changed for ever the idiom of popular music, attuned themselves to the spirit of the age. And yet they could not be at rest with the world or with their own spirits. More and more frantic grew the Beatles' search for this elusive inner peace at times taking them across the very bounds of the law, into the forbidden and exciting regions of smoking that which they were not permitted to smoke. Alas, the forbidden and exciting region visited, it turned out to be more forbidden and exciting, and the search for certainty was on again.

And so they came to the Mahirishi, plums ripe on the tree and to be collected for the shaking. The Maharishi shook . . . but . . . the idyll in the Maharishi's close-carpeted lair did not last long. Soon the Beatles . . . returned . . . some of them expressing grave disillusionment. It was never quite clear what had upset them so, but there were hints that the Maharishi's courteous request, as payment for his spiritual ministrations, for ten per cent of a week's earnings, which in the case of the Beatles and a good week could amount to several thousand pounds, might have had something to do with it; in any case the search was on once more.

Less perceptively Levin later consigns 'the bulk of the output . . . including that of the Beatles' to 'the memory hole of oblivion.'

Folk and jazz spawn their own wits. Two dicta on folk are anonymous: 'A folk song is a song that nobody ever wrote', and 'The only thing to do with a folk melody, once you've heard it, is to play it louder.' Jazz admits Wally Stott's sceptical approach: 'If you're in jazz and more than ten people like you, you're labelled commercial'; it admits Louis Armstrong's more downright, 'Hot can be cool and cool can be hot, and each can be both. But hot or cool, man, jazz is jazz'; it admits Anthony Burgess's more ambitious: 'Jazz . . . was illiterate, instinctual, impulsive, aleatoric, unscorable, unprintable – therein lay its charm'; it allows Duke Ellington to attack, by himself, in prose – 'Playing "Bop" is like scrabble with all the vowels missing' – and in a lyric, with Irving Mills – 'It Don't Mean A Thing If It Ain't Got That Swing.' Jazz is religious for Father G.V. Kennars, SJ: 'To swing is to affirm.' Paderewski saw it as 'a terrible revenge by the culture of the Negroes on that of the Whites'. To Charlie Parker it is 'Your own experience, your thoughts, your wisdom. If you don't live it, it won't come out of your horn.' Sousa, however, was dubious: 'Jazz will endure, just as long as people hear it through their feet instead of their brains.'

The most civilized and amusing contribution to popular music, and the literature which surrounds it, comes from the composers and lyricists of musical comedy of this century. In many cases they were immigrants to America – or the sons and daughters of immigrants – and the lyricists among them displayed an intoxicated delight in flourishing their prowess in an alien tongue in front of their disoriented, emigré parents. Perhaps those who were of German origin were following Goethe's dictum that 'All good lyrics must make sense as a whole yet in details be a little absurd.'

Irving Berlin, Ira Gershwin, E.Y. Harburg, Lorenz Hart, Oscar Hammerstein, Dorothy Fields, Howard Dietz, all represent this tradition of first- or second-generation delight in a new language, and colleagues with longer roots in America – Johnny Mercer and Cole Porter, as well as their successors, Alan Jay Lerner, Frank Loesser, Sheldon Harnick and Stephen Sondheim – could only catch the enthusiasm from them. In England Noel Coward kept pace – writing just as many good songs but rather more bad ones. Coward it was who pointed out 'the potency of cheap music' – that ability a tune has to evoke a never-never land as vivid but as illusory as Peter Pan's, Gatsby's or the enchanted past of *Le Grand Meaulnes*. 'When people hear good music, it makes them homesick for something they never had and never will have', observed E.W. Howe in 1911. For me, a music-hall nonsense song which I used to knock out on the piano with one finger brings back childhood in one fell swoop and still makes me smile:

> Don't cry Daddy, Mummy will soon be back
> She's only gone for a trip round the world
> In a Grimsby fishing smack
> Don't cry Daddy, she will come home from sea,
> She'll get a job at the Hotel de Lockhart
> And work for dear Daddy and me.

If Fenimore Cooper is to be believed, America was a late starter in musical appreciation. 'The Americans are almost ignorant of the art of music, one of the most elevating, innocent and refining of human tastes, whose influence on the habits and morals of people is of the most beneficial tendency', he wrote in the *American Democrat* in 1838. By the end of the century it was a different story. Irving Berlin was the first of the great songwriters to arrive, on a boat from Russia in 1892, and at a show business dinner honouring him just before the First World War, his change of name from Israel Baline was noted by George M. Cohan, in a blunt example of homespun wit which would hardly be acceptable today: 'Irving Berlin', he stated genially, 'is a Jewboy who named himself after an English actor and a German city.'

The father of the Gershwin brothers, George and Ira, arrived at the same time as Berlin. (Much comical mileage has been made out of jokes on the lines, 'George and his lovely wife, Ira'. I prefer Richard Stilgoe's suggestion that Ira is, in fact, George's Irish aunt, IRA Gershwin, who commissioned 'I Got Rhythm', as a means of popularizing an acceptable method of birth control for Catholics.) Ira Gershwin's quality of civilized, literate amusement shines through lyrics like 'They All Laughed', 'I'm Bidin' My Time', 'How Long Has This Been Going On', 'But Not For Me' –

> With love to lead the way
> I've found more skies of gray
> Than any Russian play
> Could guarantee

– as clearly as it does in his comic set pieces, 'Sam and Delilah', 'My Cousin From Milwaukee' and 'It Ain't Necessarily So'; and

> When J.P. Morgan bows, I just nod;
> Green pastures wanted me to play God . . .
> . . . But I can't get started with you.

One of their satirical musicals, *Strike Up The Band*, opened in Philadelphia. The book was by George S. Kaufman who looked like seeing his adage, 'Satire is what closes on Saturday night', proved true again. Spotting two aged gentlemen entering the theatre he asked Ira Gershwin who they could be. 'Gilbert and Sullivan, come to fix the show', Gershwin replied. 'Pity you can't get that sort of wit into your lyrics', said Kaufman. Kaufman himself was caustic on the subject of George Gershwin's fondness for playing his new tunes at parties: 'George's music gets around so much before an opening

that the first night's audience thinks it's at a revival', he said. Oscar
Levant once said to George, 'Tell me, George, if you had to do it all
over would you fall in love with yourself again?'

Lorenz Hart, along with Coward and Porter, ranks among the
most flamboyantly witty lyricists. 'Larry Hart can rhyme anything –
and does', wrote one critic. Another critic made his point by parody-
ing Irving Berlin's 'Always' in Hart's rhyming style:

> In saloons and drab hallways
> You are what I'll grab, always
> Our love will be as grand
> As Paul Whiteman's band
> And will weigh as much as Paul weighs.
> See how I dispense
> Rhymes which are immense;
> But do they make sense,
> Not
> Always.

Lorenz Hart was unmatched in the craft of telling jokes gracefully
in rhyme and then switching effortlessly to a sentimental line:

> When love congeals
> It soon reveals
> The faint aroma of performing seals
> The double crossing of a pair of heels
> I wish I were in love again . . .

or:

> You are so graceful, have you wings?
> You have a faceful of nice things
> You have no speaking voice, dear . . .
> With every word it sings.   (Thou Swell)

Hart's castles of rhymes and compendia of jokes poured out over
twenty years until his sad, neglected end. One of his most brilliant
scores came then – *Pal Joey* – which contained 'Bewitched', 'Our
Little Den of Iniquity', 'I Could Write a Book', and 'Zip', an
anthology of the pretensions of an intellectual stripper based on
Gypsy Rose Lee:

Zip! I was reading Schopenhauer last night.
Zip! And I think that Schopenhauer was right!

Once on tour, alternative lyrics were needed and Hart was not to be found. So Richard Rodgers, the composer, chimed in with a neat couplet of his own:

Zip! In England people don't say clerk (clurk) they say clerk;
Zip! Anybody who says clark is a jark!

Rodgers's work with Hammerstein, while not yielding a comparable quota of laughs, was more innovative in its approach to the dramatic aspects of musicals. And Hammerstein often raised a wry smile. In *The King and I*, Anna attacks the King on the subject of his wives:

A flock of sheep, and you're the only ram –
No wonder you're the wonder of Siam.

So successful were they that they inspired one of Cole Porter's most bitter broadsides. Basking in the success of *Kiss Me Kate*, Porter was irritated to find that *South Pacific* was an even bigger smash. Entertaining an out-of-town friend one night at the Waldorf he heard the band strike up 'Some Enchanted Evening'. The ill-informed guest pricked up his ears. 'Who wrote that?' he enquired. 'Rodgers and Hammerstein', said Porter, 'If you can imagine it taking two men to write one song.'

Like Hart's work, Porter's songs delighted both café society and the man on the sidewalk outside in a manner rare nowadays when show songs are infrequently popular hits. His forte was the inexhaustible list. 'You're the Tops', 'I Get a Kick Out Of You', 'Cherry Pies Ought To Be You', 'Nobody's Chasing Me', etc., bubble with obscure, fashionable proper names – The Duc de Verdura, Parke Bernet, Camembert and Cadillacs, Elsa Maxwell, The Comtesse di Zoppola, Wendell Wilkie, F.D.R., Mae West, the Lunts, El Morocco, The Lido, The Ritz. Porter even conceived an oyster and a gigolo as heroes. The oyster finishes up back in the sea after a heady day of social climbing:

I've had a taste of society
And society has had a taste of me.

(The society hostess who downed him had thrown him up). The gigolo is also after a society matron:

> . . Of lavender my nature's got just a dash in it;
> As I'm slightly under-sexed
> You will always find me next
> To a dowager who's wealthy rather than passionate.

George Jean Nathan wrote, 'A musical show is like another fellow's wife or sweetheart. For one man who shares his taste there are always those who wonder what he sees in her.' In spite of Cole Porter's 'caviare' style of living and writing, he was so good that the public found him irresistible. Michael Arlen summed up his social front:

> Every morning at half past seven, Cole Porter leaps lightly out of bed, and, having said his prayers arranges himself in a riding habit. Then, having written a song or two, he will appear on the stroke of half-past twelve at the Ritz where, leaning in a manly way on the bar, he will say, 'Champagne cocktail please! Had a marvellous ride this morning.' This statement gives him the strength and confidence on which to suffer this, our mortal life, until ten minutes past three in the afternoon when he will fall into a child-like sleep.

Porter and Coward, great friends, are often compared. Porter is the greater songwriter, Coward the more versatile man. 'Success took me to her bosom', wrote Coward, 'like a maternal boa constrictor.' He was photographed everywhere – 'In the street. In the park. In my dressing-room. At my piano. With my dear old mother. Without my dear old mother – and, on one occasion, sitting up in an over-elaborate bed looking like a heavily doped Chinese illusionist.' Herbert Farjeon saw Coward's life like this:

> It must be hard work throwing off a couple of lyrics before breakfast, setting them to music by eleven o'clock, finishing the big scene in Act II before dashing off to the Ivy Restaurant, appearing in a matinée, talking business with Mr Curtis Brown [his agent] between Acts I and II and letting off gas to an interviewer between Acts II and III, sketching a new revue and practising the latest step before the evening performance,

gathering copy and declaring that everything is just too mar-
vellous or just too shattering at the midnight Follies or the
Gargoyle. As I say, it must be hard work, and I hope that Mr
Coward will not suffer a nervous breakdown as a result of it.

Yet Coward's most loved and lasting comic songs, 'Mad Dogs And
Englishmen', 'Mad About The Boy', 'I've Been To A Marvellous
Party', 'I Wonder What Happened To Him', 'Poor Uncle Harry', 'The
Stately Homes of England', 'Why Do The Wrong People Travel?'
and 'Why Must The Show Go On?', and his parody versions of Cole
Porter's 'Let's Do It', show no sign of losing their appeal (although
in 1981 I did hear a Connecticut matron, who had plainly confused
him with P.G. Wodehouse, inquire, 'Who is this Noel Coward? Is he
the guy who collaborated with Hitler during the war?').

Howard Dietz, whose most famous lyrics were written for Arthur
Schwartz's music, was another deeply-dyed Broadway wit. He
combined writing lyrics with a job as a film publicist and executive,
coining the phrase, 'A day away from Tallulah is like a month in the
country.' 'I don't like composers who think', he once said, 'it gets in
the way of their plagiarism.' When he and Schwartz were asked to
supply daily songs for a long-running radio serial, he asked his
collaborator if it would not take a lot out of him. 'Yes,' replied
Schwartz, 'but it'll take a lot more out of Bach, Beethoven
and Brahms' (a sentiment echoed in Dimitri Tiomkin's famous
Oscar acceptance speech for best musical score in 1955, 'I would
like to thank Beethoven, Brahms, Wagner, Strauss, Rimsky-
Korsakov . . .'). The young Dietz was on the fringe of the famous
Algonquin set of wits: 'I didn't eat with the Round Table; I watched
the Round Table eat. Although I rubbed elbows with the famous
wits and playwrights, they didn't rub elbows with me.' When he was
promoted inside MGM he was reprimanded for arriving late.
'That's all right', he replied, 'I leave early.' One Dietz and Schwartz
song, 'I Guess I'll Have to Change My Plan', took a long time to
catch on. It was eventually exported to England and became a hit.
The writers went to a nightclub to hear it. After the show, they told
the singer how much they liked the song and disingenuously asked
who wrote it. 'Someone like Noel Coward', said the singer. 'Best
song someone like Noel Coward ever wrote', said Schwartz. Apart
from their famous ballads such as 'Dancing in the Dark' and 'That's

Entertainment', a wittier variation on the theme 'There's No Business Like Show Business' is immediately appealing:

> It might be a fight like you see on the screen
> A swain getting laid for the love of a Queen,
> Some great Shakespearean scene
> Where a ghost and a prince meet
> And everyone ends as mince-meat . . .
> . . . The world is a stage
> The stage is a world of Entertainment.

Dorothy Fields, another near-contemporary, is the only woman to hold her own in this group. At seventy she could still be vivid in modern argot in 'Big Spender' ('. . . I don't pop my cork for any guy I see . . .'). She came from a vaudeville family – 'You children must be extra polite to strangers because your father's an actor', her mother used to say. She wrote lyrics against her father's will. 'Ladies don't write lyrics', he told her. 'I'm no lady, I'm your daughter', she replied. Her initiation was in the crass school of valedictory ballads like the ludicrous:

> They needed a songbird in heaven
> So God took Caruso away . . .

and

> They needed a new star in heaven
> So God took Valentino away . . .

Her first assignment commemorated an American girl pilot's trans-atlantic flight:

> One American Girl
> You took a notion
> To fly across the ocean . . .

and a contemporary university dance-craze song contained the couplet:

> Ev'ry pedagogue
> Goes to bed agog at night –
> Doing Collegiana . . .

Like Ira Gershwin her wit colours her sentimental songs, 'I Can't

137

Give You Anything But Love, Baby', 'Sunny Side of the Street',
'Lovely to Look At' and 'A Fine Romance':

> A fine romance! with no kisses
> A fine romance! my friend this is.
> We two should be like clams in a dish of chowder
> But we just fizz like parts of a Seidlitz powder.

   People like Johnny Mercer and Frank Loesser continued the
traditon into the era of Alan Jay Lerner, Sheldon Harnick and
Stephen Sondheim (who writes lying down so that he 'can go to
sleep easily'). Here are some examples.

Frank Loesser – from 'Adelaide's Lament' in *Guys and Dolls*:

You can feed her all day with the vitamin A and the Bromo fizz,
But the medicine never gets anywhere near where the trouble is,
If she's getting a kind of a name for herself, and the name ain't his –
A person . . . can develop a cough.

Alan Jay Lerner – from 'A Hymn to Him' in *My Fair Lady*:

> Men are so honest, so thoroughly square;
> Eternally noble, historically fair;
> Who when you win will always give your back a pat.
> Why can't a woman be like that?

Sheldon Harnick – creating in *Fiorello* a Tammany Hall boss
accused of graft:

> I can see your Honor doesn't pull his punches
> And it looks a trifle fishy I admit
> But for one whole week I went without my lunches
> And it mounted up, your Honor, bit by bit.

>   MEN: Up your Honor, bit by bit . . .

Stephen Sondheim – one of the songs cut from *Follies* – an effortless
Cole Porter pastiche called 'Uptown Downtown', the story of a girl

called Harriet who finds her interests divided between uptown sophistication and downtown slumming:

> She sits
> At The Ritz
> With her splits
> Of Mum's
> And starts to pine
> For a Stein
> With her Village chums.
> But with a Schlitz
> In her mitts
> Down in Fitz –
> Roy's Bar,
> She thinks of the Ritz – oh,
> It's so
> Schizo.

Sondheim once described an unsuitable lyric of his own as having 'all the grittiness of *The Fantastics*', and admonished a recalcitrant actor who complained at an interminable dress rehearsal, saying 'Who do I have to fuck to get out of this show?' by replying, 'Same person you fucked to get in!'

However, the forthright statements of E.Y. Harburg carry a clout all their own. Harburg, immortal for his contribution to *The Wizard of Oz*, was also the author of perhaps the most surprising poetic line in popular song-writing in 'The Eagle and Me':

> Ever since the day when the world was an onion.

He was a committed campaigner, in his lyrics and in his occasional poems. While Oscar Hammerstein was watching the corn grow high as an elephant's eye, 'Yip' Harburg would have been arguing for a proper rate for the job for the men who were cutting it. His family was poor; he sought a steady living as an engineer. By the time of the Depression, he said, 'I had my fill of this dreamy abstract thing called business and I decided to face reality by writing lyrics . . . the capitalists saved me in 1929 . . . I was left with a pencil and I finally had to write for a living.' Nearly fifty years on he was to put on paper:

From Roosevelt to Nixon
From 'The Wizard' to 'The Wiz'
My God it can't be possible
But oh, my country, 'tis!

On the same theme he parodied his famous 1920s lyric, 'Brother, Can You Spare A Dime' for the *New York Times*:

Once we had a Roosevelt
Praise the Lord!
Life had meaning and hope.
Now we're stuck with Nixon, Agnew, Ford,
Brother, can you spare a rope!

Harburg was wise and witty on the subject of music and words: 'Together they go places. Words make you think a thought. Music makes you feel feelings. A song makes you feel a thought . . . The greatest romance in the life of a lyricist is when the right word meets the right note; often, however, a Park Avenue phrase elopes with a Bleeker Street chord, resulting in a shotgun wedding and a quickie divorce.' Yet with all his commitment he could send up enchanting, billowing balloons of nonsense which got the message airborne – never more vividly than in 'The Begat' – a song from *Finian's Rainbow* which takes corruption, intolerance and miscegenation in its stride:

Fat filibusterers begat,
Income tax adjusterers begat,
'Twas Natchaler and Natchaler to begat,
And sometimes a bachelor, he begat . . .

In the same vein in *The Wizard of Oz* he mischievously rhymes 'prowess' and 'mou-ess'. In *Jamaica*, in 'Push de Button', Harburg applies the same technique to dehumanized urban life on 'a little island on the Hudson . . . where . . . everyone big millionaire, with his own co-operative castle, rising in the air-conditioned air':

Push de button!
Up de elevator!
Push de button!

140

> Out de orange juice!
> Push de button!
> From refrigerator
> Come banana short-cake and frozen goose!

or, launching into the anti-nuclear debate:

> Don't get smart alecksy
> With the galaxy
> Leave the atom alone.

On those occasions when he was content with nonsense alone Harburg was equally felicitous. In 'When I'm Not Near the Girl I Love, I Love the Girl I'm Near', he found infinite variations on a whimsical theme:

> When I can't fondle the hand I'm fond of
> I fondle the hand at hand.

and likewise in another song:

> Even the rabbits
> Inhibit their habits
> On Sunday at Cicero Falls.

Bert Lahr called him 'the only lyric writer on the Broadway treadmill to get comic with the cosmic':

> No matter how much I probe and prod [he wrote]
> I cannot quite believe in God
> But oh! I hope to God that he
> Unswervingly believes in me!

'It is sobering to think', said Tom Lehrer, 'that when Mozart was my age he had already been dead for a year.' (It is sobering too, to think that Stephen Sondheim is seventeen years older than the prolific George Gershwin when *he* died.) To come back to Mozart brings us again to Beecham. At a lunch given in honour of his seventieth birthday telegrams of congratulation were read from famous composers from all over the world. To reverberating applause the chairman read them out, one after another. 'Congratu-lations', 'Greetings' – from Strauss, Stravinsky, Hindemith, Sibelius, and so on. As the cheering died down, Sir Thomas looked up to the chairman from his place at the table and asked, with a slightly pained expression on his face, 'Nothing from Mozart?'

4

POLITICS

'Politics is not the art of the possible. It consists of choosing between the disastrous and the unpalatable.' – J.K. Galbraith

A definition is a convenient corset. It can bring a certain shapeliness to wild, overblown or over-imaginative ideas. The neatness of the effect is often in direct proportion to the ease with which the thought can be stuffed into the straight-jacket. In *The Real Thing* Tom Stoppard compares the craft of writing with a properly sprung cricket bat: the beautifully made instrument sends valuable thoughts hurtling over the boundary into a debate to score six. Perhaps in politics, a divisive profession, a nicely weighted boxing glove sending a man down for the count is a more appropriate metaphor.

Not all political wit comes wrapped as a definition but the temptation to be quotable is, for many irresistible:

'All political parties die of swallowing their own lies' – Swift, *Thoughts on Various Subjects*

'In politics there is no honour.' – Disraeli, *Vivian Grey*

'An honest politician is one who, when he is bought, will stay bought.' – Simon Cameron (nineteenth-century US politician).

'How can anyone govern a country that has 246 different kinds of cheeses?' – Charles de Gaulle

'The saddest life is that of a political aspirant under democracy. His failure is ignominious and his success is disgraceful.' – H.L. Mencken, *Baltimore Evening Sun*, 1929

'The proper memory of a politician is one who knows what to remember and what to forget.' – John, Viscount Morley, *Recollections II*

'There are some politicians who, if their constituents were cannibals, would promise them missionaries for dinner.' – H.L. Mencken.

'Political ability is the ability to foretell what is going to happen tomorrow, next week, next month and next year. And to have the ability afterward to explain why it didn't happen.' – Winston Churchill.

'This is the first convention of the Space Age – when a candidate can promise the moon and mean it.' – David Brinkley, the American newscaster.

'The first requirement of a statesman is that he be dull. This is not always easy to achieve.' – Dean Acheson.

The danger with too compact a definition is that it will distort the truth. Examine a few:

What is an ambassador? 'An honest man sent abroad to lie for the Commonwealth', said Sir Henry Wotton.

A diplomat? 'A baby in a silk hat playing with dynamite,' said Alexander Woollcott. (Snappier is Sidney Brody's, 'A person who can be disarming, even if his country isn't.')

Diplomacy? 'Lying in state', said Oliver Herford (probably 'out of state' would be more precise).

Politics itself? 'Nothing more than a means of rising in the world', said Dr Johnson dismissively.

The great Doctor's definition is not, however, quite so cynical as Sir Ernest Benn's: 'Politics is the art of looking for trouble, finding it whether it exists or not, diagnosing it incorrectly and applying the wrong remedy.' Ambrose Bierce's *Devil's Dictionary* supplies cynical but neat and lasting definitions:

'A strife of interests masquerading as a contest of principles',

and:

'the conduct of public affairs for private advantage.'

To Winston Churchill politics were 'as exciting as war . . . and quite as dangerous. In war you can only be killed once. In politics – many times.' Lloyd George was more personal: 'A politician is a person with whose politics you don't agree. If you agree with him, he is a statesman.' Peter de Vries is more literary: 'A politician is a man who can be verbose in fewer words than anyone else' (an echo there of Lincoln's verdict on a certain lawyer: 'He can compress the most words into the smallest ideas better than any man I ever met').

And what is democracy? In France it is 'the name we give to the people each time we need them' (Robert de Flers, *L'Habit Vert*, 1912). But, after all, in France, according to Paul Valéry, politics is also 'the art of preventing people from taking part in affairs which properly concern them.' In America it is 'the theory that the common people know what they want and deserve to get it good and hard' (H.L. Mencken, *A Book of Burlesques*). Clement Attlee, Prime Minister from 1945 to 1951, is better remembered for brevity than for wit, but his definition of democracy sums up his own way of making it work: 'Democracy means government by discussion, but that is only effective if you can stop people talking.'

It is a happy coincidence when the *mot* embodies the man. Oscar Wilde hit a fortunate, frivolous note: 'Democracy is simply the bludgeoning of the people, by the people, for the people.' But a formula used by Wilde can be light and magical, whereas a formula introduced in desperation can soon be the death of a smile. Compare Wilde's comment with Winston Churchill's tired saw on Socialist Governments, 'Government of the Duds, for the duds, by the duds.' Churchill fortunately got onto surer ground when he, too, defined democracy: 'the worst form of Government, except for all those other forms that have been tried from time to time.'

A great deal of wit survives because it sets its own tone of graceful flimsiness and does not invite detailed examination. In politics wit can be a trap. On the old BBC 'Tonight' programme we once had to dissuade Norman St John Stevas from summing up the appointment of Lord Dilhorne as Lord Chancellor with the phrase, 'At last we have a woolsack on the Woolsack'. Cruelly accurate; but it would not have been good for Norman's career. 'Those who cannot miss an opportunity of saying a good thing . . . are not to be trusted with the management of any great question', said William Hazlitt.

Disraeli knew the dangers, too: 'Men destined to the highest places should beware of badinage . . . an insular country subject to fogs, and with a powerful middle class, requires grave statesmen.' Fortunately he continued to take the risk. Nor was he the first. Two thousand years earlier, when Demosthenes said to General Phocian, 'The Athenians will kill you someday when they are in a rage', Phocian replied, 'And you someday when they are in their senses.' The attention of Talleyrand, the French statesman, was once drawn to Fouché, who ran Napoleon's Secret Police. 'He has', said the informant, 'a profound contempt for human nature.' Talleyrand agreed: 'Of course, he is much given to introspection.'

Adlai Stevenson kept notebooks of such 'good things' over forty years of political life in America, and had certain favourites. For example:

> Alcibiades was telling Pericles how Athens should be governed, and Pericles, annoyed with the young man's manner, said, 'Alcibiades, when I was your age I talked just the way you are talking.' Alcibiades looked him in the face and rejoined, 'How I should like to have known you, Pericles, when you were at your best.'

> William Hazlitt wrote, 'Man is the only animal that laughs and weeps; for he is the only animal that is struck with the difference between things as they are, and what they ought to be.'

> When Evita Peron was in Barcelona, and complained that she had been called 'puta' (prostitute), as she drove through the streets, an old general apologised, saying, 'Why, I've been retired for twelve years and they still call me General.'

Adlai Stevenson's own most quoted epigrams include: 'An independent is a guy who wants to take the politics out of politics'; 'Someone must fill the gap between platitudes and bayonets.' Of Eisenhower's political crusade he said, 'The General has dedicated himself so many times he must feel like the cornerstone of a public building', and, 'If I talk over people's heads, Ike must talk under their feet.' On Republicans he commented, 'I like Republicans . . . I would trust them with anything in the world except public office,' and 'Whenever Republicans talk of cutting taxes first and discussing national security second, they remind me of the very tired, rich man who said to his chauffeur, "Drive off that cliff, James, I want to commit suicide".'

Cynicism is a regular ingredient of political wit – at least in the stones thrown by people who live outside the political glasshouses of Parliament and Congress. Shaw set it out clearly in *Major Barbara* – 'He knows nothing; and he thinks he knows everything. That points clearly to a political career.' Those inside may demur. 'I reject the cynical view that politics is inevitably, or even usually, a dirty business', Richard Nixon said in 1973 – only to sink in a tidal wave of jibes when he retired in disgrace to California, taking only one walk a day, 'to go and launder his money'. Even on his better days, Nixon had a bad time with wits. As far back as 1970, the critic and journalist I.F.Stone was writing: 'The Eichmann trial taught the world the banality of evil. Now Nixon is teaching the world the evil of banality.' And Adlai Stevenson's verdict was: 'Nixon is the kind of politician who would cut down a redwood tree, then mount the stump for a speech on conservation.' 'Nixon's farm policy is vague', said Stevenson on another issue, 'but he is going a long way towards solving the corn surplus by his speeches'; and in a mixture of prophetic accuracy and inaccuracy, he also commented:

> Mr Nixon's defenders insist that although there are certain things that aren't very pretty, he has, nevertheless, shown the capacity for growth and, if elected, will develop the character for the job. I think it unlikely, however, that the American people will want to send Mr Nixon to the White House just on the chance that it might do him a world of good.

At least Stevenson employed a little more art than Harry S. Truman on the subject of Nixon – 'I don't think the son-of-a-bitch knows the difference between truth and lying', said the former President. But Truman then had another go at defining Nixon – same matter, more art – 'Richard Nixon is a no-good, lying bastard. He can lie out of both sides of his mouth at the same time, and if he ever caught himself telling the truth, he'd lie just to keep his hand in' – or tongue in, to be pedantic. Nixon was such a conformer in duplicity that he now lends himself to formulae – Laurence Peter has coined 'The Nixon Political Principle: If two wrongs don't make a right – try three.' Art Buchwald was a fan of President Nixon – 'I worship the quicksand he walks in' (later, he was a fan of the luckless Jimmy Carter, using the same phrase). In the end, the bitter Nixon joke exhausted itself. As Gore Vidal said, 'Everyone is so anaesthetized by scandal that if it turned out that Richard Nixon was the illegitimate son of Golda Meir, it wouldn't make the front pages.'

The strain of political cynicism is now most marked in America. Gore Vidal discerned a difference between English and American political scandals: the English scandal involved sex, the American, money. ('Have you ever seen a candidate talking to a rich person on television?' asked Art Buchwald.) But as with most Anglo-American distinctions, there is some blurring at the edges. H.L. Mencken's view of politicians – 'A good politician is quite as unthinkable as an honest burglar' – and George Jean Nathan's opinion of the craft – 'Politics is the diversion of trivial men who, when they succeed at it, become important in the eyes of more trivial men' – still ring true. So does Mencken's more rueful observation, 'When I hear a man applauded by the mob, I always feel a pang of pity for him. All he has to do to be hissed is to live long enough.' (Churchill lived long enough to hear the newish members of Parliament whisper behind their hands, 'Poor old Winston, he's gaga'; and to turn to them and say, 'Yes, and he's deaf too.') Gary Wills, the American academic and journalist, also has a sense of pity for the profession: 'There is a kind of noble discipline in politicians, in persons prepared to devote a lifetime to discourse on a single subject, over and over, with anyone who will listen, anywhere. It inspires a goofy awe, this sight of them ringing a single bell all their lives, hammering at their own heads.'

It is in invective, though, that political wit breeds its lushest foliage. A debating chamber is a forcing house for the vivid phrase. Old chestnuts abound in the history of English political cut-and-thrust, pre-eminent among them being that eighteenth-century classic in which Lord Sandwich, mulling over his put-down for John Wilkes, said, ''Pon my honour, Wilkes, I don't know whether you'll die on the gallows or of the pox.' 'That must depend, my lord,' Wilkes replied, 'upon whether I embrace your lordship's principles, or your lordship's mistress.'

In comparing a great man to a minnow, Canning coined another famous phrase, 'Pitt is to Addington as London is to Paddington.' Five years earlier, Shelley dismissed Canning's rival, Castlereagh, after the Peterloo massacre of 1819, 'I met murder on the way! He had a mask like Castlereagh.'

Sheridan used a similar Wilkesean formula against Henry Dundas, a Privy Councillor in William Pitt's cabinet: 'The Right Honourable Gentleman is indebted to his memory for his jests and to his imagination for his facts.' Wilkes scored creditably with his rebuke to a heckler who said he'd as soon vote for the devil as Wilkes: 'And if your friend is not standing?' he inquired. And again in his dismissal of Lord Bute's ignoble Peace of Paris in 1763, 'The peace that passeth all understanding.'

Lady Astor excited Winston Churchill to one unconquerable chestnut:

Lady Astor: If you were my husband, I should flavour your coffee with poison.
Churchill: Madam, if you were my wife, I should drink it.

(Dirtier, later and less funny is the comment of the Labour MP, Jack Jones, on one of Lady Astor's passionate temperance speeches. She had taken in Jones's fat physique and made several references to 'beer bellies'. Jones rose at the end to say, 'I will tell the noble and honourable lady that I will lay my stomach against hers any day.')

Another Churchillian target was Sir Stafford Cripps: 'There but for the grace of God, goes God.' And God came into his estimate of the chances of getting through the Yalta Conference in five or six days: 'I do not see any other way of realizing our hopes about a world organisation in five or six days,' he cautioned the optimistic Roosevelt. 'Even the Almighty took seven.'

Lord Home was the unlikely source of a political classic when Harold Wilson jibed at his hereditary position as a Fourteenth Earl in 1963. Home's reply (I hope it was Home's, but tread carefully as we begin to enter the era of the speechwriter), was admirably direct: 'As far as Fourteenth Earl is concerned, I suppose that Mr Wilson, when you come to think of it, is the fourteenth Mr Wilson.'

There are degrees of invective, to be sure. Recent classic examples are much more savage. Also in 1963 Jeremy Thorpe's verdict on Harold Macmillan's night of the long knives – 'Greater love hath no man than this, that he lay down his friends for his life' – is surely destined for a classic career. Macmillan himself could coin a dismissive phrase. Of Aneurin Bevan he said, 'He enjoys prophesying the imminent downfall of the capitalist system and is prepared to play a part, any part, in its burial, except that of mute.' In 1956 during the Suez crisis, Aneurin Bevan was questioning the Foreign Secretary, Selwyn Lloyd, but stopped when he saw the Prime Minister, Anthony Eden, enter the Chamber. 'Why,' he continued, 'should I question the monkey when I can question the organ grinder?' (Presumably the organ grinder had come straight from his drawing-room through which, as his wife sadly but wittily said, 'it seemed as if the Suez Canal was running.') Bevan had a cruelly dismissive wit: Gaitskell could be 'the right kind of leader for the Labour Party . . . a desiccated calculating machine'; and Eden, so long in Churchill's shadow, was 'the Juvenile Lead'. Harold Macmillan, too, showed claws on the subject of Eden: 'he is forever poised between a cliché and an indiscretion'. Malcolm Muggeridge's verdict on Eden smells more of midnight oil: 'a benzedrine Napoleon and a pinchbeck Machiavelli all in one'. To Reginald Paget, MP, he was 'an over-ripe banana, yellow outside, squishy in'. To A.J.P. Taylor, 'Eden did not face the dictators. He pulled faces at them.'

Across the Atlantic, John Foster Dulles was not faring much better at the hands of his critics: 'A diplomatic bird of prey smelling out from afar the corpses of dead ideals', said James Cameron; while Adlai Stevenson reckoned he was an expert on 'the positive power of brinking'. (Neither remark, perhaps, was *quite* as vicious as Sam Houston of Tennessee in the nineteenth century on Thomas Jefferson Green: 'He has all the characteristics of a dog except loyalty.')

Reginald Paget's rebuke to Lord Hailsham for his holier-than-thou attitude to John Profumo's frailties was magisterial (in an atmosphere precisely prophesied by Macaulay in 1843 – 'We know no spectacle so ridiculous as the British public in one of its periodical fits of morality'). 'From Lord Hailsham', said Paget, 'we have had a virtuoso performance in the art of kicking a fallen friend in the guts . . . when self-indulgence has reduced a man to the shape of Lord Hailsham, sexual continence requires no more than a sense of the ridiculous.'

Lord Hailsham is not, however, a regular target for wit. Some politicians automatically attract abuse because they are too ineffectual, too shifty, too unlucky, too mediocre or too sanctimonious.

Winston Churchill said of Stanley Baldwin, 'He occasionally stumbled on the truth, but hastily picked himself up and hurried on as if nothing had happened', and said on Baldwin's retirement '. . . Not dead. But the candle in that great turnip has gone out.' Lord Curzon dismissed Baldwin as being 'not even a public figure'; while the pseudonymous Kensal Green wrote in *Premature Epitaphs*:

> His fame endures; we shall not forget
> The name of Baldwin until we're out of debt.

Harold Wilson was usually assailed for his sharpness – on TW3 David Frost compared him and Sir Alec Douglas Home: 'Dull Alec versus smart Alec'. Duncan Sandys was Minister of Defence and it was at him that Wilson pointed as he said, 'We all know why Blue Streak was kept on although it was an obvious failure. It was to save the Minister of Defence's face. We are, in fact, looking at the most expensive face in history. Helen of Troy's face, it is true, may only have launched a thousand ships, but at least they were operational.' (Helen of Troy had been used before in the House of Commons when Florence Horsbrugh, Minister of Education, was accused of being 'the face that lost a thousand scholarships'.) Wilson's open admiration for Harold Macmillan's style was saved for Macmillan's retirement. Earlier he had given currency to 'Mac the Knife' as a nickname and borrowed Disraeli's attack on Lord Liverpool: 'The archmediocrity who presided, rather than ruled, over a cabinet of mediocrities . . . not a statesman, a statemonger, peremptory in little questions, the great ones he left open.' Harold Wilson's own favourite example of political invective is reported to be John Burns's dismissal of Joseph Chamberlain: 'To have betrayed two leaders – to have wrecked two historic parties – reveals a depth of infamy never previously reached, compared with which the Thugs of India are faithful friends and Judas Iscariot is entitled to a crown of glory.'

In more recent years the journalist Hugo Young found James Callaghan 'living proof that the short-term schemer and the frustrated bully can be made manifest in one man'. While in Australia, Gough Whitlam's politicking was neatly encapsulated by a local politician, Barry Jones, who said, with uncharacteristic Australian understatement, 'He is not well suited to the small-scale plot.'

The mediocre certainly get short shrift in politics, and often the modest and unassuming are mistaken for the ineffectual. Churchill delighted in building the myth of Attlee as a nonentity. His phrase, 'A sheep in sheep's clothing' – sometimes surely misquoted as 'a sheep in wolf's clothing' – quickly gained currency while 'An empty taxi arrived and Mr Attlee got out' was usually attributed to Churchill and was always good for a laugh in the right club. There was also, 'A modest little man with much to be modest about'. Attlee seems invariably to have been unmoved. On one occasion his simple retort to a Churchill broadside was, 'I must remind the Right Honourable Gentleman that a monologue is not a decision.' Of Kenneth Harris's biography of Attlee in 1982, John Vincent was to write, 'The result is a well-proportioned portrait of an annoyingly uninteresting paragon. Blamelessness runs riot through six hundred pages.' Attlee's own epitaph on himself was terse and neat:

> Few thought he was even a starter.
> There were many who thought themselves smarter.
> But he ended PM, CH and OM.
> An Earl and a Knight of the Garter.

The Chamberlain family provide rich pickings – Neville especially. 'In the depths of that dusty soul is nothing but abject surrender', said Churchill. 'A good Lord Mayor of Birmingham in a bad year'; closely akin to Lloyd George's verdict, 'He saw foreign policy through the wrong end of a municipal drainpipe.' Aneurin Bevan in 1937 found him a handy target: 'Listening to a speech by Chamberlain is like paying a visit to Woolworth's; everything in its place and nothing above sixpence.' A few years later he added: 'The worst thing I can say about democracy is that it has tolerated the Right Honourable Gentleman for four and a half years.' Another Churchill verdict, this time on Joseph Chamberlain – if it was original then – has become a joke-book regular for countless politicians: 'Mr Chamberlain loves the working man – he loves to see him work.' Lord Birkenhead set his sights on Austen Chamberlain: 'Austen always played the game and always lost.'

Mediocrity has this happy knack of bringing out wit in those confronted by it. President Warren G. Harding was 'not a bad man, just a slob', according to Alice Roosevelt Longworth. But H.L. Mencken's verdict was much more considered:

He writes the worst English that I have ever encountered. It reminds me of a string of wet sponges; it reminds me of tattered washing on the line; it reminds me of stale bean soup, of college yells, of dogs barking through endless nights. It is so bad that a sort of grandeur creeps into it. It drags itself out of the dark abysm of pish, and crawls insanely up the topmost pinnacle of tosh. It is rumble and bumble. It is flap and doodle. It is balder and dash.

Ramsay Macdonald drew dismissive epithets from Churchill's tag, 'The Boneless Wonder', inspired by a boyhood visit to the circus, through to Lloyd George's pot-calling-the-kettle-black – 'He has sufficient conscience to bother him, but not enough to keep him straight' – back to Churchill again, after a string of defeats which still left Ramsay Macdonald in power, who said, 'He is the greatest living master of falling without hurting himself.'

Calvin Coolidge is another American President whose mediocrity made him a target. Walter Lippman's comment was formal and considered: 'Mr Coolidge's genius for inactivity is developed to a very high point. It is far from being an indolent inactivity. It is a grim, determined, alert inactivity which keeps Mr Coolidge occupied constantly . . . Inactivity is a political philosophy and a party programme with Mr Coolidge.' Alice Roosevelt Longworth, as usual, shot straight from the lip: 'Though I yield to no one in my admiration for Mr Coolidge, I do wish he did not look as if he had been weaned on a pickle.' (Alice Roosevelt Longworth's best put-down was, perhaps, her rebuke to Senator Joseph McCarthy: 'The policeman and the trashman may call me Alice. You cannot.') The Coolidge chestnut, of course, variously attributed to Wilson Mizner and Dorothy Parker, when one or the other heard he had died, is, 'How do they know?'.

In recent years, Gerald Ford has been the undisputed champion butt. Here again the chestnuts ripened early for the accident-prone President: 'Jerry's the only man I ever knew who couldn't walk and chew gum at the same time', said Lyndon Johnson; and on another occasion, 'Jerry Ford is a nice guy, but he played too much football with his helmet off.' The New York politician, Bella Abzug, neatly tarred Nixon and Ford in one phrase; 'Richard Nixon impeached himself. He gave us Gerald Ford as his revenge.' But the amiable Ford, or one of his writers, hit back: 'Ronald Reagan doesn't dye his hair', he said in 1974, 'he's just prematurely orange' – a complement to Gore Vidal's description of Reagan as 'a triumph of the embalmer's art'. Ford's verdict on Nixon in 1974 was, I am sure, unconscious humour: 'President Nixon', he intoned, 'represents a cross-section of American ethics and morality.'

Like the mediocre politician, the holier-than-thou politician quickly breeds in his opponents an instinct for the jugular. 'I don't object to Gladstone always having the ace of trumps up his sleeve', spluttered Labouchère, 'but merely to his belief that God Almighty put it there.' Holier-than-thou carries its own booby traps. How quickly a chestnut loses its conquering power. Once 'The Church of England was the Tory Party at prayer'; not in the 1980s after the Falklands Thanksgiving Service, the revised National Anthem and the Church report on Nuclear Disarmament.

Eugene McCarthy, one of Jimmy Carter's opponents in the 1976 campaign for the democratic nomination, had two bites at the vein: 'I would not want Jimmy Carter and his men put in charge of snake control in Ireland'; and 'Jimmy Carter has the potential and proclivity of a despot.' Carter came to the presidency as an obscure Georgia politician whose heart appeared to be in the right place. His emphasis on human rights, nuclear arms control, world peace, honesty and a more humble Oval Office was immediately popular. Before long 'humble' became Uriah Heepian and Carter began to show that 'he knew a lot about how to get there, but not much about why he wanted to, or what to do when he did'. 'I have seen Mr Carter's future,' Barry Goldwater prophesied, 'it is Lyndon Johnson's past.' 'We're realists,' said the trade union leader, Lane Kirkland. 'It doesn't make much difference between Ford and Carter. Carter is your typical smiling, brilliant, backstabbing, bullshitting, Southern nut cutter.'

Woodrow Wilson had the aura of sanctity. Lloyd George referred with despair to his position at the negotiating table with Wilson and Clemenceau: 'Well, it was the best I could do, seated as I was between Jesus Christ and Napoleon.' J.M. Keynes also had a disrespectful view of Wilson: 'Like Odysseus, he looked wiser seated.' And Clemenceau, not to be left out, said, 'Mr Wilson bores me with his Fourteen Points. Why, God Almighty has only ten.'

The tradition of political wit goes back a long way. In the eighteenth century Sheridan set standards difficult to surpass. No politician since then could have written *The Rivals* or *The School for Scandal* or even *The Critic*. 'There is no possibility of being witty without a little ill-nature; the malice of a good thing is the barb that makes it stick', he wrote in *School for Scandal*. Having heard that a judge had slept through his play, *Pizarro*, a piece of tub-thumping, patriotic fustian, Sheridan shrugged and said, 'Poor fellow, I suppose he fancied he was on the bench.'

Sheridan's long flights of invective, especially his five-hour speech against Warren Hastings, alleging his disgraceful treatment of the Begums of Oude, were admired by Pitt, Byron, Fox and Burke; 'the most astounding effort of eloquence, argument and wit united'. But his rhetoric is not as easily remembered as his off-the-cuff quips. Queried about a reference to Gibbon as the 'luminous author of *The Decline and Fall . . .*', he recovered quickly, 'Luminous! Oh, of course, I meant voluminous.' He drank a great deal and was told that wine and spirits would ruin the coat of his stomach: 'Then my stomach must digest its waistcoat.' Accused by Pitt of being drunk in the House of Commons, he recalled an epigram written to commemorate an occasion on which Pitt and Henry Dundas staggered into the House together – both incapacitated,

> 'I can't see the Speaker,
> Pray, Hal, do you?'
> 'Not see the Speaker, Bill!
> Why, I see two.'

Two dukes told him one day in St James's that they had been trying to decide if he was a greater fool or rogue. Sheridan took each by the arm and said solemnly, 'Why, o'faith, I believe I am between both.' His son announced his intention of entering the House and proclaiming his independence of party by writing clearly on his forehead the words 'To Let'. 'And, under that, Tom,' Sheridan suggested, 'write "unfurnished".'

His wit was as bright in dire adversity. Always in debt he once mused on why, since he was Irish, he was not O'Sheridan – 'For in truth we owe everybody'; but his bravest retort was in the House of Commons in 1809, when it was announced that his theatre, Drury Lane, was on fire. He opposed a motion to adjourn the House:

'Whatever the extent of the private calamity, I hope it will not interfere with the business of the country.' Watching his property burn he accepted sympathy with a drink in his hand, saying, 'A man may surely be allowed to take a glass by his own fireside.' He spent his last years in dire poverty and was then buried in great style in Westminster Abbey. 'France', commented a French newspaper, 'is the place for a man of letters to live – England is the place for him to die.'

Sheridan's most flamboyant successor was Disraeli. In Disraeli's case as in Sheridan's, a bad beginning in the House of Commons heralded a brilliant career. Disraeli started his career as though he was an out-of-town try-out for Oscar Wilde. He was both dandy and novelist: 'Let me die eating ortolans to the sound of soft music', will do for dandy; the fledgling author supplied, 'A want of tact is worse than a want of virtue', and, 'I rather like bad wine, one gets so bored with good wine'; not so far from his 'I am one of those to whom moderate reputation can give no pleasure.' However, his early affectation had an original voice. He went to Gibraltar: 'I have the fame of being the first who has passed the Straits with two canes, a morning and an evening cane . . . it is wonderful the effects that these magic wands produce . . . I also have a fan which makes my cane extremely jealous.' The observations come from a man who decided early that 'affectation tells . . . here better than wit'; and would soon find, like Wilde, that affectation was a way of making people pay attention. In *Coningsby* he introduced Taper (a politician who was to lend his name to Bernard Levin when he became political correspondent of the *Spectator*). For Disraeli, Taper was a convenient mouthpiece: 'I am all for a religious cry,' said Taper, 'It means nothing, and, if successful, does not interfere with business when we are in.'

In Parliament after his notorious debut (he was howled down and retired shouting, 'Gentlemen, the time will come when you will hear me!'), Disraeli developed a talent for sustained invective, with Peel as his first whipping-boy. He cut his teeth on the Free Trade debates with an elaborate metaphor in which the inconsistency of Peel's policy in power was contrasted with his protestations in opposition. He was represented as a suitor whose behaviour in 'the hours of possession' contrasted unfavourably with his previous conduct 'during the hours of courtship'. As the debates continued Disraeli found new similes. Peel was Lord High Admiral of the Turkish Navy betraying his Sultan: 'organised hypocrisy'; a nurse dashing out the brains of her charge in 'a patriotic frenzy'; and his change of policy was matched only by 'the conversion of the Saxons by Charlemagne'. Nor did he confine himself to Peel's policy. He was happy to be personal: 'The Right Honourable Gentleman's smile is like the fittings on a coffin . . . The Right Honourable Gentleman is reminiscent of a poker. The only difference is that a poker gives off occasional signs of warmth.'

It was his opposition to Peel which brought Disraeli to the unfavourable notice of Queen Victoria. When he came to power his first task was to win her confidence with flattery. 'Everyone likes flattery', he said to Malcolm Arnold, 'and when you come to Royalty you should lay it on with a trowel.' He joined her in a reference to, 'We authors, Ma'am', after the publication of her *Highland Journal* and told her she was 'the head of the literary profession'. He defined his formula for handling her: 'I never deny, I never contradict: I sometimes forget.' Gladstone, she complained, addressed her as a public meeting; Disraeli treated her 'with the knowledge that she was a woman'.

Disraeli knew the value and the danger of wit: 'Next to knowing when to seize an opportunity, the most important thing in life is to know when to forego an advantage.' When Lord Palmerston became his target, he launched a different attack: he went for his opponent's age – 'at the best only ginger-beer and not champagne, and now a very old painted pantaloon, very deaf, very blind, and with false teeth which would fall out of his mouth when speaking if he did not hesitate and halt so in his talk.' However, when a colleague suggested that one of Palmerston's affairs which had come to light might be used to discredit him, Disraeli was immediately on his guard: 'Palmerston is now seventy. If he could prove evidence of his potency in his electoral address he'd sweep the country.' (I heard an echo of this attitude in 1963 at the height of the Profumo scandal. A taxi-driver on Fifth Avenue was misunderstanding the finer points of the affair. He was convinced that Harold Macmillan was the adulterous Minister. 'I don't see the trouble,' he said, 'at his age it's to his credit.')

Disraeli was unique in combining an orchidaceous style with the responsibilities of the highest office. 'Life is too short to be little', he said, and 'Revolutions are not made with rose-water.' Disraeli's grapeshot, in speeches, conversation, letters and novels, splatters the nineteenth-century institutions: 'I believe that nothing in the newspapers is ever true . . . and that is why they are so popular, the taste of the age being decidedly for fiction' (*Endymion*); 'The fun of talk is to find what a man really thinks, and then contrast it with the enormous lies he has been telling all dinner, and, perhaps, all his life'; 'depend upon it, when a man or a phrase is much abused there is something in both'; 'No man is regular in his attendance at the House of Commons until he is married.' When asked to speak up in the House, he retorted calmly, 'What I say is to enlighten you. If I bawled at you, you would leave this place as great a fool as you entered it.' To a Tory who threw his Radical roots in his face, he said, 'We all sow our wild oats and no one knows the meaning of that phrase better than you.'

Disraeli, 'the great panjandrum', in Alfred Munby's phrase, had to take insults more than once. 'He is a self-made man and worships his creator', said John Bright, while Carlyle called him a 'Hebrew conjuror' and inquired, 'How long will John Bull allow this absurd monkey to dance on his chest?' As proud of his Jewish ancestry as he was protective of the Church of England, he responded to Daniel O'Connell's slur by saying, 'Yes, I am a Jew, and when the ancestors of the Right Honourable Gentleman were brutal savages in an unknown Island, mine were priests in the Temple of Solomon.'

To a heckler who shouted that Disraeli's wife had picked him out of the gutter, Disraeli was more predictable: 'My good fellow, if you were in a gutter, no one would pick you out.' More reflectively, he coined a string of fine remarks: 'I have always thought that every woman should marry and no man'; 'He who anticipates his century is generally persecuted when living and is always pilfered when dead'; 'There are exceptions to all tales but it seldom answers to follow the advice of an opponent'; 'Something unpleasant is coming out when men are anxious to tell the truth'; 'My idea of an agreeable person is a person who agrees with me'; and 'What we call public opinion is generally public sentiment.'

The climax to Disraeli's career was his confrontation with Gladstone. His invective was still spirited but his years, his honours, and his increased responsibility, confronted by his monumental, solemn, and righteous opponent, contrived to turn his sallies from glancing

wit to a head-on assault. When he came in for the kill, he characterized Gladstone as 'intoxicated by the exuberance of his own
verbosity'. He conjured up a triumphant simile for Gladstone's
dying ministry out of 'those marine landscapes not very unusual
on the coast of South America', with their 'range of exhausted
volcanoes. Not a flame flickers on a single, pallid crest'; and
privately he could turn lightly to Gladstone's daughter and refer to a
diplomat as 'the most dangerous man in Europe, myself excepted –
as your father would say; your father excepted – I should prefer to
say'. Gladstone had not, in Disraeli's public phrase, 'a single re-
deeming defect'. Another Disraeli chestnut has been liberally puréed
for other politicians since: 'If Gladstone fell into the Thames,
that would be misfortune, and if anybody pulled him out, that, I
suppose, would be a calamity.' It is a neat formula, the double
definition – a sort of nineteenth-century 'good news – bad news'
joke.

Disraeli's dying, though not his last, words, as he corrected the
proofs of his final speech – 'I will not go down to posterity talking
bad grammar' – retain to the end the light, dilettante, detached wit
which he did not allow to sabotage his other achievements.

'Party is', in Disraeli's words, 'organized opinion'; or, as Gilbert
rhymed it more forcefully fourteen years later in *HMS Pinafore*:

> I always voted at my party's call,
> And I never thought of thinking for myself at all.

A party is often a label of convenience rather than a statement of
principle. Disraeli could turn on Peel's sort of conservative government and accuse Peel of adopting Whig measures: 'The Right
Honourable Gentleman caught the Whigs bathing and walked
away with their clothes. He has left them in full enjoyment of their
liberal position and he is himself a strict conservative of their garments.' Disraeli identified 'the closest thing to a Tory in disguise' as
'a Whig in power'. And Ambrose Bierce's definition of a conservative is on similar lines: 'A statesman who is enamoured of existing
evils as distinguished from the Liberal who wishes to replace them

with others.'

The party conflict is often reduced to a set of poses – Mencken's definition is perhaps the most apt: 'Under democracy one party always devotes its energies to trying to prove that the other party is unfit to rule – and both commonly succeed and are right.' Attlee was characteristically laconic on the subject of Conservatives. 'If we have to have Tories, at least they should be gentlemen' (a remark he would feel like making more frequently if confronted by the Tory party of the 1980s. Austin Mitchell defined the state of party leadership in 1983 in his book, *Westminster Man*: 'Labour is led by an upper-class public school man, the Tories by a self-made grammar school lass who worships her creator, though she is democratic enough to talk down to anyone.') The subject of class was encapsulated as wittily by Wilde as by anyone: 'Really, if the lower orders don't set us a good example, what on earth is the use of them?'

Liberals, with 'ls' of any size, take a good deal of stick; partly because the creed of liberalism should embrace turning the other cheek, partly because the convinced liberal feels a responsibility to dish it out all around. Compare the worthy attack of a right-wing, nineteenth-century American on the Democratic party – 'A mule without pride of ancestry or hope of posterity' – with Lenny Bruce's cameo of benign intolerance – 'The liberals can understand everything but people who don't understand them', Robert Frost's gentler phrase – 'A liberal is a man too broadminded to take his own side in a quarrel', and Heywood Broun's funny, but less fair summary – 'A liberal is a man who leaves the room before the fight begins'. Michael Frayn summed up the dilemma of the small 'l' liberal in the *Observer* in 1963: 'To be honest, what I feel really bad about is that I don't feel worse. That is the intellectual's problem in a nutshell.'

Liberals with a big 'L' have also had to get used to the big stick. 'As usual', said Harold Macmillan, 'the Liberals offer a mixture of sound and original ideas. Unfortunately, none of the sound ideas is original and none of the original ideas is sound.' And on an occasion when a failed Tory tried to stand as a Liberal, Churchill commented, 'The only instance in history of a rat swimming *towards* a sinking ship.' Lloyd George led the Liberal counter-attack in the early years of the century, inspired or perhaps challenged by Margot Asquith's description of his methods, 'He could not see a belt without hitting below it.' One of his targets was Joynson-Hicks, who only added Joynson to his original Hicks when he married Miss Joynson, an heiress. Joynson-Hicks mocked Lloyd George's phrase, 'unearned increment', in the House of Commons. Lloyd George, challenged to define it, said, 'On the spur of the moment I can think of no better example of unearned increment than the hyphen in the Right Honourable Gentleman's name.' (Joynson-Hicks, incidentally, went on to crusade for an early ecumenical movement in the 1920s. He proposed a conference to innumerable London churches. Only St Mary's, Bourne Street, very high and Anglo-Catholic, responded. Hicks was enthusiastically invited to a Sunday service. Red carpets were rolled out for him and Lady Hicks. The uncongenial scent of incense hit them hard but they ploughed on. The congregation was an odd mixture of Belgravia socialite and Pimlico working class. Hicks coughed through the fumes to a pew. He and his wife were soon out of synchronization with the up-and-down choreography of the service. After a while, Hicks decided to stand firm and hissed at his wife to do the same. They held their ground at one of the most critical moments for a high churchman to kneel and Hicks was given a sound thump on the shoulder by the Anglo-Catholic Pimlico labourer behind him – accompanied by the loud instruction – 'Bow, you bugger, bow!'. Little more was heard of Hicks's move towards ecumenicalism for some years.)

Of the criticism Lloyd George attracted, as opposed to the criticism he handed out, the retort which left him bereft of words was Wedgwood Benn's. Benn had abandoned Lloyd George to join the Socialist government. Lloyd George fulminated against 'this little pocket Moses who is going to lead the people to a new Jerusalem'. Benn, recalling Lloyd George's well-known profitable traffic in peerages, simply said, 'Anyhow, I have never bowed down to the Golden Calf.' Lloyd George did not relish remarks which pointed out how small he was. He told one Liberal Chairman whose introduction he disapproved, 'In North Wales we measure a man from his chin up. You evidently measure from his chin down.'

It is hard to be funny about fascism though it was poetically dismissed by Aneurin Bevan as 'Not in itself a new order of society. It is the future refusing to be born'. In 1934, an English diplomat, Sir Eric Phipps, who had to entertain Herman Goering to dinner, found to his annoyance that his guest was late. Goering's excuse was a shooting party. 'Animals, I hope', muttered Sir Eric.

The regular reporting of politics requires sharpness to make interesting the oceans of banality that pour from politicians who daily have to make a statement, take an attitude, mount a platform or champion a cause. In Parliament the entertainment is offered daily and here there parades a rich cast of pundits, boobies and holy fools, providing the commentator with plenty of sitting ducks. The plot is more repetitious than any soap opera and the urge to supply in the prose a vivacity missing from the proceedings is often irrestible. The art of the sketchwriter is a long and noble one, frequently underrated.

In 1982 Colin Welch, who many years ago reported Parliament in the *Daily Telegraph*, joined the *Spectator* to confront two phenomena, the Liberal party, not much changed from the old days, and the Social Democrats, who were new to him. He sighted the Liberals at Bournemouth:

> 'We always hope that the voice of reason will prevail,' declared Councillor Meadowcroft, prospective Liberal candidate for Leeds West. Outside, the elephantine elements mocked him: wind gusts like bombs, horizontal rain, the Bournemouth hotels shaking and banging as in an earthquake, wheelchairs flying like skiffs before Fastnet gales, nurses, cloaks and skirts over their heads, brollies inside out. One expects the Liberal Assembly to bring a little excitement to somnolent Bournemouth. As it is, their arrival is as if, after 'The Flying Dutchman' overture, at the height of the storm, a peaceful punt had appeared, its merry occupants in boaters and picture hats, listening to The Arcadians on a hand-cranked gramophone.

Welch then tackled the new Social Democratic Party, sketching in the process by which, after a long absence from the House, he got his bearings again:

> When I did report Parliament years ago, it was my good

fortune to witness the Profumo affair – you remember, when Sir Harold Wilson and the rest of us were all so high-mindedly concerned solely about the security rather than the more prurient aspects of the unfolding drama. Drawn doubtless by the loftiest curiosity, my old and revered editor, Maurice Green of *The Daily Telegraph*, visited the Press Gallery. He leant forward over the rail, subjecting the members below to a minute scrutiny, his lips working appreciatively as if he were inspecting some particularly ripe, active and odoriferous cheese. 'Ye'es, ye'es', he finally observed with a certain dry relish, 'ye'es, I think I see some adulterers down there.'

Mr Welch then abandons nostalgia for the present:

Among the many changes which have taken place while my back was turned is the emergence of the Social Democrats. Not all of them, mercifully, have marked their defection from Labour with a book. If it were obligatory to do so, one would beg further potential defectors for the love of God to stay where they are. But books by Dr Owen, Mr Rodgers and Mrs Williams I have manfully perused – and this, mark you, on holiday in Carinthia. With every page the mountains, the lake, the sun, the waitresses, seemed to sparkle more alluringly. The attention wandered irresistibly, resting now on beer bottle labels, now on regulations governing the entry of drunkards, the lousy and indecently dressed to the swimming pool. Yet resolutely I struggled on – about 1,000 pages in all, with never a laugh nor a smile, save those involuntarily evoked, nothing novel, witty or profound, only the sluglike onward movement of progressive bureaucratic prose, 'enlightened', 'compassionate', cliché-infested, leaden, 'moderate', abstract, heavy with all the quasi-modish cant, clap-trap, errors and half-truths supposedly current in Hampstead. Dr Owen's book gives the false impression of being written not by a machine but by a whole committee of machines . . . it often suggests an almost Hamlet-like indecision, a Hapsburgian hesitancy and taste for conflicting half-measures. It is as if he had a 'hung' mind (in the sense of a 'hung' Parliament), equally divided within itself, with nothing to hold the balance or tip it this way or that.

Colin Welch stands in a long tradition of witty British political commentators. Alan Watkins, among the survivors, has a gift for period parody and pastiche, after Pepys or after Aubrey, which serves as a vehicle for sharp contemporary jabs. 'David Steel, not as nice as he looks'; 'Peregrine Worsthorne, adept at losing his temper if he considered such a course suitable'; 'Sir Ian Gilmour, a highly strung man at the best of times'. Watkins, too, finds inspiration in the SDP – 'One cannot imagine Mr Jenkins sending a task force anywhere except to a good restaurant' – and his journalist's eye view of a Conservative Cabinet Minister (not yet a protected species), at a party conference is beautifully sustained:

> Conservatives come to praise and love to applaud: just as Labour delegates come to blame and love to quarrel . . . there are, it is true, exceptions to this general principle of Conservative charity. One of them is Mr William Whitelaw. There he sits, like a very old beast of the jungle or veldt, turning his great sad eyes now this way, now that, in an attempt to locate his enemies, and contemplating the while whether to take evasive action or mount a counter-attack. The conference organisers, those mysterious creatures who emerge from the Conservative undergrowth once a year, were shrewd enough to hold the law-and-order debate first thing in the morning. The proper, the appropriate time for this traditional occasion is first thing in the afternoon, when the representatives are heated by gin-and-tonic.

The extreme right recently collected a body blow from Alan Coren in *Punch*. Coren's premise was the predicament of Jeremy Isaacs, the Controller of Channel 4. According to Isaacs his channel, under attack for its left-wing bias, wanted more right-wing programmers. In a sustained exercise in witty, selective name-dropping Coren produced a page of right-wing programmes for the *T.V. Times*. Transmission was to start at 5.30 with David Irving's *A Full Life*: 'David Irving, historian wit, humanitarian, talks to Jill Cochrane about his unrivalled collection of Himmler hankies, his disillusion with the Ayatollah Khomeini's wets, and his own work on the revolutionary chicken-strangling machine to which so much of his leisure time has been dedicated.' *Big Strong Bugger* at 6.00 is a portrait of Jack Anderson ('Research: Giant Haystacks. Director:

Loni Riefenstahl – An LWT Argentina Rundfunk Co-production'). At 7.00 *Channel Four News*: Peter Sissons and Sarah Hogg . . . 'Trevor McDonald accompanies them on the Banjo.' At 8.00 *Brookside* under a new production team – Writer: Richard Ingrams, Producer: Colin Jordan – has an intriguing synopsis: 'A snivelling wimp from the local Labour Party attempts to canvas Number 14 and is dragged around the estate behind Rodney's Jag. Fenella comes home with a new dress from Ikey Modes, and when it turns out not to be crease-resistant hubbie Peregrine and some of his old rugger chums trot round to the shop and prove to the wily Levantine that British Petroleum lives up to its name.' *Films for Women* features *The Dam Busters* and 'amateur naturalist General Zia of Pakistan' puts the anti-conservationist case on *Nature Watch*. In *Jazz on Four* at 11.30 the Band of the Second Battalion, the Parachute Regiment, plays more favourites, including Tipperary, Goodbye Dolly Gray, Maggie's Tune, etc. Programmes for Channel 4's Asian viewers are not neglected. At 12.00 in *Somewhere East of Suez*, 'R.D. Mukerjee, Narasimha Singh, and Ram Chaudhury recite Kipling's *Barrack-Room Ballads* at gunpoint.' 12.15 *Lights out!*

Unlike liberalism, which we celebrated a paragraph or so back, definitions of socialism usually provoke dour determined prose and few ripples of wit, either from friend or foe. Socialism as a concept inspires wild and whirling phrases – Lord March thinks that 'As far as socialism means anything, it must be about the wider distribution of smoked salmon and caviar', and Norman Mailer, briefer than is his wont, but no more precise, says 'The function of socialism is to raise suffering to a higher level.'

The Left needs a jollier device than a definition to become the occasion of wit. I have not been able to discover what was in King Edward VII's mind in 1895 (he was still Prince of Wales then) when he said at a Mansion House dinner, 'We are all socialists nowadays.' But there is no doubt what Frank Johnson of *The Times* meant, reporting from the 1981 Labour Party Conference in Blackpool, when he said, 'Being defence spokesman in the Labour party is rather like being resident chaplain in a bordello.' The same year Johnson cast a quizzical eye on Labour Election Manifestos:

Who should read them? Normal people, such as a majority of Labour MPs and successive leaders of the party, do not need the stimulus provided by this sort of lurid, occasionally violent literature. But a minority in our society, as was all too evident by some disturbing cases on view yesterday, are unable to lead such fortunate lives.

What the conference should have established was whether such sad people could somehow be *helped* by being shown, under suitably controlled conditions, such material hour after hour. None of this is to deny that it degrades women. But is not censorship also an obscenity?

At the closing session Johnson – and the Labour Party – really came into their own with:

> ... those final Labour conference rituals which, even for an opponent of socialism, always have a curiously moving quality: 'The Red Flag', 'Auld Lang Syne', the chairman's farewell address, the translation of the chairman's farewell address from the Glaswegian, the nostalgic row over whether a frightful young man in T-shirt and jeans has a right to put a point of order virtually after the conference has ended and a closing debate accusing the police of brutality ... this final session, then, shows the Labour Party at its best. It must never be forgotten that, whatever they say, the things that divide the party are much greater than the things that unite it.

Mr Johnson discerned a difference in the Tory conference the same year:

> ... the conference is not changeless. The changes, however, are almost imperceptible year by year to all but the trained eye. This year's chairman was a trade unionist called Fred . . . Some of the traditional conference cries were still sounded. Young women, catching up on the latest developments in modern Conservatism, could still be heard calling to one another 'Did Jessica marry Desmond in the end or did she go off with that frightful American?' But, sadly, there seemed fewer of them this year. The SDP could be making inroads here . . .

Frank Johnson approaches his subject like a theatre critic and is

166

undoubtedly at his best at Party Conferences. The daily routine of parliament is clearly not such attractive fodder to him as the eccentricities thrown up by the annual bouts of hysterics observed in overcrowded seaside towns.

When the SDP met in Salford in 1983 Johnson chose to see Roy Jenkins as a political prisoner finally due for release by his party so that he could 'get back to his loved ones in his native Kensington, forget Salford and pick up the shattered pieces of his lifestyle.' He went on, 'His captors had treated him with courtesy. But he had been subjected to psychological torture. He had been forced to sit for hours on end on a raised platform in a depressing hall built in the 1960s and listen to dozens of speeches by middle-class progressives on such subjects as the need for a more positive approach to the problems of the inner city.'

Arthur Scargill himself starred in several of Johnson's accounts of the TUC conference in Blackpool that year. The revelation that his wispy back combings were secured by a Brut hairspray had been the sensation of the week and Johnson's last report harked back to 'a shock *Which* report which showed that, under capitalism, there was no known cure for baldness'.

When the Liberals met at Harrogate Johnson, again structuring his review of the assembly by referring to the most widely received reports of events which had preceded it, saw David Steel's key speech in the light of the much publicized sabbatical which had preceded it:

> Mr David Steel took a complete rest from politics during quite a long part of his speech to the Liberal Assembly yesterday.
>
> This was the part about who would actually provide the money for all the full employment, public works, roof installation (a Liberal and an SDP obsession that one) and other joys that he was promising. He avoided talk of the more specifically political subject of taxation. Thus no votes were lost, no one offended.
>
> At the end of this passage during which he was able to avoid all work connected with politics, Mr Steel emerged looking fit and refreshed.

In his introduction to his book *Out of Order*, a collection of his parliamentary reports, Johnson finds that journalism and politics have much in common: 'Journalists and politicians are as one in their search for recognition, status, praise.' He also encapsulates the art of political writing for the *Sun* (his job before transferring to the *Daily Telegraph* in 1972) in a sentence: 'I had written scarcely anything other than "Premier Ted Heath lashed Labour leader Harold Wilson in a new Commons storm last night", which is the other main language of the profession.' From the *Telegraph* Johnson moved on to Sir James Goldsmith's *Now*: 'It was an unreal existence. We were people most of whom had not previously known each other, on a voyage to we knew not where, though most suspected that it would not be a long trip. Collections of science fiction or ghost stories are full of such situations'; and eventually to *The Times*. It is not easy to make an impressive debut on a new page in a new paper but Johnson's witty observation had a field day with Lord George Brown canvassing for the SDP in Islington in Chapel Market 'one of the last of the romantically proletarian London street markets':

Admittedly, George was subdued compared with the by-election monster of his great days. But there was still The Voice. This, contrary to some popular belief today, was never a proletarian roar, more a honeyed, pleasantly strangulated tenor similar to that of Sir Peter Pears. Moreover, the vowels are pronounced with that beguiling imitation, indulged in by many Londoners, of what is assumed to be toff speech. It is the sound favoured by regimental sergeant majors and commissionaires at the Royal Opera House, Covent Garden. Thus, George replied to a stallholder who suggested that his visit to the market from the House of Lords was a bit of slumming. 'New, new. Note at all.'

Television cameras were present and a few of us pencil men. So everybody started acting in the way in which they had read or viewed, that they should act. So chirpy Cockneys behaved like chirpy Cockneys. Stallholders with crab-apple faces started to look even more so. The decades slipped away and one was suddenly among the fantasized working class of Noel Coward's *Cavalcade* or *This Happy Breed* . . .

. . . Eventually we reached Manze's pie and eel shop, a strategic stop this. For the GLC Social Democratic candidates are out to prove that they are more working-class than the Labour Left: prolier than thou . . . Matters were not initially helped by the fact that George was wearing a royal blue cashmere overcoat with an elegant velvet collar. He might at least have added a Stanley Holloway-type flat cap. No matter. He seized a plate of pie and mash. In the media age, a celebrity, a number of cameras, some lights and a bazooka-shaped sound device, all intruding themselves into a confined space, seem not to arouse the slightest interest or disturbance in the citizenry originally occupying that space. They regard it as one of the hazards of shopping, like the presence of West Indian lads on roller skates. So the folks carried on munching the pies or torturing the eels. . . . 'Better than the stuff in the House of Lords, this meal . . . Not that I eat there much . . . tuppence each, they were in my day . . . tuppence ha'penny for the large ones' . . . Soon George's day was over. He disappeared in the direction of Central London where there are fewer pie shops, but more velvet collars. What a superb campaigner! But his present role in the new movement is not consistent with his dignity and talents. Why should George Brown play second to David Owen? The situation in which George finds himself is similar to that adumbrated in a song of his cockney youth – a song almost Schubertian in its suggestion of disappointment stoically borne:

> 'Please don't tell my Mother,
> I'm half of a horse in a panto,
> Never let her know that I'm a sham,
> But if she learns in due course,
> That I'm only half a horse,
> Please don't let her know which half I am.'

If Frank Johnson is the Dramatic Critic in the political Press Gallery (was, I should say, since he has now moved on to report from Paris), then Simon Hoggart, particularly in *Punch*, is the Gossip Columnist. (Re-reading some of Hoggart's collected paragraphs reminds me that I have made no mention of two other parliamentary commentators, Pepys (unofficial) who wrote in 1661 that the young men who sat in Parliament were 'the most profane swearing fellows that I ever heard in my life, which makes me think they will spoil all and bring things into a warr if they can,' and Dickens (accredited) who found it the noisiest, most confused place he knew, 'not excepting Smithfield on a market day, or a cockpit in all its glory'.)

Hoggart's ear is for revealing tittle-tattle set in a sparse commentary occasionally spiked with sharp remarks of his own. Like Alan Watkins he has specialized in anthologizing Lord Whitelaw's eccentricities. 'When you collect Willie-isms, the death-defying logical leaps made by the Home Secretary (as he then was) there is nothing more horribly frustrating than seeing someone else get into print first with a new and classic addition to the *oeuvre*. You feel as Vladimir Nabokov might on watching a particularly rare and beautiful butterfly climb into another's formaldehyde bottle.' Hoggart caught Whitelaw talking about the problems of the TV Licence fee. 'Another MP asked whether, in view of the various anomalies, he would examine alternatives. Willie replied with firmness and vigour. "We are examining alternative anomalies", he said.' At a press conference on law and order answering a question about a report specifically recommending shorter sentences Willie, 'in his usually waffly speech', could dimly be perceived to be agreeing with it:

> 'That's funny', said one of the journalists present, 'your candidate here' – a right-winger – 'said that it should be screwed up and thrown into the wastepaper basket'.
> Willie didn't hesitate an instant.
> 'That's right', he said, 'It should be thrown into the wastepaper basket, then taken out and carefully re-examined.'

Classic was Whitelaw's response to the problem of overcrowding in Britain's prisons. 'Willie made his position absolutely clear on this urgent issue. "I can assure you that I definitely might take action," he said.'

Hoggart has neatly compared two styles of American President:

> Jimmy Carter used to get up at 5am. Reagan's chief aides don't meet until 7.30am when the President is still snoozing. He turns up around 8.45am most days and, after a rough morning's decision-taking, goes back for a nap. If it's a

working afternoon, which it often isn't, he'll be back in the Residence at 6pm for some much-needed rest before facing a strenuous reception or dinner party. Then he's back home to greet the sandman for the final visit of the day . . . He is the first man for 20 years to make the Presidency a part-time job, a means of filling up a few of the otherwise blank days of retirement.

But Hoggart's heart is really nearer home:

Conservatives . . . are highly suspicious of all bills to do with animals. I think they suspect that any piece of legislation, whether it is meant to end vivisection or protect some endangered species such as the natterjack toad, is in some subtle way a stalking horse, a harbinger of the bill which will one day seek to abolish fox-hunting . . . or interfere with the God-given right to blaze away at anything that has four legs or feathers.

However, this is but a prelude to an exchange which delighted the political Gossip Columnist. Lord Houghton supported the Laboratory Animals Protection Bill. He sent a ten-page letter to the chairman of the Tory Party, Lord Thorneycroft, 'outlining his massive campaign to put Animals into Politics. The reply was a polite but remarkably brief letter from Thorneycroft which read: "Dear Douglas, Thank you for your letter about animals. I do think that the poor creatures have enough to put up with without being put into politics. Yours Sincerely . . ." '

Tony Benn's eating habits became a source of concern on an occasion when he was admitted to hospital and rumour had it that malnutrition was at the root of the problem (not only physical depletion attacks Benn. Neil Shand once wrote him off for television as 'The Incredible Shrinking Name'):

It seems almost unimaginable that a well-to-do politician with a rich wife, and as many opportunities to eat at someone else's expense as a wine merchant has to drink, should have such a complaint. There are MPs at the House who eat three square meals a day, plus innumerable canapés, biscuits and dry roast peanuts, and never once spend a penny of their own. There are whole tribes in the Amazon basin who survive on less than is thrown away from PR functions at the Commons.

But this is less surprising in Mr Benn's case. When he was in the Cabinet he is thought to be the only Minister in history to survive on an exclusive diet of Department of Energy sandwiches . . . This would consist of those tiny, wrinkled, institutional sandwiches, quarters of Mother's Pride smeared thinly with meat paste or soggy with inadequately dried lettuce, washed down by mugs of tea. Mr Benn is also an obsessively hard worker, and would never waste time eating properly if it meant an hour away from some cherished speech or position paper. It could be that Michael Foot tried stuffing him with truffles and duck in orange sauce as a last desperate means of shutting him up.

Hoggart has a low opinion of House of Commons wit – citing an occasion soon after Marcia Falkender's 'lavender' honours list: 'Dennis Skinner, the left-wing Beast of Bolsover, stood up and said to James Callaghan: "When my right honourable friend comes to write his own honours list, will he take a piece of clean paper, not lavender coloured, and write upon it the following" . . . at which point two Tories interrupted simultaneously with a single word: "Skinner!" They were still laughing at that one six months later.'

A delightful vignette was the result of Bill Pitt's election as Liberal MP for Croydon in 1981.

A third man told me that it had been fascinating, on the Friday after Pitt's election, to watch him being transformed from human being to Member of Parliament. 'It's the self-assurance they get from people being nice to them and treating them with unaccustomed respect. After all, if you do fifteen radio and TV interviews in one day, you actually come away with the impression that what you say really matters. The Jimmy Young programme sent a Mercedes to pick him up that Friday morning. 'Gosh, do all MP's get this treatment', he asked. 'Only on the day after they are elected,' a Liberal official said drily.

In Ted Heath Hoggart goes so far as to discover a sense of humour. 'It's not what you would call a gossamer, elfin-footed sense of humour and it is often disconcertingly confused with extreme rudeness . . . When he made his crack at the Tory conference about "Don't clap me, it might annoy your neighbour," even Mrs Thatcher turned to *her* neighbour on the platform and muttered "that's a good one".'

Sleeker was the snatch of gossip he picked up about a 'clever young diplomat in our German Embassy'. James Callaghan, then Prime Minister, spotted his exceedingly smart Parisian-designed silk tie . . . Callaghan peered myopically at the tie. 'What on earth does "YSL" stand for?' he asked. Quick as a flash the youth replied: 'Young Socialist League, Prime Minister'.

Hoggart has an ear for a phrase. He quotes Alastair Burnet's description of the Mall as 'the ceremonial asphalt of Old England'. I like his label for Dennis Thatcher, 'Britain's first spouse'; but how sad the gossip in him must have been to see the departure in March 1982 of the master of indiscretion, Rab Butler. Hoggart therefore recorded a few in his valedictory piece: 'At the Carlton Club a fellow-diner rose to say goodbye after a long and friendly conversation. "Who was that?" asked someone else. Butler raised his voice a notch to become audible to the parting guest, "Oh, that's X", he said. "He's of no significance".' And of Eden, Butler would say, 'And then of course dear Anthony will make the speech he *always* makes so well.' Hoggart pinpoints Rab's formula as a mastery of 'the insult cast as a compliment'. As Leader of the House he could keep MPs happy by pausing gravely and saying, 'I have this matter at the front of my mind', where of course it remained forever. When a reporter aksed him if Eden was the best Prime Minister we had he replied notoriously 'Yes'. Asked who it was who asked the question, he would always say, 'I have his name'. Another verdict on Eden was prompted by the story that he was the son of a mad baronet and a beautiful woman. Butler did not ponder the information for long. 'That's the trouble with Anthony – half mad baronet, half beautiful woman.'

There is a whole vein of political wit, which I find tedious, but which is the stock-in-trade of the populist politician. In England it always gets a laugh and a respectful round of applause on *Any Questions*. It is the wit which hopes to ingratiate the speaker with a large 'no-nonsense' audience, who love such nonsense. It is home-spun and corny, and it flowers most sumptuously in America on the lips of crackerbarrel philosophers. Abraham Lincoln found it necessary to defend his excursions into the genre. In 1863 *Harper's Weekly* lampooned him in a cartoon in which 'Columbia' inquired, 'Where are my fifteen thousand sons murdered at Fredericksburg?', to which Lincoln answers, 'This reminds me of a little joke'. His justification was simple: 'They say I tell a great many stories. I reckon I do, but I have found in the course of a large experience that common people, take them as they run, are more easily informed through the medium of a broad and humorous illustration than in any other way; as to what the hypercritical few may think, I don't care.'

Sometimes the most such wit can hope to be is defensive and disarming. Jimmy Carter or his writers used a lot of this in trying to divest his relations of their inbred offensiveness. Of his brother he joked: 'Billy's doing his share for the economy. He's put the beer industry back on its feet.' And in much the same popular vein he accounted for his ancient mother and his wife: 'We're having the President of Mexico here for a State dinner in a few days and Rosalynn and I have never been to a State dinner, so we're going to look at movies of past State dinners to see how it's done.'

John F. Kennedy developed a curious rich man's equivalent, a sort of inverted snobbery of cornball humour, with the same intention of disarming criticism. At election time: 'I have just received the following telegram from my generous Daddy. It says, "Dear Jack, Don't buy a single vote more than is necessary. I'll be damned if I'm going to pay for a landslide." ' On his aggressive brother Bobby: 'My brother Bob doesn't want to be in government – he promised Dad he'd go straight.' Another version of his recurring theme was: 'Mothers all want their sons to grow up to be President but they don't want them to become politicians in the process.' When he appointed Bobby Attorney-General, he tried yet another folksy joke: 'I don't see what's wrong with giving Bobby a little experience before he starts to practise law.' Kennedy could also speak American in its most simple, artless guise. 'I didn't think John Diefenbaker was a son of a bitch. I thought he was a prick.' Adlai Stevenson commented on the Kennedy phenomenon when he was given a thankless supporting role in the 1960 campaign. He told a story 'about Jimmy, aged eight, who went over to play with his friend, Bill. "Let's play cops-and-robbers", he proposed. "I'll be the good guy and you can be the bad guy." Bill's little brother Tommy, aged four, said eagerly, "Can I be the commercial?" '

In its simplest form cornball humour is best represented by Will Rogers, the folksy American humourist; 'I don't make jokes; I just watch the government and report the facts'; 'Politics has got so expensive that it takes a lot of money even to get beat with'; 'You can't say civilization don't advance . . . for every war they kill you a new way.' Harry S. Truman often found it convenient to be a political Rogers: 'I never gave them hell. I just give 'em the truth and they think it's hell.'

Often it is simply bluntness for effect. Jimmy Hoffa, the American teamster union boss who disappeared in gruesome circumstances, said, 'I do unto others what they do unto me, only worse.' His biographer's epitaph for him had a similar directness: 'Jimmy Hoffa's most valuable contribution to the American labour movement came at the moment he stopped breathing – on July 30th 1975.' Lyndon Johnson (whose 'instinct for power was as primordial as a salmon's going upstream to spawn') was a recent master of the genre, pushing it well beyond the bounds of drawing-room taste. His images are bracingly open-air. On J. Edgar Hoover: 'I'd rather have him inside the tent pissing out, than outside pissing in.' Richard Nixon said, 'People said that my language was bad, but Jesus, you should have heard LBJ.' LBJ once gave his frank opinion of a Nixon speech: 'Boys, I may not know much, but I know chicken shit from chicken salad!' On Senator Fulbright, LBJ's verdict was, 'You know when you're milking a cow and you have all that foamy white milk in the bucket and you're just about through when all of a sudden the cow switches her tail through a pile of manure and slaps it into that foamy white milk? Well, that's Bill Fulbright.'

Barry Goldwater was another presidential candidate who could find the lowest common denominator when it suited him: 'Hubert Humphrey talks so fast that listening to him is like trying to read *Playboy* magazine with your wife turning over the pages.' On Senator William Scott in 1975, Goldwater remarked that, 'If he were any dumber, he'd be a tree.' I.F. Stone had a look-alike phrase for Goldwater himself: 'It was hard to look at Goldwater and realize that a man could be half Jewish and yet sometimes appear twice as dense as the normal Gentile.' Reagan has his folksy streak too. It is fairly revolting. Asked a hostile question about the effect of his policies on the poor, he replied, 'How can you say that about a sweet guy like me?'

In a country full of people proud of their identity as the Americans, folksy prarables have had a potent appeal. Lincoln told so many stories that not only did nuns (as well as cartoonists) complain of his lack of seriousness, but he was credited with innumerable jokes which were not his – just as Coward, Wilde, Shaw and others have been since. Long before *The Wit and Wisdom of Prince Philip*, and similar collections, America was peddling *Old Abe's Jokes* or *Wit at the White House*. Unofficially he was 'the American Aesop'. Lincoln was also a tireless re-treader of old tales to run the road in his latest campaigns. Caught in debate by a hell-fire opponent who asked everyone to rise who would follow him, give their hearts to God and go to heaven, and then observed Lincoln sitting alone and asked where he was going, Lincoln was quiet, brief and reasonable: 'I am going to Congress', he said, which is where he went. His speech-making stock-in-trade was sows and pigs and ten dollars a day and two stacks of hay, travelling preachers and Mississippi steamboats, chin-flies and whiskey. Early in his career he was worsted by Senator Douglas who recalled his first speech in the Illinois legislature, during which Lincoln said three times, 'I conceive . . .' and got no further. 'Mr Speaker', Douglas pointed out, 'the Honourable Gentleman has conceived three times and brought forth nothing.' Lincoln got his own back some years later when Douglas referred to Lincoln's store-keeping days. Lincoln had sold Douglas whiskey, and was not above a low blow: 'Many a time have I stood on one side of the counter and sold whiskey to Mr Douglas, but the difference between us now is this. I have left my side of the counter, but Mr Douglas' (whose fondness for drink was well-known) 'still sticks to his as tenaciously as ever.' Impatient with a tardy General, Lincoln replaced him with another who mailed a despatch from his 'Headquarters in the Saddle'. Lincoln, who was beginning to regret the substitution, snapped, 'The trouble with Hooker is he's got his headquarters where his hindquarters ought to be.' Even sharper was his response to a judgment on another public figure. 'It may be doubted', pontificated the proposer, 'whether any man of our generation has plunged more deeply into the sacred fount of learning'; Lincoln was unimpressed. 'Or come up drier', he added.

Senator Henry Clay of Kentucky once interrupted a long dull speech by an American General who turned on him to say, 'You, sir, speak for the present generation; but I speak for posterity.' 'Yes,' said Clay, 'and you seem resolved to speak until the arrival of your audience.' Clay clashed with John Randolph of Roanoake on occasion. A story, perhaps apocryphal, commemorates their encounter on a narrow pavement – mud seeped all around. 'I, sir,' said Clay, loftily, 'do not step aside for a scoundrel.' Randolph took his cue and stepped straight into the mud, saying, 'On the other hand, I always do.' It is fair to say that partisans of Clay and Randolph claim the last word for their champion and award the feed line to the man for whom they have less sympathy.

Back in the twentieth century, Hunter S. Thompson somehow managed to mix the corny with the sick in his vignette of Ed Muskie on the campaign trail in 1972: 'Muskie talked like a farmer with terminal cancer trying to borrow on next year's crop.' Thompson was as bluntly rude to Hubert Humphrey: 'A treacherous, gutless old ward-heeler who should be put in a bottle and sent out with the Japanese current.' Occasionally, the 'folksy' can be used constructively, as in Gerald Gardner's verdict on Robert Kennedy's methods: 'That was the Kennedy way; you bit off more than you could chew, and then you chewed it.' Mark Twain, however, ground the corn more smoothly. Of a dead politician he wrote, 'I did not attend his funeral, but I sent a letter saying I approved of it.'

Just as those who hold political office are targets for wit, so are the offices and institutions themselves:

'The Treasury are never happy; even in Paradise they will be worried about excessive imports' – A.P. Herbert.

'The House of Lords is the perfect eventide home' – Baroness Stocks.

'Think of it, a second chamber selected by the Whips – a seraglio of eunuchs' – Michael Foot.

'The House of Lords has a value . . . it is good evidence of life after death – Lord Soper.

A.P. Herbert risked a defence of the Lords:

> We don't represent anybody it's true,
> But that's not a thing to regret;
> We can say what we think – and I know one or two
> Who've never said anything yet.
> While the Commons must bray like an ass every day
> To appease their electoral hordes
> We don't say a thing till we've something to say,
> There's a lot to be said for the Lords.

Not even the office of Prime Minister is safe – as *The Times* put it in 1967: 'High politics are unsuitable for ordinary man. Great Prime Ministers Winston Churchill and William Pitt were sociable drinkers, Lloyd George and Palmerston could not be trusted with women, Chatham, perhaps greatest of all, was actually mad.'

In America the Presidency is almost as popular a target as the President. '. . . Any boy may become President and I suppose it's just one of the risks he takes,' said Adlai Stevenson. 'If Presidents don't do it to their wives they do it to the country,' Mel Brooks has said. Earlier Oliver Wendell Holmes Jr found another way of putting the office in its place: 'It takes me several days, after I get back to Boston, to realize that the reference "the President" refers to the President of Harvard and not to a minor official in Washington.' Anthony Burgess has written that 'The U.S. Presidency is a Tudor Monarchy plus telephones.'

The Vice-Presidency is even more vulnerable – less important and so more potentially risible. The classic dismissal of the office by Thomas Marshall echoes an old show-business joke, 'Once there were two brothers; one ran away to sea, the other was elected Vice-President – and nothing was ever heard of them again.' Hubert Humphrey's Vice-Presidency was dismissed by the journalist Murray Kempton – he 'has no function in any game his government plays, except to lead the cheers'.

In England a similar contempt has been reserved for the office of Speaker. Its importance is much overrated, particularly by its incumbents. Lord Rosebery put the record straight for Queen Victoria's benefit: 'There is much exaggeration about the attainments required for a Speaker. All Speakers are highly successful, all Speakers are deeply regretted, and are generally announced to be irreplaceable. But a Speaker is soon found, and found, almost invariably, among the mediocrities of the House.'

In recent years the man who did more than any other to emphasize the importance of wit in politics – and who made sure that he had a ready supply to hand – was Franklin Roosevelt. Roosevelt was an innovator. If he was not the first to use a speechwriter, he was certainly a pioneer in relying on the breed extensively. Regular radio appearances heard throughout the country demanded new scripts. In the glare of the modern media old political treatises must be re-vamped as relentlessly as old vaudeville acts exposed on television for the first time. Roosevelt realized the value of wit, humour and especially ridicule as a weapon.

Roosevelt's writers are said to have included Judge Samuel Rosenman, Harry Hopkins, Robert E. Sherwood, Archibald Macleish and academics like Raymond Moley, Rexford Tugwell, Adolph Berle and others. Rosenman claims to have coined the phrase 'New Deal' and that neither he nor the future president had any idea of its potency as a rallying cry. Other favourite expressions – 'a rendezvous with destiny', 'economic royalists', 'I hate war' – can be traced to other sources, and the thundering phrase 'arsenal of democracy' was borrowed for Roosevelt from Jean Monnet by Felix Frankfurter. Ridiculing businessmen who attacked his economic measures, Roosevelt reminded them of the state in which they had been a few years earlier – besieging Washington like some vast emergency hospital. 'The distinguished patients wanted two things – a quick hypodermic to end the pain and a course of treatment to cure the disease. They wanted them in a hurry. We gave them both. And now some of the patients seem to be doing very nicely. Some of them are even well enough to throw their crutches at the doctor!' His speechwriters occasionally tried practical jokes on him – since practical joking was the President's favourite form of humour. In a speech which started, 'In the polling booth we are all equals', they continued, 'In the polling place, as in the men's room, all men are peers'. Trying his speech out on his mother, Roosevelt saw the trap in time to skip the sentence. It was not Roosevelt, but a member of his Cabinet, Harold Ickes, who found dismissive phrases for two of Roosevelt's opponents. Wilkie was 'the rich man's Roosevelt, the simple barefoot boy from Wall Street'; and, when Dewey announced his candidacy, 'Dewey has thrown his diaper into the ring.' He later characterized Dewey as looking 'like the little man on top of a wedding cake'. Like Nixon and 'Chequers', Roosevelt also had his 'dog' speech. He was accused of sending a destroyer at enormous expense to bring back his dog, Fala, left behind in Alaska by mistake. In a climactic paragraph, written this time by himself, not by his speechwriters, for a key rally in Madison Square Gardens, Fala became a magic red-herring to distract voters from worrying about Roosevelt's third term. 'I don't resent attacks, and my family doesn't resent attacks, but Fala *does* resent them. Fala is . . . a Scottie . . . and as soon as he learned that Republican fiction writers had concocted a story – of a cost to taxpayers of two or three or eight or twenty million dollars – his Scotch soul was furious.' The speech was an overwhelming success and radio commercials played it round the clock introduced by the song, 'They Gotta Quit Kickin' My Dawg Around'.

Nowadays politicians' speeches are invariably in the earnest, verbose, humourless monochrome which is the sign of the speechwriter. It is hard to believe that Kennedy was not speaking someone else's platitude when he said: 'If we cannot now end our differences, at least we can help make the world safe for diversity.' One of Kennedy's speechwriters, his Press secretary, Pierre Salinger, made his own bid for verbal freedom. Salinger was named 'Plucky Pierre' by Kennedy and when he refused to depart from a prepared and authorized text insisted, 'I am not a textual deviate'. Off the cuff, when questioned about the escape of the (then) very young Caroline Kennedy's hamsters, he said, with all the seriousness of a man used to coping with questions of heavy secrecy, 'Our security is very tight but these were extremely intelligent hamsters.' Mrs Thatcher's annual joke at the Tory party conference is supplied by a 'safe' playwright whose strong point is not humour – yet 'The Lady's not for turning' was probably right for the audience to which it was addressed: a playgoer I overheard at the National Theatre looked forward to a new play at the Haymarket: 'It's by the man who writes Mrs Thatcher's speeches – so it must be good.'

Consider the predicament of the presidential or prime-ministerial jokester. Peter Stone, the distinguished Broadway playwright and movie scriptwriter, was from time to time telephoned from Airforce One and asked to supply a gag which would leaven one of the holier-than-thou, mawkish sermons Carter was about to deliver. Having hit the desk hard for a half an hour, Peter would risk his quip over the air on an aide, be thanked and wait for the live broadcast. Invariably he would see the President approach the appropriate paragraph, shy at the *mot* and plough on into convinced, gauche, man-of-the-people simplicity. The writer saw only one joke actually used, and relished the look of surprise on the President's face when the laugh came.

Perhaps it is appropriate to wind up political wit with a selection of snipings from the touchline of the most recent General Election in Britain – for the plethora of pictures on television and the interminable interviews on the radio opened up the field to witty commentators. It is difficult to improve on some of the moments so generously offered up. I remember a brief glimpse of Sir (sic) Ronald Millar, standing by an upright piano, sipping a clear, brown liquid and singing his Tory campaign song 'Maggie for Me' in a style best described as posthumous Jack Buchanan. Mrs Thatcher was confronted by two other Iron Ladies on a TV phone-in – the intrepid Sue Lawley, the referee, and a prodigious West Country battleaxe, a Mrs Gould, who had briefed herself – or been briefed – carefully about the 280-degrees bearing which the *Belgrano* was following *away* from the Falklands when she was sunk. Mrs Thatcher refused to answer the question as put, point-blank, three times. At one stage she even looked at the icy Lawley in desperation and got no help. Then there was the annihilation of Michael Foot – the only leading politician who had been a television star thirty years ago. Now his suitability for the box was being questioned by whippersnappers who would not have rated a vox-pop appearance in front of Thomas T. Crapper's Kings Road emporium in the fifties. Presumably it had to do with changing styles.

In the *Sunday Telegraph* Anthony Quinton addressed himself to the subject of the physical appearances of Michael Foot, Margaret Thatcher and Dennis Healey:

Mrs Thatcher started her campaign with a cold, which seemed still just audible up to Williamsburg, but there has been no doubt of her general bodily vigour. She has developed a powerful, crouching style of movement, like Groucho in pursuit of a rich widow or a submarine commander coming on deck after surfacing. Mr Foot, however, despite the nice new dark suit, still looks like an English toy in which a crucial part has been put in upside down.

Mr Healey's appearance, to which we have been exposed quite a lot, faute de mieux perhaps, has become increasingly garish. His skin shines, the copses of hair on various parts of his face seem to grow as one looks at them.

Since most of us saw the election at second hand, here is Frank Johnson, in *The Times*, observing Mrs Thatcher at close quarters:

One of the happiest moments of Mrs Thatcher's election campaign of 1979 was her visit to the Cadbury's factory in a Birmingham marginal.

There, balancing on the brink of successive vats of whirling chocolate, with the crush of photographers threatening to propel her downward at any moment, she narrowly missed being incorporated in a range of delicious walnut whips. The history of Britain over the last four years could have been so different.

Many of us interpreted that visit as the turning point of the 1979 campaign – there being more pigs among the electorate than joggers.

Yesterday, just over four years later, she kept faith with the pivotal 'fat vote' by visiting a marzipan factory in a south London marginal.

'11.00 Arrive John F. Renshaw Ltd, Lock Lane, Mitcham. Manufacturers of marzipan', said the sheet of paper issued to those of us travelling with the Prime Minister. Please note: very limited press facilities because of hygiene regulations'.

This was rather offensive, since some of us reporters are a good deal less filthy than some politicians.

Three coaches, one of them containing the Prime Minister, descended on the factory. Then, as in Act Two of *The Nutcracker*, we children were led by her through the Kingdom of Sweets ...

... The machinery clattered. The marzipan churned and gurgled. Women continued to stuff chunks of it into brown boxes. Mrs Thatcher started to make full use of her gift of being piercingly interested in whatever is being explained to her on an election tour.

Unlike the sadly limited Mr Foot, she has many roles which, depending on the role of the person whom she is addressing, she can assume at will – politician, wife, mother, shopper, marzipan-maker.

On this occasion she was all five. 'Making marzipan with almonds is a brute of a job', she told a group of women, referring to her own experience of the process.

Meanwhile Mr Denis Thatcher, whose mastery of factory-visit conversation is now the equal of the Duke of Edinburgh's, could be heard in the background working away at the firm's executives: 'Do you buy your almonds from the almond people overseas? . . . I see, yes . . . you make the cherries, d'you?' Back to the Prime Minister, still working the women. 'I don't like too much of it because it is VAIRY, VAIRY rich. . . .'

Clatter-clatter, continued the machines. Gurgle-gurgle, continued the marzipan. The Prime Minister sat down at a conveyor belt with some more women and joined in the sorting of dark almonds from light. Whereupon, the photographers started climbing up the adjacent walls, and indeed each other.

'By law, you can only make marzipan with almonds,' an executive was at the same time explaining to Mrs Thatcher, which is in itself an astonishing piece of information.

Excitement mounted. 'You skin them and grind them yourself,' the Prime Minister could be heard bafflingly telling some of the executives at one stage. This turned out to be a further reference to her way with nuts, when marzipan-making, rather than to her way with Cabinet colleagues.

A joyous occasion, then. Sadly it was time to go.

Reluctantly, we took off the long white coats, and the white hats, which all of us – including the Prime Minister – had had to wear for hygiene reasons.

Mr Thatcher had looked in his like a reassuring surgeon in a private hospital catering for senior businessmen.

'Nothing wrong with a medium sherry now and then, old boy,' one could imagine him advising after an op. 'But I'd go easy on stuff like marzipan if I were you.'

One of the shrewdest and funniest television critics of the 1983 election was Julian Barnes – he seemed to be finding his length in the *Observer* after a shaky start. 'Politics increasingly comes down to style, and style increasingly comes down to plausibility on television,' wrote Barnes. He was much concerned by the eclipse of Michael Foot:

> It is a continuing curiosity that Mr Foot, orator and literateur, has lost his grasp of words. Watching him manage a sentence is like watching a novice blackbird pulling on a worm: there's a complete lack of confidence about where the thing in his mouth will ever end. It was, we can now see, clearly a mistake on Mr Foot's part to abandon that handy boned corset known as punctuation: the gay release of flesh in his sentences may make the speaker himself feel more relaxed, but it has the viewer averting his eyes.
>
> Worse, even his control of cliché – which every politician sucks in with his mother's milk, swallows as the staff of life and leans on like a crutch – has deserted him. On Panorama (BBC1) he condemned the election as 'the Gadarene stampede of the Conservative Party to gain an advantage' – as if the Biblical swine somehow did well out of their foray into the sea.

From Barnes too, comes a final word on the victor:

> Another four years of Matron. The cold showers, the compulsory cod-liver oil, fingernail-inspection, and the doling-out of those vicious little pills which make you go when you don't want to. No wonder the sick bay's over-populated. In some places this might indicate failure; but in Britain, mysteriously, it's held to be a sign of success.
>
> The only difference in Matron as she freewheeled to victory this time was her hairline. Of late it's been distinctly higher, with the tresses swept resolutely back off the forehead. After the Churchillian voice, the Shakespearean hairdo. The only comparable coiffure in recent times was that worn by Glenda Jackson, who had a hairline-shave to play Elizabeth I. Perhaps this was the final Saatchi gag of the campaign: Matron plays the Virgin Queen in the school pageant.

And on the bet-hedging of the losers:

> Preparing most busily was Shirley Williams, with her repeated

claim through Thursday night that the Alliance would provide 'the moral opposition' in the new parliament. A few years ago Dr Owen, while TV punditing for the Labour Party at a by-election, came up with the phrase 'differential abstention'. A 'differential abstention', it turned out, was a posh way of saying that most of your supporters had either stayed at home or voted for your opponents. Similarly, a 'moral opposition', we can now appreciate, is what arises when your party loses 78½% of its seats.

Now the cast is changing, the old actors are wandering into the wings, good for no more than the occasional off-stage whisper. Will the take-over players sharpen their wits for our delight or keep any instinct for levity safely under wraps? We wait to see. Meanwhile, we could leave the last word to one whose political wit may yet shine through the rest of the century – the new boy, Neil Kinnock, elected in Michael Foot's place to lead the Labour Party. Shortly after the General Election of 1983 he was perceptive enough in a newspaper interview to see the similarities between politics and sport. 'I think Ian Botham is the stuff of which heroes are made', he said. 'I have a certain soul sympathy for him, because sportsmen and politicians suffer the same fate. All their successes are written in sand, and their failures are carved in stone.'

5

SPORT

'I hate all sports as rabidly as a person who likes sports hates
common sense' – H.L.Mencken

The nature of competitive games breeds a deal of heroism on the
field and the occasional felicitous understatement off. Witty sportsmen are witty in spite of their prowess, but the literature of sport
tends towards celebration, rhetoric, overstatement and tub-thumping and, occasionally, insult, not towards sharp, purposeful, amusing and elegant economy.

On *That Was the Week that Was*, in the early 1960s, Peter Cook
and David Frost captured the overheated prose of contemporary
sports journalists: Frost's character – Desmond—there will be dancing in the streets of Bogata tonight—Packet – used to mail des-
patches from exotic datelines:

> On the red shale track, it was a black, black day of gloom,
> despair and despondency for the British lads and lasses who
> ran their hearts into the ground in the sizzling cauldron that is
> Rome! Rome? I prefer to call it the muddle city of all time. In
> the farcically run 10,000 metres, the British contingent, upset
> by the sounds of Italian love-making in their nearby cubicles,
> looked tired and drawn at the start . . .

> 'If the British girls are men, then I'm a Dutchman,' declared
> Hugo Van Der Huyst, the prominent Amsterdam businessman.

> Meanwhile in this seething Rome – Rome? I prefer to call it the
> Terrazzo of Tittle Tattle – rumours fly like bees round a glass
> of milk . . .

> Heinrich Gestetner is the mysterious German behind Britain's
> failure in the track events. Gestetner, incidentally, went to
> school with the Duke of Edinburgh, but that was before the
> outbreak of the ghastly war which was to overwhelm Europe,
> and bring an end to organised athletics as we knew it . . .

Meanwhile, on the sunbaked soccer fields of Rome – Rome? I prefer to call it Sodom and Gomorrah in sheep's clothing – British prestige has sunk to an all-time low . . .

This British soccer blues day – there is no other word for it – drove another nail into the tottering coffin of Britain's Barons of Ball and Caliphs of Kick, who, if they do not yield to the public demand for a floodlit Asian Super League, must surely kiss goodbye to Alf Ramsey and his pipe-dreams of a world soccergarchy.

Witty parody of this sort of sports writing has done nothing, however, to stem its flow. Nor did Bernard Levin's sceptical examination of the reaction of press and public to World Cup fever in 1966. 'The Trophy, one of the most hideous artifacts Western Man has ever produced in his long history of bad taste, had been stolen before the competition began, but unhappily recovered before it ended', remarked Levin. Then he went on to examine the patriotic frenzy aroused in the breast of the leader-writer for *The Times* – 'it being accepted that in a fair contest England must either win the match or, in the parlance that the sportsmen had picked up from the politicians, "gain at any rate a moral victory".' Levin then considered the aftermath of soccer hooliganism:

As the streets of London seethed and heaved with a marching, cheering, flag-waving, horn-blowing, rattle-wielding, bell-ringing, drum-banging, cymbal-clashing, traffic-jamming, glory-remembering, victory-celebrating crowd, who at last had something to march, cheer, wave, blow, wield, ring, bang, clash, jam, remember and celebrate about . . . the nation that chooses to live by football shall perish by the trade gap, the sterling crisis, the failure of national purpose, the loss of identity, the cohesion and determination of her enemies and commercial rivals.

Perhaps this is the moment for the great World Cup chestnut inspired by England's defeat by West Germany in 1970 – German fan: 'You see, we have beaten you at your national game!' Disgruntled Englishman (remembering two World Wars): 'Yes, well, we beat you twice at yours!'

Sports commentators are a relatively new and fertile source of laughter. The wit involved here is often in spotting those inadvertent howlers and slips made under pressure, the kind which have been immortally anthologized by *Private Eye* under the title *Coleman-balls*. The Master, David Coleman himself, leads off:

> The pace of this match is really accelerating, by which I mean it is getting faster all the time.

> Football is football; if that weren't the case, it wouldn't be the game it is – Garth Crooks (LBC).

> The only thing that Norwich didn't get was the goal they finally got – Jimmy Greaves (Central TV).

> Ian St John: Is he speaking to you yet?
> Jimmy Greaves: Not yet, but I hope to be incommunicado with him in a very short space of time. (ITV)

> There's been a colour clash: both teams are wearing white – John Motson (BBC).

Julian Barnes, when TV critic for the *New Statesman*, was vigilant regarding 'commentatese':

> Ron Pickering continued to overheat as usual. The mockery of my confrères had chided him out of saying 'he's pulling out the big one', and even, 'he's whacking in the big one'. But the National Viewers and Listeners Association will cut off his tail with a carving knife for his new and shameless variant: 'If she hits the board and bangs a big one, that'll put her in the bronze medal position'.

But we should spare some sympathy for the sports commentator. It can't be easy in the heat of the moment to speak proper English, and without sounding trite or even suggestive. As Russell Davies puts it in *The Sunday Times*:

> They know their stuff – even if David Coleman, in particular, has trouble in actually expressing it without mangling a couple of syllables per sentence. Living with the producer's voice permanently murmuring inside his ear is very gradually robbing him of the power of speech. But some things never

change. Plainly no way has yet been found to stop long-jump commentaries sounding like naughty stories after lights-out in the dorm ("Oooh, it's *enormous!* it was *so long!*").

Another lapse, unmonitored by *Private Eye*, but gleefully seized on by American addicts, was Phil Rizzuto's impromptu remark during a baseball commentary which had been interrupted by the news of the pope's death: 'This puts a damper even on a Yankee win', he intoned.

Sports-*writing* is a bastard business at best or, as Jimmy Cannon, a witty American sportswriter who died in 1973, put it, 'A sports-writer is entombed in a prolonged boyhood.' Nevertheless, Cannon himself came up with many phrases good enough for the grown-up section: 'Philadelphia is an old wino sleeping it off in a doorway littered with busted dreams. Its teams are doomed to lose and its fans are cruel and crabbed.' He was against the romantic school: 'Sports-writing survives because of the guys who *don't* cheer'; and, 'Hemingway was a sportswriter . . . he was the only guy who could make fishing sound interesting to me. Fishing, with me, has always been an excuse to drink in the daytime.' Cannon had a healthy contempt for sportsmen, too: 'Let's face it, sports-writers, we're not hanging around with brain surgeons.'

American sports-writers are more prone to self-examination than their English counterparts (but then so are all Americans). Ring Lardner was convinced that 'there isn't anything on earth as depressing as an old sports-writer'. (He also found the Americas Cup 'as exciting as watching grass grow'. Tell that to Peter de Savary; the 1983 event did a lot to shake Lardner's chestnut off the tree for good.) One of America's most versatile and stylish sports-writers, Red Smith, is also defensive: 'The public can't tell good writing when they see it and neither can plenty of editors and publishers. Still the good writers become popular. I guess they succeed for the same reason that the jury system succeeds. Somehow Eugene O'Neill and Hemingway and W. Shakespeare managed to make it.' Red Smith occasionally casts a beady eye on the purple passages of his colleagues. Back in 1924, Grantland Rice, another revered American sportswriter, had rhapsodized about an American football game between the Army and the University of Notre Dame:

Outlined against a blue-gray October sky the Four Horse-
men rode again. In dramatic lore they are known as Famine,
Pestilence, Destruction and Death. Their real names are
Stuhldreyer, Miller, Crowley and Layden. They formed the
crest of the South Bend cyclone before which another fighting
Army football team was swept over the precipice of the Polo
Grounds yesterday.

Coolly examining this famous piece of sporting prose, Red Smith
wondered at 'What angle "Granny" watched the game from if he
could see them outlined against the blue-gray October sky.'

William Saroyan, on the other hand, considered baseball writing
to be among the 'best folk-writing of our nation'. He should have
told that to Robert Lipsyte who complained that 'Well-meaning
people often ask sports-writers, even middle-aged sports-writers,
what they are going to do when they grow up.'

The war between sports-writers and sports stars or managers
never lets up. A college football coach in America, Bo Schenbechler,
said, 'I don't have anything against media people. I just don't want
my daughter going to school with them.' Jim Murray, another
American sports-writer, opined, 'By and large baseball writers and
baseball managers get along like man and wife. They respect each
other, but not much. . . . To me, sports-writing has never been a
matter of schools. When a guy is wonderful you can say he is
wonderful. When he isn't, just say that he stinks.' Dick Young from
the New York *Daily News* is yet more jaundiced: 'Every young
sports-writer starts out writing about black athletes in the ghetto.
They come back saying how articulate the black athlete is. What
does that mean? That they can speak words?' Fred Trueman, the
cricketer, once proposed the toast to sports-writers at an annual
dinner. 'I'm here to propose the toast to sports-writers', he glower-
ed, 'it's up to you if you stand up.' An American greyhound owner,
Ralph Ryan, was once accused of using live rabbits for his grey-
hounds to practise on in training. He denied it vehemently: 'No,
I use sports-writers like you. And when we get a broken-down dog
we give him a typewriter.' Jimmy Breslin, the volatile New York
columnist, sympathized with his ex-colleagues in a nostalgic look-
back at his days as a sports-writer:

You find yourself covering the Kentucky Derby for the third time and you realise there's nothing new to write. You sit through a Sunday double-header and you want to kill yourself. You get extra innings and you're ready for an observation ward. Football is the worst of all. They're killing the game with this phoney mystique. Telling people that a guy needs the abilities of a brain surgeon to play left guard for the Colts. Football is a game designed to keep coal miners off the streets.

A notorious American sports-announcer, Bill Curry, famous as 'The Mouth of the South', had no high opinion of his younger colleagues:

Sports-announcers nowadays are about as colourless as a glass of gin . . . Most of them are like a bunch of barbers cutting each other's hair. They emulate each other and fawn over each other on the air. The same dull, successful ones show up everywhere . . . The broken-down old ball-players are the worst, but almost all are equally appalling.

One former baseball star, Don Drysdale, bewailed his fate on turning sportscaster in 1973: 'Interviews are the hardest for me. I felt so damn funny asking players questions when I already knew the answer.' I once booked Danny Blanchflower – still a football player at the time but disgracefully articulate – to be interviewed on television. The interviewer failed to show so Blanchflower easily and wittily interviewed himself for five minutes!

In his short stories, Damon Runyon evokes wonderfully the games, the characters, the atmosphere of the crummy sports hangers-on around the seedier cross streets off Broadway:

It is really surprising to see how many college guys do not care to see large football games, even after they get their duckets, especially if a ticket spec. such as Sam the Gonoph (the same Sam who 'long ago came to the conclusion that all life is six to five against') comes along offering them a few bobs more than the duckets are worth. I suppose this is because a college guy figures that he can see a large football game when he is old, while many things are taking place around and about that it is necessary for him to see while he is young enough to enjoy them, such as the Follies.

191

Runyon is famous on boxing: 'While Spider McCoy manages a number of fighters, he never gets excited about anything but a heavyweight and this is the way all fight managers are. A fight manager may have a lightweight champion of the world but he will get more heated up about some sausage who scarcely knows how to hold his hands up, if he is a heavyweight.' (An anonymous rhyme makes the same point: 'You've heard about the bees and the honey? The lightweights do the work and the heavies get the money.') On a certain heavyweight Runyon remarked: 'He was once known along Broadway as a heavyweight fighter and he was by no means a bad fighter in his day, and he now has a pair of scrambled ears to prove it. Furthermore he is bobbing slightly, and seems to have a few marbles in his mouth, but he is greatly pleased to see me.'

And then there is Runyon, inevitably, joyously, and equally famously, on the gee-gees:

> A handicapper being a character who can dope out from the form what horses ought to win the races, and as long as his figures turn out all right, a handicapper is spoken of most respectfully by one and all, although, of course, when he begins missing out for any length of time as handicappers are bound to do, he is no longer spoken of respectfully, or even as a handicap. He is spoken of as a bum.

and:

> It seems that one spring day, a character by the name of Nicely-Nicely Jones arrives in a ward in a hospital in the city of Newark, N.J., with such a severe case of pneumonia that the attending physician, who is a horse-player at heart, and very absent-minded, writes 100, 40 and 10 on the chart over Nicely-Nicely's bed. It comes out afterwards that what the physician means is that it is 100-1 in his line that Nicely-Nicely does not recover at all, 40-1, that he will not last a week, and 10-1 that if he does get well he will never be the same again.

Runyon's genius was eccentric and unique. Another American sports veteran, John Tunis, considered his more typical colleagues: 'Most sports-writers are dopes. They get their egos hepped up. They are guilty of overblowing everything. Absolutely every game is the most important, most vital, most exciting, most dazzling, most beautiful they've ever seen. Some of them say this through necessity. If they admit that many of the games and the athletes are dull, they're fearful of losing their jobs. But . . . I suppose the spectators, the fans, don't want to be told, either. They may not like it if you tell them sport is unimportant.'

However, do not despair. Sport does not produce only rampant illiteracy in those who comment upon it. Not all the humour is homespun or hearty, and the palm goes to the greatest of cricket-writers, R.C. Robertson-Glasgow. Wit so often flourishes in the cause of criticism that it is remarkable to find it so eloquently employed by Robertson-Glasgow as the servant of enthusiasm. Page upon page of his prose is crammed with respect and yet his approval is given in a style as subtle, pleasing and glancing as an almost imperceptible deflection to leg executed by the Nawab of Pataudi. Hear him on Frank Woolley:

> . . . easy to watch, difficult to bowl to, and impossible to write about. When you bowled to him, there weren't enough field-ers; when you wrote about him there weren't enough words. In describing a great innings by Woolley, and few of them were not great in artistry, you had to go careful with your adjectives and stack them in little rows, like pats of butter or razor blades. In the first over of his innings, perhaps, there had been an exquisite off-drive, followed by a perfect cut, then an effortless leg-glide. In the second over the same sort of thing happened; and your superlatives had already gone. The best thing to do was to presume that your readers knew how Frank Woolley batted and use no adjectives at all.

On Herbert Sutcliffe:

> He sets himself the highest available standard of batting and deportment. If he is bowled he appears to regard the event less as a human misfortune than some temporary, and reprehens-ible, lapse of natural laws. There has been a blunder, to which he is unwillingly privy and liable. The effects of this blunder will be entered, with other blunders, in a score-book, and the world may read of it in due time. He does not regret that it has occurred for he is never sorry for himself; but he is sorry that Nature should have forgotten herself. To the latecomers to the

ground he would, so to speak, announce: 'Mr Sutcliffe regrets he's unable to bat today, being, ludicrously enough, already out'.

On George Gunn (who approached faster bowlers walking 'sideways towards them like a grimly playful crab'):

He mocked equally the rules of batting and the Rules of Cricket. He was silently and exquisitely amused at cricket's precise measurements and its neat pomps. Why twenty-two yards? Why not an acre or so? Wherein a man might stroll about with bat and pads and play any ball jerked along by unseen agency, backhand or forehand, cutting half-volleys square to the boundary and driving long-hops for a single over mid-off's head. Why not? And in these genial wanderings, he should have come upon Edward Lear, looking as usual, perfectly spherical and wearing a runcible hat; and there should have been a single-wicket match of no time, no dimension and no result; then an argument over a glass of ale on whether Aunt Jobiska was exactly right in her argument that a Pobble is better without his toes, as everyone knows. Then they should have pledged a return match, to be played three weeks earlier, with Lewis Carroll as umpire . . .

On E. Oldroyd (Yorkshire):

One of those small, tough, humorous, militant men who make the comedy and the greatness of a country . . . they are to be found answering back something or somebody, which may or may not have existence, fate, a tax-collector, Monday morning, a bus conductor, thirst or a Hyde Park orator. They bounce and argue down time's corridors. And they generally win the battle.

On Harold Gimblett, the great Somerset opener, sometimes accused of being 'too daring for the greybeards':

He is also too daring for the majority of the black-beards who sit in judgement on batsmen; in short, too daring for those who have never known what it is to dare in cricket. Only for those who have not yet grown to the tyranny of the razor is Gimblett possibly not daring enough.

There is a sad echo of Gimblett in Harold Pinter's precise and charming profile of Arthur Wellard, the other memorable Somerset hitter of the '30s, '40s and '50s (and fast bowler to boot). Pinter and Wellard appear to share a prose style, clipped, practical, understated. Pinter is reporting Wellard (readers should insert their own pauses). 'All the old stagers were dropping like flies. Harold Gimblett had topped himself. He was always a nervous kind of man, highly strung. Remember his first knock for Somerset. Made a hundred in just over an hour. He did it with my bat. I lent it to him, you see. He was only a lad'.

Pinter was reporting Wellard in his seventies. Robertson-Glasgow saw him, as I did, in his heyday:

> . . . he does what most young cricketers would like to do and most spectators long to see; he is a fast bowler and a hitter. Pretend as we may to delight in subtlety, spins, deflections and defence, our keenest pleasure is in the sight of a stump madly wheeling or a ball soaring over the sight screen.

Robertson-Glasgow is the Ken Tynan, the James Agate, the Bernard Levin, the H.L. Mencken of cricket. But I must stop quoting him before he elbows other writers from this book as well as from this chapter. When I first started to work with Caryl Brahms it was accepted between us that I knew about cricket and she knew about music. After a few years, we discussed Neville Cardus. 'The highly respected cricket writer', she said. 'No', I corrected her, 'the well regarded music critic.' Since bringing in those rash verdicts we revised her view of Cardus on music; but not mine on Cardus as the second string among cricket writers. (This may well say more about Caryl's flexible mind than my judgment.) But I defy anyone to read *Summer Game*, *Days in the Sun*, *Close of Play* and *Cricket*, and match them against Robertson-Glasgow's *Cricket Prints* and its sequel, without conceding victory by an innings to the latter. Yet one must give Cardus his due. He it was who made this eloquent plea:

> When I get to heaven I shall produce on my behalf, in hope of salvation, my stock of failures and frustrations. My attempt to become a leader writer on the Manchester *Guardian*, my attempts to sing the Abschied of *Wotan*, my attempts to under-

195

stand Hegel, my attempts to spin a fast ball from the leg to the off stump.

And his last words in *Cricket*, culled from a letter dated September 1739 and written by Mary Turner, of East Hoathly, Sussex, to her son, are also charming: 'Last Monday, you're Father was at Mr Payns and plaid at cricket and come home pleased anuf, for he struck the best Ball in the Game and whished he had not annything else to do he would play Cricket all his life.' And perhaps only Cardus could have found the sight of Wally Hammond taking a slip catch 'as lively as any ballet dancer', or have thought that Keith Miller, 'the greatest match-winner in contemporary history', was 'as much an Australian as God'.

Today most of the wit in cricket writing comes from Alan Gibson. Take, for instance, this brief piece from the *Spectator*:

> Eyes are unpredictable things. Some years ago I had some bother with mine, and wondered if I might have to give up cricket-writing. Friends were kind after their manner. One said he thought that being blind would make no difference to the quality of my reports, and another, who had just had two unlucky leg-before decisions, said I could always take up umpiring.

Cricket as a metaphor is no longer as powerful as it once was. Who would say, as did the Duke of Dorset in 1777, 'What is human life but a game of cricket?' No, the Duke was as wide of the mark, albeit in the opposite direction, as was Archbishop Temple in his schoolmastering days when he dismissed cricket to a parent as 'organised loafing'. Lord Mancroft could have put the Archbishop right. 'Cricket', he said, 'is a game which the English, not being a spiritual people, have invented to give themselves some concept of Eternity.' A concept of Eternity has little to do with fast bowling today of course – Mike Brearley is vivid on the subject of Jeff Thomson's 90-mile-an-hour onslaughts in Australia: 'Broken marriages, conflicts of loyalty, the problems of everyday life fall away as one faces up to Thomson.'

The most touching remark provoked by cricket came appropriately from the lips of W.G. Grace. In his last season the elderly Grace felt the need to apologize for his inept fielding – 'It is the ground,' he moaned, 'it's too far away.' The Oscar Wilde of cricket is Fred Trueman – again a magnet for apocrypha, a creator of chestnuts and a skilled reteller of other cricketers' wit. Batting with Cowan, a fine quick bowler, and appalling batsman, for Yorkshire against the West Indies, they were faced by a fast bowling onslaught. Wes Hall sailed in to Cowan. Cowan's bat prodded to leg, the ball rocketed past the off stump. 'I think this fella has found my weakness, Fred', said Cowan. The next delivery encouraged Cowan to play to the off side. The errant ball shot over the leg stump. 'It looks to me he's found both of 'em now', said Trueman. Reporting Emmott Robinson, Trueman evokes the era of Amateur and Professional when the two classes were required to converge on to the ground from the pavilion through different entrances. The occasion was an early appearance by A.E.R. Gilligan, future amateur Captain of England – done up to the nines. As he approached the wicket a fellow-professional came up to Robinson. 'What's this fella doing then?' he asked. 'I don't know', said Emmott, 'but he smells nice.' He proceeded to bowl Gilligan comprehensively first ball. Gracious, gentlemanly and condescending, Gilligan deigned to speak to him on the way back to the pavilion. 'Well bowled, indeed, Robinson. That was a great ball.' 'Aye,' said Robinson, 'but it were wasted on thee.'

Trueman tells of the time when Washbrook and Wharton were opening for Lancashire, with Washbrook on 90 and Wharton on 99, and Washbrook called a quick single. Wharton refused to move and Washbrook barely regained his ground in time. 'It is a well known fact', he snarled, the next time they met in the middle of the wicket, 'that I am the best judge of a single in all England.' 'Yes', Wharton concurred, 'and it's a well known fact that when I'm on 99, I'm the best judge of a run in all the bloody world.'

On one occasion Trueman entered an opposing team's dressing room breathing fire and slaughter. 'I need nine wickets from this match', he announced, 'and you buggers had better start drawing straws to see who I don't get.' Reproving Subba Row in the West Indies, after Subba Row had dropped a slip catch that led to four runs off his bowling, Trueman received the apology ungracefully and asked about the four runs. 'I'm sorry about that', said Subba Row, 'it might have been better if I'd kept my legs together.' 'Yes', Trueman agreed. 'it's a pity your mother didn't.'

Australian cricket produces more verbal slapstick than wit. But

Thomas Keneally, in *Summer Days*, has written wryly on the subject:

> We may be a small and callow race, but there is a divinity to
> our cricket. There are profound social and cultural reasons for
> it. As late as the 1930s, the curriculum in Australian schools
> was identical to that of an English grammar school. Poetry cut
> out at Tennyson. The only history was European history.
> When we spoke of literary figures, we spoke of Englishmen.
> But when we spoke of cricket, we spoke of our own. Cricket
> was possible! We knew why it was. We had more sunshine, we
> ate more protein, we washed more regularly than the Poms!
> ... Cricket was the great way out of Australian cultural
> ignominy. No Australian had written *Paradise Lost*, but Bradman had made 100 before lunch at Lords.

Cricket sets poets off quicker than does any other sport. Apart
from that 'breathless hush in the close' that night, and Kipling's brief
but memorable excursion:

> Then ye returned to your trinkets:
>   then ye contented your souls,
> With the flannelled fools at the wickets
>   or the muddied oafs at the goals;

there is Gavin Ewart's Ogden Nashian poem – a wailing and
gNashing of rhymes:

'Not Quite Cricket?'

Watching cricket is habit-forming, it can become habitual,
It's a kind of long-lasting white-robed ritual;
and (until recently) it's been a male prerogative,
played by big hairy bowlers and blacksmiths who were
    slogative.
And in village cricket, which was where it all began,
it was a straightforward matter (as in Milton) between
    God and Man –
in spite of the bumpy pitch and the blinding light
the idea was that, if you tried hard, the Deity would see you
    right.

The ladies just watched – in crinolines that were both broad
   and high,
which would have made the l.b.w. law hard to apply.
Notice, by the way, that cricket doesn't have Rules,
   like any ordinary game; it has LAWS
and many a staunch cricketer is ready to die for the Cause.
In low-grade cricket they sometimes get hit on the head
and left on the field (as at Eton and Waterloo) for dead.
Personally I think you don't have to be much of a detective
to work out that all those devices categorised as protective,
gloves, pads, boxes, helmets, are a good thing. Though
   the fans, stiff-upper-lipping and bobbysoxing,
consider it should be A Man's Game and lethal – like boxing.

You can imagine cricket going on eternally in Heaven.
Perhaps the Devil would be allowed to bowl, with the Seven
   Deadly Sins all clustered around the bat, fielding.
They once had Demon Bowlers and 'fast' meant yielding
(in the case of young ladies) to a sexual attraction;
but I think the Devil would bowl leg-breaks with an
   off-break action,
the classical googly, as invented by Bosie.
Such games, going on for ever, could get quite cosy.

Or perhaps the angels would be fielding, in their white
   flannels.
And it would be compulsory viewing on all the heavenly
   channels.
Certainly many Englishmen are so enamoured of cricket
that in Paradise, rather than a pretty girl, they'd like to see a
   wicket.

There are some well-known pieces of cricket writing which, alas, I
have never smiled at much, perhaps because their familiarity breeds
a certain amount of contempt. I do not, for instance, smile much at
A.G. Macdonnel's great village cricket match set-piece in *England
Their England*; or at A.P. Herbert's 'Cricket in the Caucasus' – 'A
big wolf runs out of the wood and takes the ball in its mouth. "Run

Volodja, the wolf has the ball. Follow and help him, Boris Borisovitch" '; or at the wild juxtapositions in Peter Tinniswood's recent *Tales from the Long Room* – though here I do have to confess a fondness for, 'I except from these strictures, of course, Mr John Inman, brother of that fine Pakistani test cricketer, Mr Inman Khan'; and for Sibson's (Ibsen's) ignominious end, yorked sixth ball by Lord Harris: 'Sibson had not troubled the scorer. And as he stormed back to the pavilion swinging his bat angrily, muttering dark Scandinavian curses and grinding his remaining Nordic teeth (the two front ones went with the fifth ball), we realise now only too well the origin of his most celebrated play. I refer, of course, to *The Wild Duck*.'

The new cricket literature lingo is not much to write home about: it is just amiable mumble from the radio commentator's high-slung hutch, sporting disc-jockeys filling silences. Peter Baxter, a BBC producer and sometime commentator, once dismissed his team of Test Match commentators, their efforts and, particularly, their audience in two sentences: 'I think that for a lot of people listening, the cricket is incidental. If the team were talking about rabbit-keeping, people would probably be just as happy.'

I have included so much cricket writing here simply because it is the best game played by the best people in front of the best crowds. But all good things must come to an end. Let me finish with a piece from *The Times* gossip column in the summer of 1983, a neat and witty reversal of the standard cricketing tradition:

A sharp dispute has arisen between the leading auction houses and the Victoria & Albert Museum. It concerns the latter's cricket team, which is alleged to be full of ringers. The V & A recently played Sotheby's, and hammered them. Tomorrow they meet Christie's, and the antecedents of their team will be closely scrutinized. 'It is no good playing febrile types who turn out in Fiorucci track suits and stand on the boundary remarking the too, too Turneresque sky, oblivious to the ball flying past them', says the V & A's captain, Nicky Bird. 'Our players all have a connexion with the Museum. Our opening bowler, for example, sheltered in the doorway during a shower. We feel it is not how you play the game that matters, but whether you win or lose'.

Yes, there are other games, with their own brands of wit amongst those who watch as well as those who participate. There is golf for a start – 'A good walk spoiled', as far as Mark Twain was concerned. Not so to Bob Hope: 'If you watch a game, it's fun. If you play it, it's recreation. If you work at it, it's golf.' To O.K. Brand, an American sports-writer, it was 'Cow pasture pool'. A.A. Milne knew the secret of golf's popularity: 'Simply it is the best game at which to be bad.' Golf is, of course, an international game. 'I learn English from American pros', said Roberto de Vicenzo, 'that is why I speak it so bad. I call it P.G.A. English.' Another professional on the American circuit, Chi Chi Rodriguez, was also disarmingly frank: 'I'm playing like Tarzan and scoring like Jane.' H.G. Wells was merely an observer: 'The uglier a man's legs are, the better he plays golf – it's almost a law', he wrote, before the days of televised golf where elegant young men, in immaculately pressed pastel flannels, now stroll confidently from tee to green, unruffled by the distractions which so disturbed one of P.G. Wodehouse's characters – 'The least thing upset him on the links. He missed short putts because of the uproar of butterflies in the adjoining meadow.'

Wodehouse's man would have been ill at ease on Alan Coren's golf course of the immediate future, conjured up after reading an advertisement in *Esquire* for a 'Cushman Electric Golf Car', a Fort Knox putter of 14-carat gold and a Hooch handle – a 'fine golf umbrella with a special handle that unscrews to reveal a flask'. Coren's imaginary car had 'steel chassis, Italian styling, real imitation pigskin seats, automatic transmo, air conditioner. Imported'. The clothes for golf à la Coren are similarly sumptuous:

'Those', he said, 'I like. The mohair plus-fours. Style!'
'I gotta nanorak to match', said Sorfik, excitedly. 'Hold on fellas, this ya haveta see!'
The driver is "alligator-handled", the caddy "the best . . . Scotch. Imported." Say something Angus'.
'It's a braw, bricht, moonlicht nicht, tonicht,' said the caddy.
'Fantastic!' cried Hummer. 'The genuine article!'
'I've always had coloured', said Belt, grudgingly, 'You know where you are with coloureds'.

The instinct to hunt, shoot and fish is usually stronger than the instinct to write amusingly about it. 'I always like the outdoor life', brags an open-air character in a Monty Python sketch, 'out there with the guns slaughtering a few of God's creatures, tramping about the moors blasting their heads off.' Fortunately there are honourable exceptions to this attitude. 'It aren't,' wrote Robert Surtees, in *Mr Sponge's Sporting Tour* 'that I loves the fox less; but that I loves the 'ound more'; and, 'Women never look so well as when one comes in wet and dirty from hunting'; and, 'No man if fit to be called a sportsman wot doesn't kick his wife out of bed on a haverage once in three weeks' – presumably practising to measure up to Wilde's chestnut description of fox-hunting as the 'unspeakable in full pursuit of the uneatable'. Doctor Johnson had similar views on angling: 'I can only compare it to a stick and a string with a worm at one end and a fool at the other.' 'It is very strange and very melancholy', reflected the Doctor on another occasion, 'that the paucity of human pleasures should ever persuade us to call hunting one of them.' Asked Byron: 'For what were all those country patriots born? To hunt and vote and raise the price of corn.'

George Bernard Shaw focused on tiger hunting: 'When a man wants to murder a tiger he calls it sport; when a tiger wants to murder him, he calls it ferocity.' P.G. Wodehouse considered that 'the fascination of shooting as a sport depends almost wholly on whether you are at the right or the wrong end of the gun', a slightly more genial summary than the dismissal of a sportsman as 'a man who, every now and then, simply has to get out and kill something'. 'The Rolls-Royce and Runny Nose Brigade', Phil Drabble, passionate and professional countryman, has called the modern shooting syndicates, 'They shoot as a status symbol . . . (and) don't go into the country except to exterminate everything to get to the last pheasant.'

In *Decline and Fall* Evelyn Waugh provides a link to the next sport: 'I have observed in women of her type a tendency to regard all athletics as inferior forms of fox hunting.' Athletic prowess did not impress Winston Churchill either: 'In my experience officers with high athletic qualifications are not usually successful in the high ranks.' Nor was the playwright Dennis Potter over-impressed as he watched the sport dragging itself into the sponsored 1970s at the Crystal Palace track: 'The BBC cameras picked up a solemn lady called Paula Fudge as she pounded along . . . with "British Meat" written across her understandably heavy bosom. Sponsorship in

sport is one thing but this was altogether a different kettle of offal.'
A.P. Herbert was more impressed by the great Czech runner:

> Vladimir, Vladimir, Vladimir Kuts
> Nature's attempt at an engine in boots.

One of Miles Kington's wilder flights of fancy in *The Times* was
inspired by the ever-present rumour of athletic sex changes behind
the Iron Curtain:

> Controversy still surrounds the 1,500-metre runner from
> Russia, Ilf Simonov, who surprised everyone by coming last
> but one in his semi-final. He had been fully expected to come
> last. Simonov, a slim, petit, slightly gamin figure, is not every-
> one's idea of the average Russian runner; not to put too fine
> a point upon it, many people suspect Simonov of being a
> woman. His previous results, which are uniformly disappoint-
> ing, certainly bear this out. But as sex tests have always until
> now been applied to women, there is no way of finding out.
>
> At the after-match press conference one daring American
> journalist asked Simonov if there was any truth in the rumours
> that he was not as other men, and perhaps more like other
> women. Simonov burst into tears and said he was interested
> only in building world peace, also in tennis, horse-riding and
> knitting, and that he wanted to open a boutique in Moscow
> after this was all over. As he was led away, dabbing at his
> mascara, another journalist managed to ask the Russian coach
> why on earth a woman would want to go in for men's events.
> To his surprise, the coach winked and said: 'Why do you
> think?'

Robert Benchley and Douglas Jerrold represent the other side of
the medal. Benchley looked on his study couch as 'the track'. 'Guess
I'll take a couple of turns around the track', he would say when he
felt like a nap. Jerrold's verdict was final – 'The only athletic sport I
ever mastered was backgammon.' Ring Lardner once told George S.
Kaufman that 'the only exercise he got was when he took the
cuff-links out of one shirt and put them in another'. Kaufman
added, 'That goes for me too.'

Boxing produces rather more flashes of eloquence from both

promoters and practitioners before punch-drunkenness sets in. 'The bigger they are the harder they fall', said Bob Fitzsimmons memorably before he faced the enormous Jim Jeffries in 1902. 'Tall men come down to my height when I hit 'em in the body', said Jack Dempsey some eighteen years later. Asked by a lady reporter once whether he watched an opponent's eyes or his gloves, Terry Downes flashed back in reply: 'His gloves, dear: never been 'it by an eye in me life.'

As David Belasco, then a promoter, put it, 'Boxing is show-business with blood'. It readily provides a powerful image. P.G. Wodehouse described one of his characters in these terms: 'He was built on large lines and seemed to fill the room to overflowing. In physique, he was not unlike what Primo Carnera would have been if Carnera had not stunted his growth by smoking cigarettes as a boy.'

When Theodore Roosevelt asked one Frank Moran why he had given up dentistry to box, the ex-dentist knew exactly why: 'It pays me better to knock teeth out than put them in.' Floyd Patterson's contempt was for boxing's hangers-on: 'I don't have many acquaintances. You get an acquaintance and the first thing they start doing things for you, favours for you, and the next thing they want to borrow.'

The champion of off-the-cuff boxing chat is undisputed – from his days as Cassius Clay when he said, 'I figure I'll be champ for about ten years and then I'll let my brother take over – like the Kennedys down in Washington', to his manifesto as Muhammad Ali, 'Float like a butterfly, sting like a bee. His hands can't hit what his eyes can't see.' (Was Ali's couplet, incidentally, an echo of the 'Ballad of Joe Louis', lyrics by Richard Wright, music by Count Basie, sung by Paul Robeson in 1942:

> Rabbit say to the bee 'What make you sting so deep?
> The bee say, 'I sting like Joe and rock 'em all to sleep'.)

Ali was particularly hard on Joe Frazier: 'He's so ugly they ought to donate his face to the Wild Life Fund'; and, 'That man can't sing – he's the only nigger in the world ain't got rhythm.' Ali was also a source of wit in others. 'I'd like to borrow his body for just 48 hours', said Jim Murray in 1964 (when Ali's body was in better shape) – 'There are three guys I'd like to beat up and four women I'd like to make love to' (reminiscent of the old joke about the elderly man who, when he went romancing, always took along a younger man and a pair of jump leads). Even Ali's doctor could be quotable: 'They're selling video cassettes of the Ali–Spinks fight for $89.95. Hell, for that money Spinks will come to your house'.

Among boxing managers Jack Hurley, whose character is summarized by the title of his autobiography, *Don't Call Me Honest, You'll Ruin Me*, best typifies the mean, sub-Runyon literature of boxing disenchantment. When one of his fighters, Vince Foster, was killed in a car crash in 1949, Hurley said, 'At his funeral in Omaha he filled the church to capacity. He was a draw right to the finish.' (An echo here of the last word on Harry Cohn, the Hollywood mogul, of whose well-attended funeral innumerable comedians have since said, 'Give the public what they want and they'll turn out for it.') Hurley is relentlessly quotable: 'Looking at a fighter who can't punch is like kissing your mother-in-law'; 'Putting a fighter in the business world is like putting silk stockings on a pig'; 'I think every young man should have a hobby. Learning to handle money is the best hobby'; and 'I've had more operations than any human being alive. I've had twenty-seven sinus operations and now they say you shouldn't have any. That's how they found out.'

Angelo Dundee, Muhammad Ali's trainer, runs Hurley a close second:

> Tired is a disgusting word. You never say tired to a fighter, even if he's ready to drop from exhaustion. Even if he *thinks* about being tired you're dead . . . I always give my fighters a little life, it encourages them . . . I drop ice down their pants, pinch the flesh about the waist or slap them high on the inside of the thigh. You get to be too homey with a fighter it's no good.

One famous bout in recent years was not a professional contest but an epic encounter between the literary giants Gore Vidal and Norman Mailer, 'after a brief verbal exchange at a Manhattan party for the rich and famous'. I include it here because the flurry of punches sent Russell Baker of the *New York Times* off on a parody excursion into the boxing career of Henry James:

> They were calling him an old man now. Henry James could take that. He was old, old in the bone, old in the spirit. All

those years of brooding about the significance of the American heiress in Europe had taken it out of him. But, by George! he was still Henry James, The Master. And he could still raise a lump on the jaw of any writer who stepped into the same party with him.

His agent didn't believe it. 'Henry', he had said, 'It's time to hang up the gloves.' By way of reply, Henry James had given him a smart uppercut toward the jaw which missed and struck a chandelier, damaging James's middle finger, the one he relied on to start his famous 'which' clauses.

'Look what you've done', said his agent. 'Now you won't be able to write any "which" clauses for a month. You'll start writing like that new Hemingway kid'. (After that it is all downhill in the fight game for Henry.) . . . For one thing Henry James was a name that spelt floperoo at the box office – even though he had once 'gone a few rounds with Mr Tolstoy'. Joseph Conrad cracked three of Henry's ribs with an indolent left hook one evening in the Boston Atheneum, and A.E. Housman came all the way from England to raise a mouse under James's right eye at a black-tie dinner the Fricks gave for Nellie Melba. James finally retired from pugilism after Edith Wharton knocked him out for thirty-five minutes with her famous powder-puff uppercut at Alice Roosevelt's coming-out party. With James's retirement the great era of two-fisted *belle lettres* was almost at its end. With World War One and the Twenties, a new generation began to dominate American literature, a desperate lost generation which was to abandon the manly art of self-defence and make alcoholism the principal sport of their profession.

Wit in soccer slips most readily off the lips of no-nonsense managers. 'Some people think football is a matter of life and death', said Bill Shankly of Liverpool. 'I don't like that attitude. I can assure them it's much more serious than that.' Shankly on particular matches was just as caustic. 'I'm not giving away secrets like that [his team line-up] to Milan', he said, before one encounter. 'If I had my way I wouldn't even tell them the time of the kick-off.'

A jaundiced view of a manager came easily to the footballer Stan Bowles when Don Revie did not pick him for England: 'Maybe he thinks the gypsies have put a curse on me. He's very superstitious, you know.' In 'The English People' George Orwell had a clear idea why football was so significant in England – an evaluation which is only just beginning to lose its contemporary accuracy.

> The English themselves are not outstandingly good at all games but they enjoy playing them, and to an extent that strikes foreigners as foolish they enjoy reading about them and betting on them. During the between-war years the football pools did more than any one thing to make life bearable for the unemployed.

Inter-team soccer loyalties find expression in folk poetry, bawled to well-known tunes from terraces. For instance, to the tune of 'My Bonnie Lies Over The Ocean', Chelsea fans have been known to sing:

> If I had the wings of a sparrow
> If I had the arse of a crow
> I'd fly over Tottenham tomorrow
> And shit on the bastards below.

For every ten soccer fans there are only a couple of rugby supporters. In Australia an adolescent Clive James played rugby football with a team clad in yellow shirts:

> Dyed at home by mothers commanding various techniques and materials. The singlets covered the range of all possible yellows from fresh butter to old urine . . . The moment the whistle blew, thirty small boys would gather around the ball, forming a compact, writhing, many-legged mound which, during the course of what seemed like hours, would transfer itself at random to different parts of the field. I was somewhere in the middle, praying it would end . . . The real nightmare was when the First Grade side turned up. The star of the First Grade was Reg Gasnier . . .
>
> I can well remember the first time I was deputed to tackle Gasnier. He was three times as heavy as I was, although, density having the relationship it does to dimensions, he was of course only twice as high. There were only a couple of hundred people watching. Gasnier appeared out of the distance like an

express train moving unhampered by rails. I ran at him on a despairing collision course. Casually he put his hand in my face. My head stopped while the rest of me kept going, so that I spent a certain amount of time supine in mid-air before deftly falling on my back. While I was being resuscitated on the sidelines, Gasnier kindly materialized in my blurred vision and explained that the thing to do was keep my head so low that he could not palm me off. The next time I tackled him I kept my head low. Side-stepping with uncanny ease, he put his hand on the back of my head and pushed my face into the ground. So much for friendly advice.

Clive James's rugby career ended much sooner than George Mooney's. George who? In *The Times* in March 1983, there appeared Michael Stevenson's vignette (displaying more matter but perhaps less art than Clive James) of George Mooney, the fanatical 66-year-old still playing rugby for West Park:

> The average rugby man longs for his game in his twenties, wonders how long he should continue with it in his thirties and retires around the age of forty.
>
> George Mooney's devotion to physical fitness and the game of rugby football makes most of us appear self-indulgent to the point of downright decadence. Any sceptic, still doubtful about Mooney's sterling qualities, might reflect on the words of an official of the Halton Club, near Widnes: 'George Mooney? Of course I remember him. He played here recently. I knew he was something special when he ate one of our pasties without any teeth.'

Michael Stevenson concluded his piece in this way: 'Gentle and relaxed, grey hair straggling and the eyes full of integrity, George Mooney cannot help suggesting values and preconceptions that have long since been consigned to the realms of period script-writers.' There must be a lesson to us all there?

American participation in the world of rugby is a very recent event, but it gave rise to a delightful anecdote reported on radio following the 1983 Cathay Pacific Sevens tournament, in which there was the somewhat bizarre spectacle of a match between America and Japan. The huge and small men confronted each other. The American team kicked off, the Japanese caught the ball, interpassed at lightning speed, and scored. Again the Americans kicked off, again the Japanese interpassed and scored a breathtaking try. And again a third time. As the US team coach put his head in his hands he was heard to mutter, 'Pearl Harbour I can forgive. But not *this*!'

The longer history of American football has inevitably given rise to more transatlantic wit than has soccer in the States. Attitudes to American college football range from T.A.D. Jones's, 'Gentlemen, you are about to play football for Yale against Harvard. Never in your life will you do anything so important', to the contemptuous President of Cornell who said, 'I shall not permit thirty men to travel four hundred miles [to Michigan] to agitate a ball of wind.' As in so many other sports, football-writers tend to wax lyrical. As Bob Zuppke, a realistic sports-journalist, put it: 'Often an All-American hero is made by a long run, a weak defence and a poet in the press box.' But, once again, the practitioners share a wry sense of disenchantment. 'Life is a shit sandwich and every day you take another bite', said one Joe Schmidt, employing a now-popular American metaphor. 'If I had gone into pro-football the name Jerry Ford might have been a household word today', said President Gerald Ford. And the mood is occasionally caught by the fans. 'Once my wife was crying', said Charlie Winkler, self-billed as America's number one sports fan, 'and she said, "You love football more than me". And being honest I said, "Well, that's true; but I love you more than baseball".'

Baseball, however, brings out the best on all sides. Ogden Nash couldn't wait for the start of play:

All winter long I am one for whom the bell is tolling
I can arouse no interest in basket ball, indoor fly casting or bowling.
The sports pages are strictly no soap
And until the cry of 'Play Ball', I mope!

John F. Kennedy was philosophical: 'Last year, more Americans went to symphonies than to baseball games. This may be viewed as an alarming statistic – but I think both baseball and the country will endure.'

Dick Gregory knew the score: 'Baseball is very big with my people. It figures. It's the only way we can get to shake a bat at a white man without starting a riot.'

Paul Gallico had it in a nutshell: 'No game in the world is as tidy as dramatically neat as baseball, with cause and effect, crime and punishment, motive and result so clearly defined'.

Ring Lardner saw off one aspiring player: 'Although he is a bad fielder, he is also a very poor hitter' – a sentence balanced very much like one of Runyon's.

And Robert Benchley worried about the quality of the spectator: 'One of the chief duties of the fan is to engage in arguments with the man behind him. This department of the game has been allowed to run down fearfully.'

This attitude that things are not as they were, common in all sports, is particularly prevalent in baseball. Bigger money breeds discontent. Reggie Jackson struck out at white-collar interference in the game: 'The way things are going the faces on next year's bubble gum cards will be lawyers.' Realistically, he also pointed out, 'Fans don't boo nobodies.' Owners, on the other hand, tell rueful stories about the riches of players. A young player Wayne Garland, telephoned his mother. 'I told her, "Mom, I didn't get my million". And she said, "Well, son, money isn't everything". Then I said, "No, I got two million".' But it works the other way round, too. Harold Parrott once said, 'When you get right down to it the baseball owners are really little boys with big wallets.'

Baseball legends abound. The legendary Joe Di Maggio ('Where are you now, Joe Di Maggio? A nation turns its lonely eyes to you', wrote Paul Simon in *Mrs Robinson*) married Marilyn Monroe and in the course of time visited Korea with her and duly returned. When they got home an enormous crowd had gathered. 'Joe, you never heard such cheering', said the astonished film star. 'Yes, I have', said the idol of the ball-parks, quietly. (On the announcement of the marriage, incidentally, the legendary Yogi Berra had said, 'I don't know if it's good for baseball but it sure beats the hell out of rooming with Phil Rizzuto!') The legendary baseball manager, Casey Stengel, had a simple formula for success: 'All you have to do is keep the five players who hate your guts away from the five who are undecided.' Yogi Berra had the same attitude to games as Isaac Stern has to concerts: 'If people don't want to come to the park, nobody's going to stop 'em.' Of the legendary and literate pitcher, Tom Seaver, the legendary Reggie Jackson said, 'Blind people come to the park just to listen to him pitch.' The legendary Dizzy Dean advertised a breakfast cereal and said, 'Sure I eat what I advertise. Sure I eat wheaties for breakfast. A good bowl of wheaties with bourbon can't be beat.' The legendary Babe Ruth was famous for breaking the curfew imposed on players before a game. 'I don't room with him. I room with his suitcase', said a colleague.

The sportsman's renowned sexual drive is not confined to baseball players. In later years the handsome football player, Joe Namath, had quite a reputation. Mike Royko, the Chicago sportswriter, took a dim view of this: 'In another century someone with his chronic droop-eyed leer would have been pegged the village idiot. I remember when a quarterback's most famous appendage was his arm.'

Soccer also produces its quota of sex symbols. According to the former England player, Rodney Marsh, women do not go to football to watch the goals: 'They come to watch the men's legs.' Marsh, a broadminded man, even condoned the kissing congratulations that follow a goal: 'Cuddling is part of the game.' George Best got even more attention than Marsh in his day: 'It's always the same. When they're taking off their clothes, they say they hope I don't think they're doing it just because I'm George Best. . . People always say I shouldn't be burning my candle at both ends. Maybe because *they* don't have a big enough candle.'

Motor cars are powerful sex symbols, too. Jackie Stewart used one to describe the other. 'Cornering is like bringing a woman to a climax. Both you and the car must work together. You start to enter the area of excitement at the corner, you set up a pace which is right for the car and after you've told it it is coming along with you, you guide it along at a rhythm which has now become natural. Only after you've cleared the corner can you both take pleasure in knowing it's gone well.'

I am reminded of a David Nobbs' sketch for *That Was the Week That Was* that explored the sexual symbolism of cars. Driver, 'he', and vehicle, 'she', are having a dialogue:

She: (Car): (coyly)   I like it when you move the gear lever and close the switch, thus energising the solenoid and causing the left hand side of the piston to be exposed to the partial vacuum in the reservoir.

He: (Driver): (suspiciously)	You've been driven by other men.
He:	It's not the same thing.
She:	Why are you stopping? I'm not going in a lay-by with a strange man.
He:	I'm not stopping.
She:	What are you doing?
He:	Reversing.
She:	Pervert!

Perhaps the saddest of the sex-searching sportsmen is Bobby Fischer, the chess player. His tragedy is summed up in three sentences:

'I like vivacious girls with big breasts', he said. His lawyer muttered, 'Bobby is desperate to get laid, but socially he is so inept he can't even get to meet girls.' And after the breakthrough, Fischer remarked sourly, 'Chess is better.'

But of course there are other sports, with their own attitudes and anecdotes, their own wit and wisdom. Here are a few choice remarks:

Croquet:	'The game is passionate enough without money.' – Richard Rodgers
Skating:	'You've got so much ice on your hands I could skate on them.' – John Curry to Liberace
Angling:	'It is to be observed that "angling" is the name given to fishing by people who can't fish.' – Stephen Leacock
Rodeo:	'Rodeoing is about the only sport you can't fix. You'd have to talk to the bulls and horses and they wouldn't understand.' – Bill Lindeman, cowboy
Bullfighting:	'The matadors I knew had souls of Toledo for the bull, but they were terrified of their impresarios, pulp in the hands of their critics and avaricious beyond belief. Perhaps they gave the audience a little courage of a certain

kind but not the kind the world needed and needs. I have yet to hear of a bullfighter who has taken a dangerous political stand, who has fought a moral battle unless its horns were shaved. It seems to me that this superb courage could be put to better use than the ritual slaughter of bulls in the afternoon.' – John Steinbeck

Basketball: 'Nothing there but basketball, a game which won't be fit for people until they set the umbilicus high and return the giraffes to the zoo.' – Ogden Nash

Racing: 'My immediate reward for increasing the tax on book making was major vilification. It was confidently asserted in the bookmakers' circles that my mother and father met only once and then for a very brief period.' – Lord Wigg, on his work as Chairman of the British Betting Levy Board

Tennis: 'Nastase rarely just grins and bears it. More commonly he grins, groans, shrugs, slumps, spins around, shakes his head, puffs out his cheeks, rolls on the ground and bears it. Even more commonly, he does all that and doesn't bear it.' – Clive James

'Nastase came over to me when I called the score and asked "Why you say Nastase? Why don't you call me *Mr* Nastase?" I didn't say anything then but when he came to the chair at the changeover I said, "Look, Nastase, we used to have a famous cricket match in this country called Gentlemen versus Players. The Gentlemen were put down on the scorecard as 'Mister' because they *were* gentlemen. By no stretch of the imagination can anybody call *you* a gentleman." ' – Trader Horn, umpiring at Wimbledon.

213

Swimming: 'Since the water was confined and remained
             unchanged for days on end, Mr Meldrum
             had frowned on the Ramsgate Baths as un-
             healthy. He was, of course, absolutely right.
             The water in each pool would be green on
             the first day, orange on the second day and
             saffron on the third. The whole place was
             one vast urinal. But there were diving
             boards, sand pits and giggling swarms of
             girls wearing Speedo swimming costumes.
             The Speedo was a thin, dark blue cotton
             one-piece affair whose shoulder straps some
             of the girls tied behind with a ribbon so as
             to tauten over their pretty bosoms. On the
             correctly formed pubescent girl a Speedo
             looked wonderful. When it was wet it was
             an incitement to riot.' – Clive James, again,
             Down-Under again.

And this anonymous verse:

Mother, may I go out to swim,
Yes, my darling daughter.
Hang your clothes on a hickory limb
But don't go near the water.

No consideration of wit in sport is complete without reference
to Gamesmanship, Stephen Potter's examination of 'The Art of
Winning Games Without Actually Cheating'. Potter wrote his book
in response to a real need. 'There have been five hundred books on
play and the tactics of play . . . not one on the art of winning'.
Potter's road to Damascus was the tennis court of Birkbeck College,
London, on 8 June 1931. Playing with 'C. Joad, the celebrated
gamesman', he found himself confronted by 'a couple of particularly tall and athletic young men . . . from University College'.
Fighting a hopeless challenge the gamesmen were in a desperate
plight when Joad saw another ace flash off his racquet and high into
the stop-netting. He advanced to the net and called across the net
in an even tone: 'Kindly say clearly, please, whether the ball was
in or out.' Crude to our ears, perhaps, but beautifully accurate

gamesmanship for 1931. For the student must realize that 'these two young men were both, in the highest degree, charming, well-mannered young men, perfect in their sportsmanship'. Potter calls them Smith and Brown:

Smith stopped dead.

Smith: I'm so sorry – I *thought* it was out (*the ball had hit the back netting twelve feet behind him before touching the ground*). But what did you think Brown?

Brown: I *thought* it was out – but do let's have it again.

Joad: No, I don't want to have it again. I only want you to say clearly, if you will, whether the ball is in or out.

'There is nothing more putting-off to young university players than a slight suggestion that their etiquette or sportsmanship is in question . . . [Their confidence destroyed they lose the match comprehensively] . . . That night I thought hard and long. Could not this simple gambit of Joad's be extended to include other aspects of the game – to include all games? For me it was the birth of gamesmanship.'

The *Henry Root Letters* of 1980 have done something to bring gamesmanship kicking and screaming into the new brutalism of the 1980s; and though Root's message is the antithesis of good sportsmanship the letter-writer's style often catches the breathless excitement of sportspeak. For the uninitiated, Mr Root fires off impudent messages to unsuspecting targets and then sits back and waits for them to make fools of themselves in their replies. For example, he writes to Brian Clough, manager of Nottingham Forest, after a successful encounter in Europe:

Dear Mr Clough,
    So you stuffed the Swiss! Magic! Mustard! You and the lads must be over the moon! [Root goes on to oppose the idea of buying a foreign player – one, Sulser] . . . I'm talking about being a credit to the game on and off the field. Short hair, smart appearance, train hard, no cussing or monkey-business in the changing room and just one holiday a year with the wife and kiddies in Majorca . . .
    Anyway, here's a pound for Sulser's fee. In spite of my

reservations [about foreign players] expressed above I recognise that you're the boss and whatever you say goes.

You'll never walk alone!   etc.

A month later, having no reply, Mr Root writes to Clough again:

Dear Mr Clough,

Did you get my letter . . . enclosing a pound for the boy Sulser? Since you don't strike me as being the sort of man who'd pocket a pound without so much as a 'ta very much, lad', I assume my letter must have gone astray. In the circumstances, here's another pound. Let me know if this one doesn't arrive either . . .

He then goes into a concentrated bout of advice couched entirely in sporting clichés:

Drop the Big Man, Shilton! Let's face it, he failed to dominate 'the box' in the first leg and I ask myself whether he's got the bottle for the big occasion. . . As for the two big centre-backs, well, one of them's got to go. Why don't you buy Toddy? I don't have to tell you of all people that he's still the most cultured No. 6 in the world . . . You could probably pick him up for a song . . . Some of us haven't forgotten how, against Arsenal last season, he saved a certain goal by knocking the opposing No. 9 as cold as a stoat with an Army-surplus sandbag he'd taken with him onto the park.

This time Henry Root – signing himself 'your pal in the stands' – got a terse reply accepting the first pound and returning the second.

Root's cricket victim was Ted Dexter who had been doing a television commentary:

It seemed to me that after lunch in the last Test you had difficulty getting your tongue round the names of our Indian friends. Here's a tip. Don't bother with their names. Just say, 'Oh dear, the ball went straight through the little sooty's legs!

He goes on to attack Mike Brearley:

I appreciate that he's an intellectual and as such will not wish to have his brains rattled too often by a piece of hard leather travelling at speed, but how many of those under him are intellectuals? . . .

. .I'm not too happy either about all the pansy kissing and hand-holding which now takes place in the middle, particularly at the fall of a wicket. The photo above Brearley's article in yesterday's *Observer* of Botham clasping the boy Gower to his bosom might well have been misconstrued by those who have a mind to do so . . .

. . Could you oblige with a photo? I'd like to stick it up in my boy Henry Jnr's room as an example of what can be done with an upright stance and a straight bat. . . some of your drives. . . would have loosened a rhino's balls. Of how many can one say that these days?

Dexter regretted that he didn't 'keep pics about the place these days' – very sensible – and hoped Root's 'lad goes the right way with his cricket. Keep him sideways both batting and bowling.'

Root cannot lose. A rude reply, a non-committal reply, or no reply at all, he is still one up and can deliver his book to his publisher for the agreed advance – Perfected Gamesmanship. But is gamesmanship worthwhile without financial reward? Indeed, are games worthwhile? Robert Lynd's airy dismissal of the whole business deserves the last word: 'Games are the last resort of those who do not know how to idle.'

6

THE HUMAN APPETITES

'Subdue your appetites, my dears, and you've conquered human
nature.' – Mr Squeers, *Nicholas Nickleby*

No doubt unfortunately in the eyes of some, mankind has not
achieved a dazzling success in following Mr Squeers's maxim. As
M.D. O'Connor reminds us, the excesses of our natural appetites
gave us a shaky send-off from the very beginning: 'It was not the
apple on the tree but the pair on the ground, I believe, that caused
the trouble in the garden.'

Our appetites have pursued us ever since, but few of us would
choose to be free of them, though many might wish that others were;
'Other people's appetites easily appear excessive when one doesn't
share them,' wrote André Gide. But our excesses are a fertile
breeding-ground for wit especially when they are carried to
extremes. Love is a lunacy and a suitable target. Henry Fielding saw
it as the catch-all for man's most basic cravings: 'Love: a word
properly applied to our delight in particular kinds of food; sometimes metaphorically spoken of as the favourite objects of all our
appetites.' John Webster describes Vittoria, the *femme fatale* in his
The White Devil, as a sweetmeat 'that rots the eater'. And Ring
Lardner, sounding a less strident, but no less jaundiced, tone once
remarked, 'He gave her a look you could have poured on a waffle.'
To Mencken love was 'man's delusion that one woman differs from
another – still, man is better off than women; he marries later and
dies sooner.' Disraeli shared his scepticism: 'the magic of first love is
our ignorance that it can ever end.' 'Love,' commented Richard
Garrett, 'is immanent in nature, but not incarnate.' While the
Countess of Blessington found a neat analogy when she observed,
'Love matches are made by people who are content, for a month of
honey, to condemn themselves to a life of vinegar.' Love is blind, but
the blindness is all too often curable – and all too quickly.

Many of the most telling commentaries on love have been made
by women. Helen Rowland worked overtime at the subject, but

allow me to quote two examples: 'Love is woman's eternal spring and man's eternal fall', and, 'Love, the quest; marriage, the conquest; divorce, the inquest.' Madame de Staël had no illusions either. Love, she defined as, 'self-love à deux'. 'Love's a disease, but curable,' wrote Rose Macaulay in *Crewe Train*, '. . . Did you ever look through a microscope at a drop of pond water? You see plenty of love there. All the amoebae getting married. I presume they think it very exciting and important. We don't.' Peter de Vries offered a shorter but similarly biological description of love: 'They made love as though they were an endangered species!' And I like Lily Tomlin's wary approach: 'If love is the answer, could you rephrase the question?'

The confusion that exists between love the emotion and love the act does at least provide a convenient ambiguity for those engaged in either. The eighteenth-century German satirist, Georg Christoph Lichtenberg, may not have been fooled – 'What they call "heart" is located far lower than the fourth waistcoat button', – but as far as most men are concerned love is an obsession only satisfied with expansion and growth. 'Make love to every woman you meet', advised Arnold Bennett. 'If you get five percent on your outlay it's a good investment.' Taken too far, this recalls Ambrose Bierce's definition of a debauchee as: 'One who has so earnestly pursued pleasure that he has had the misfortune to overtake it.' Appetites like these can be self-defeating. Here's the actress Colleen Dewhurst sounding a warning against the permissive seventies in the middle of that decade: 'We're living in a kind of pallid emotional time, we're so jaded we've almost managed to make sex boring; when somebody new approaches you, you're afraid you're being approached according to page 136.'

The philosopher Sir A.J. Ayer applied logic to love-making: 'If you spend X hours making love you have Y minus X hours left.' Others took a more casual approach. In Heywood Broun's opinion, 'the ability to make love frivolously is the chief characteristic which distinguishes human beings from beasts.' (Not that this ties in exactly with the *Book of Common Prayer*, which expressly warns against entering marriage 'unadvisedly, lightly, or wantonly, to satisfy men's carnal lust and appetites, like brute beasts that have no understanding.') David Cort, writing in *Social Astonishments*, stands up for Broun's happy-go-lucky approach: 'Sex is the great amateur art. The professional, male or female, is frowned on; he or she misses the whole point and spoils the show.' Woody Allen brought it back to basics: 'Sex is like having dinner: sometimes you joke about the dishes, sometimes you take the meal seriously.' Only the diminutive but distinctive actress Denise Coffey seems able to distance herself from the current sexual climate, and then by default. 'I am that twentieth-century failure, a happy undersexed celibate', she once confided to the *News of the World*.

In *Six Curtains for Stroganova*, Caryl Brahms and S.J. Simon considered the no-man's land between love and marriage – the honeymoon: 'Vladimir,' said Natasha, 'do you love me?' 'Toujours,' said Stroganoff with wariness. An unusual emotion for a honey-mooning husband when this particular question crops up. But Stroganoff was lying in the upper berth of the railway compartment and Natasha was in the lower berth so the question could not be an overture to a delightful interlude but merely the prelude to some less delightful demand.'

'Sex in marriage', Peter de Vries observed, 'is like medicine. Three times a day for the first week. Then once a day for another week. Then once every three or four days until the condition clears up.' Marriage, on the face of it, an upright institution, has indeed had its share of knocks, although, according to Corinthians I, chapter 8, verse 9, 'It is better to marry than to burn.' Tertullian agreed but pointed out that to do neither was better still. An anonymous sixteenth-century English poet in *The Schoolhouse of Women* rhymed an unfavourable comparison with hanging:

> To hang or wed: both have an hour;
> And whether it be, I am well sure.
> Hanging is better of the twain;
> Sooner done and shorter pain.

Marriage is even pictured as a response to baser appetites. 'If it were not for the presents, an elopement would be preferable', said the ubiquitous George Ade. Bernard Shaw, of course, viewed marriage as being 'popular because it combines the maximum of temptation with the maximum of opportunity'. And drawing the closest parellel with eating, Charles Caleb Colton remarked, 'Marriage is a feast where the grace is sometimes better than the dinner.' Of course marriage brings its own rewards – the indefatigable Helen Rowland again, 'When you see what some girls marry, you realize how they must hate to work for a living.' Claire Trevor, the actress (or her scriptwriter) pointed to another advantage of marriage, value for money: 'What a holler would ensue if people had to pay the minister as much to marry them as they have to pay the lawyer to get them a divorce.' Oliver Herford came up with the solution: 'Bigamy is one way of avoiding the painful publicity of divorce and the expense of alimony.'

And so the catalogue of pert criticism proceeds down the centuries – John Heywood's 'He that weddeth ere he be wise shall die ere he thrive', is more a refinement of the old proverb, 'Marry in haste, repent at leisure', or Shakespeare's, 'A young man married is a man that's marred.' Robert Burton in the *Anatomy of Melancholy* was an all-round pessimist: 'One that was never married and that's his hell; another is and that's his plague.' While in his *Notebooks* he ventured the question, 'Marriage is distinctly and repeatedly excluded from heaven. Is this because it is thought likely to mar the general felicity?' Seventeenth- and eighteenth-century writers could not hold their peace on the subject. To Shadwell, in *The Sullen Lovers*, 'Marriage is good for nothing but to make friends fall out.' Dryden, speaking through a character in *Marriage à la Mode* bemoaned, 'I am to be married within these three days; married past redemption.' Congreve associated marriage with foolishness. In *The Country Wife*, he wrote, ' 'Tis my maxim, he's a fool that marries: but he's a greater that does not marry a fool'; while in *The Old Bachelor*, 'Every man plays the fool once in his life, but to marry is playing the fool all one's life long.' In another context, Congreve summed up both marriage and courtship: 'Courtship is to marriage as a very witty prologue is to a dull play.'

Anon was back at his desk in 1690, railing against marriage:

> By day 'tis nothing but an endless noise
> By night the echo of forgotten joys;
> Ye Gods! that man by his own slavish law,
> Should on himself such inconvenience draw.

Vanbrugh, in *The Provoked Wife* argues both sides of the case. On the one hand the drunk says, 'If I were married to a hogshead of claret, matrimony would make me hate it'; but, on the other hand, we get, 'Tho' marriage be a lottery in which there are wondrous many blanks, yet there is one inestimable lot in which the only heaven on earth is written.' Vanbrugh's colleague, Farquhar, in *The Twin Rivals*, did not 'think matrimony consistent with the liberty of the subject'. And John Gay, in *The Beggar's Opera*, has Peachum say to Polly, 'Do you think your mother and I should have lived comfortably so long together if ever we had been married?' Pope was just as jaundiced: 'They dream in marriage but in wedlock wake.' Similar sentiments were expressed by Lady Mary Wortley Montagu – not to Pope, who would have loved to hear them, but to her future husband, Edward, in a charming and witty letter:

> Very few people have settled entirely in the country but have grown at length weary of one another. The lady's conversation generally falls into a thousand impertinent effects of idleness; and the gentleman falls in love with his dogs and horses, and out of love with everything else.

'It goes far toward reconciling me to being a woman,' she had written earlier, 'when I reflect that I am thus in no danger of marrying one.' Or, in Thomas Fuller's words in 1731, 'Keep thy eyes wide open before marriage and half shut afterward.'

Boswell reports Johnson in cynical mood:

> It is so far from being natural for a man and woman to live in a state of marriage that we find all the motives which they have for remaining in that connection, and the restraints which civilised society imposes to prevent separation, are hardly sufficient to keep them together . . .

and again:

> I believe marriages would in general be as happy and often more so, if they were all made by the Lord Chancellor, upon a due consideration of the characters and circumstances, without the parties having any choice in the matter.

Sheridan continues the dramatist's tradition of firing grapeshot at the institution of marriage, first obliquely, in *The Rivals* – ' 'Tis safest in matrimony to begin with a little aversion', – and then head-on in *The School for Scandal* – 'Zounds! Madam, you had no taste when you married me!'

Coming into the nineteenth century there is the poignant letter in support of marriage by Elizabeth Patterson Bonaparte who married Jerome of that ilk in 1803 and wrote to a friend: 'It appears to me that even quarrels with one's husband are preferable to the ennui of a solitary existence.' Their marriage had lasted less than two years. Byron gets us back on a more familiar tack, in *Don Juan*:

> Wishing each other, not divorced but dead;
> They live respectably as man and wife.

and:

> All tragedies are finished by death,
> All comedies are ended by a marriage.

Shelley declared, in the 'Letter to Maria Gisborne':

> When a man marries, dies or turns Hindu,
> His best friends hear no more of him.

Balzac was sharper in prose: 'No man should marry until he has studied anatomy and dissected at least one woman.' Coleridge could only envisage a *happy* marriage between a deaf man and a blind woman. In *Punch* in 1845, Mayhew offered 'advice to persons about to marry – don't.' For those who ignored his advice, Samuel Rogers and Benjamin Franklin dispute the credit for, 'It doesn't much signify whom one marries, for one is sure to find next morning that it was someone else.' Wilde and Shaw were, of course, prolific on the subject. In *The Picture of Dorian Gray*, Wilde writes, 'A man can be happy with any woman as long as he does not love her': in *Lady Windermere's Fan*, his studied perversity progresses to: 'The world has grown suspicious of anything that looks like a happily married life.' In *A Woman of No Importance*: 'Twenty years of romance make a woman look like a ruin, but twenty years of marriage make her look like a public building'; and 'The happiness of a married man depends on the people he has not married.' This oddly unsatisfactory play contains more than its measure of good Wildean reversals. 'Women have become so highly educated that nothing should surprise them except happy marriages'; and, 'Men marry because they are tired, women because they are curious: both are disappointed.' Then there is Wilde, the romantic: 'One should always be in love. That is the reason one should never marry'; and

Wilde, disenchanted, 'Niagara Falls is only the second biggest disappointment of the standard honeymoon.'

'It's a woman's business to get married as soon as possible,' wrote Shaw in *Man and Superman*, 'and a man's to keep unmarried as long as he can.' In *Maxims for Revolutionists* he argued that 'Home is a girl's prison and a woman's workhouse.'

Another old warhorse, Ambrose Bierce, rhymed his dismay,

> They stood before the altar and supplied
> The fire themselves in which their fat was fried.

Goethe was jaundiced: 'Bachelors know more about women than married men. If they did not they would be married too.' Chekhov was bleak: 'If you're afraid of loneliness, don't marry.' Voltaire considered marriage, 'the only adventure open to the cowardly.'

Thomas Hardy provides a charming excuse for a rural bridegroom arriving late for his wedding: 'You can marry a woman any day of the week, but a hive of bees won't come for the asking.' Saki wrote that he disliked the idea of wives about the house – 'they accumulate dust'. A Mexican proverb describes marriage as 'the only war where one sleeps with the enemy'. Developing the metaphor, Cyril Connolly defined the choice of arms: 'In the sex war, thoughtlessness is the weapon of the male, vindictiveness of the female.' Thurber decreed that, 'A husband should not insult his wife publicly, at parties. He should insult her in the privacy of their home.' An impertinent Welsh question inquires, 'Why buy a book when you can borrow one from the library?'

Ogden Nash had more than one go at versifying the marriage dilemma:

> To keep your marriage brimming
> With love in the loving cup,
> Whenever you're wrong, admit it,
> Whenever you're right, shut up.

He also defined the Perfect Husband:

> He tells you when you've got on too much lipstick
> And helps you with your girdle when your hips stick.

A more English approach comes from P.G. Wodehouse:

> Chumps always make the best husbands. When you marry, Sally, grab a chump. Tap his forehead first and if it rings solid, don't hesitate. All the unhappy marriages come from the husbands having brains. What good are brains to a man? They only unsettle him.

It would never occur to a chump to react in the classic manner of the American husband who was asked if he had ever contemplated divorce during his thirty years of marriage. 'Divorce? Never! Murder – frequently.'

Anon is not only the most prolific commentator on marriage, but the most jaundiced. 'Bigamy is having one wife too many. Monogamy is the same'; 'Marriage begins with a prince kissing an angel. It ends with a bald-headed man looking across the table at a fat woman'; 'Love is the star all men look up to as they walk along, and marriage is the coal-hole they fall into'; 'Marriage is a condition most women aspire to and most men submit to'; 'Marriage is a romance in which the hero dies in the first chapter'; 'Marriage is not a word but a sentence'; 'The Gods gave man fire and man invented the fire engine. They gave him love, and he invented marriage.'

Coming nearer to present-day animadversions on marriage, Mencken, once again, has a word or three to say on the subject: 'A man may be a fool and not know it, but not if he is married'; and, 'No matter how happily a woman may be married, it always pleases her to discover that there is a nice man who wishes she were not.' How far was Harold Nicholson's highly original marriage to Vita Sackville-West based on his theory that 'the great secret of a successful marriage is to treat all disasters as incidents and none of the incidents as disasters'?

A more public late twentieth-century jester, Billy Connolly, considers marriage 'a wonderful invention', adding, 'but then again, so is the bicycle repair kit'; while Woody Allen, whose nose is permanently poked into the neurotic by-ways of modern American romance, can not only deliver the witty, characterized joke – 'Basically my wife was immature. I'd be at home in the bath and she'd come in and sink my boats' – but also sustain a beautifully wry description of the ecstatic beginning of a doomed romance in his short story 'Retribution':

That Connie Chasen returned my fatal attraction toward her at first sight was a miracle unparalleled in the history of Central Park West. Tall, blond, high cheek-boned, an actress, a scholar, a charmer, irrevocably alienated, with a hostile and perceptive wit only challenged in its power to attract by the lewd, humid eroticism her every curve suggested, she was the unrivaled desideratum of each young man at the party. That she would settle on me, Harold Cohen, scrawny, long-nosed, twenty-four-year-old, budding dramatist and whiner, was a *non sequitur* on a par with octuplets. True, I have a facile way with a one-liner and seem able to keep a conversation going on a wide range of topics, and yet I was taken by surprise that this superbly scaled apparition could zero in on my meagre gifts so rapidly and completely.

'You're adorable', she told me, after an hour's energetic exchange while we leaned against a bookcase, throwing back Valpolicella and finger foods. 'I hope you're going to call me.'

'Call you? I'd like to go home with you right now.'

'Well great,' she said, smiling coquettishly. 'The truth is, I didn't really think I was impressing you.'

I affected a casual air while blood pounded through my arteries to predictable destinations. I blushed, an old habit.

Love flourishes, but dies when Connie begins to think of Harold as her brother. Harold promptly proposes to her mother, to the consternation of his family:

My parents . . . proceeded directly to the window of their tenth-story apartment and competed for leaping space.

'I never heard of such a thing,' my mother wailed, rending her robe and gnashing her teeth. . . .

'His girlfriend's mother he's marrying?' Aunt Tillie yelped as she slid to the floor unconscious.

'Fifty-five and a *shiksa*', my mother screamed, searching now for the cyanide capsule she had reserved for just such occasions. . . . In the far corner, Aunt Rose was down on her knees intoning Sh'ma Yisroel.

'God will punish you, Harold', my father yelled. 'God will cleave your tongue to the roof of your mouth and all your cattle and kine shall die and a tenth of all thy crops shall wither and. . . .'

Nonetheless, Harold marries Connie's mother, Emily ('My folks could not make it, a previous commitment to sacrifice a lamb taking precedence.') Since he has now technically become Connie's father (instead of her brother) he becomes attractive to her again. 'Don't worry, Dad,' she says menacingly, 'there'll be plenty of opportunities.'

> I sat on the bed and stared out of the window into infinite space. I thought of my parents and wondered if I should abandon the theatre and return to rabbinical school . . . all I could mutter to myself as I remained a limp, hunched figure was an age-old line of my grandfather's which goes, 'Oy Vey'.

If Woody Allen's wit leads us into wild, neurotic, Jewish couplings in Manhattan, Gore Vidal opens up even less conventional (or do I mean 'more unconventional'?) frontiers of sexual compatibility in his essay 'Sex is Politics'. (Though not as unconventional as the idea James Agate floated when reviewing *The Barretts of Wimpole Street*: 'What is wrong with a little incest? It is both handy and cheap'.) Vidal only *seems* to write as often as Bernard Levin; but as he is not simply a charming, observant, prolific, lightweight journalist, as Bernard is, his polemic is more passionate and more thoughtful and the attractive frivolity which they share is supported by more concerned and cogent argument. In the work of the more serious man, the wit is set off to better advantage. For example, in 'Sex is Politics':

> The sexual attitudes of any given society are the result of political decisions. In certain militaristic societies, homosexual relationships were encouraged on the ground that pairs of dedicated lovers (Thebes' Sacred Legion, the Spartan buddy system) would fight more vigorously than reluctant draftees. In societies where it is necessary to force great masses of people to do work that they don't want to do (building pyramids, working on the Detroit assembly line), marriage at an early age is encouraged on the sensible ground that if a married man is fired his wife and children are going to starve, too. That grim knowledge makes for docility.
>
> Although our notions about what constitutes correct sexual behaviour are usually based on religious texts, those texts are invariably interpreted by the rulers in order to keep control

over the ruled. Any sexual or intellectual or recreational or political activity that might decrease the amount of coal mined, the number of pyramids built, the quality of junk food confected, will be proscribed through laws that, in turn, are based on divine revelations handed down by whatever god or gods happen to be in fashion at the moment. Religions are manipulated by those who govern society and not the other way around. This is a brand-new thought to Americans whether once or twice or never bathed in the blood of the Lamb. . . .

He goes on to explain that,

Traditionally, Judaeo-Christianity approved of sex only between men and women who had been married in a religious ceremony . . . The offspring would provide more and more . . . Loyal workers and dutiful consumers . . . Fortunately, nothing human is constant . . . For one thing, workers are less obedient than they used to be. If fired, they can go on welfare – the Devil's invention . . . Homosexuality also threatens that ancient domination, because men who don't have wives or children to worry about are not as easily dominated as those men who do . . . To divert the electorate, the unscrupulous American politician will go after those groups not regarded benignly by Old or New Testament. The descendants of Ham are permanently unpopular with white Americans. Unhappily for the hot-button pusher, it is considered bad taste to go after blacks openly . . . Jews are permanently unpopular with American Christers because they are forever responsible for Jesus's murder, no matter what those idolatrous wine-soaked Roman Catholics at the Vatican Council said.

'There is', Vidal acknowledges, 'a new grudging admiration for the Jews as bully. Nevertheless, in once-and-twice-born land, it is an article of faith that America's mass media are owned by Jews who mean to overthrow God's country. Consequently, "mass-media" is this year's code phrase for get-the-kikes, while, "save our children" means get the fags. But politics, like sex, often makes for odd alliances . . .' The alliance Vidal identifies is the union of militant 'Christer' and militant 'Jew' to 'firm up the family'. He quotes an investigation in Bensenville, Illinois:

Family saviours support 'The death penalty, Laetrile, nuclear power, local police, Panama Canal, saccharin, F.B.I., C.I.A., defence budget, public prayer and real estate growth.'
Family saviours view darkly 'busing, welfare, public-employee unions, affirmative action, amnesty, marijuana, communes, gun-control, pornography, the 55 mph speed limit, day-care centres, religious ecumenism, sex education, car-pools and the Environmental Protection Agency.
Now, suddenly, it has occurred to people, in England as well as America, that a 'pro-family' movement might be politically attractive . . . A state of constant quiet in the citizenry is a good thing for rulers who tend not to take very seriously the religions they impose on their subjects. Since marriage is the only admissible outlet for the sexual drive, that institution was used as a means of channelling it in a way that would make docile the man, while the woman, humanly speaking, existed only as the repository of the sacred sperm (regarded as a manifestation of the Holy Ghost).

Vidal goes on to consider the problems raised for advocates of the traditional marriage by woman's quest for Equal Rights and Male and Female Homosexuality: 'Today Americans are in a state of terminal hysteria on the subject of sex in general and homosexuality in particular . . . for two millennia women have been treated as chattels; while homosexuality has been made to seem a crime, a vice, an illness . . .' He quotes a critic, whose name he wickedly pretends to misconstrue, in the *Partisan Review*:

What I take to be a Catskill Hotel called the Hilton Kramer wants to know why the New York intellectuals are not offering the national culture anything 'in the way of wisdom about marriage and the family' . . . The hotel is worried . . . I assume the hotel disapproves of me because (I am) not Jewish. The hotel then goes on to characterise me as 'proselytising for the joys of buggery'. Needless to say, I have never done such a thing, but I can see how, to a superstitious and ill-run hotel, anyone who has worked hard to remove consenting sexual relations from the statute books (and politics) must automatically be a salesman for abominable vices, as well as a destroyer of the family and an eater of shellfish.

In another essay – 'Pink Triangle and Yellow Star' – Vidal demonstrates again how powerful witty invective can be. This time his target is not the conspiracy to conserve marriage but the anti-gay lobby. He quotes Christopher Isherwood memorably on the derivation of the title. 'I was present when Christopher Isherwood tried to make this point [in German concentration camps, Jews wore yellow stars while homosexualists wore pink triangles] to a young Jewish movie producer. "After all," said Isherwood, "Hitler killed six hundred thousand homosexuals." The young man was not impressed. "But Hitler killed six *million* Jews," he said sternly. "What are you?" asked Isherwood, "in real estate?" ' (Irene Handl used to recall sadly a dresser whose attention was drawn to a headline at the time of the Eichmann trial. 'Six million Jews murdered', it ran. 'Oh yes,' said the dresser phlegmatically, 'I thought I 'adn't seen so many around lately'.)

Vidal himself dismisses a 'fag-baiter', Mrs Norman Podhoretz, who writes under the scarcely more accessible name of Midge Decter, with the supremely sour compliment, 'She also writes with the authority and easy confidence of someone who knows that she is very well known indeed to those few who know her.' He also captured her parading with her husband at The Pines, a partly homosexualist community on Fire Island, and going on record as not liking what she saw: 'There were also homosexual women at The Pines, but they were, or seemed to be, far fewer in number. Nor, except for a marked tendency to hang out in the company of large and ferocious dogs, were they instantly recognisable.' 'Well,' adds Vidal, 'if I were a dyke and a pair of Podhoretzes came waddling towards me on the beach, copies of Leviticus and Freud in hand, I'd get in touch with the nearest Alsatian dealer pronto.'

The sharp edges of gay wit cut fellow-homosexualists as readily as they do the straight community. Vidal is tongue-in-cheek about Truman Capote in the same essay: 'Although I would never suggest that Truman Capote's bright wit and sweet charm would not easily have achieved for him his present stardom had he been a *hetero*sexualist, I do know that if he had not existed in his present form another would have been run up on the old sewing machine because that sort of *persona* must be, for a whole nation, the stereotype of what a fag is.' (A sentiment which sends us back to that early gay graffito – 'My mother made me a homosexual – If I give her the wool, will she make me one?')

'Gays are to sex what blacks are to music', James Leverett writes in his introduction to Harvey Fierstein's *Torch Song Trilogy*, three expert plays which include the memorable camp lines, 'There are a lot of easier things in this life than being a drag queen, but I ain't got no choice. The fact is I just can't walk in flats'; and, 'I want more in life than meeting a pretty face and sitting down on it.' 'How time flies when you're doing all the talking,' the 'hero' says at another point, neatly spearing homosexual garrulity (or anyone else's, for that matter).

Camp humour can be bitchy, defensive, self-deprecatory or simply flamboyant. Leaving Oscar Wilde aside for once – apart from his reputed last words, 'This wallpaper is killing me. One of us will have to go' – Ronald Firbank is the epitome of one school of exotic hothouse camp humour. 'How rare, how precious is frivolity!' wrote E.M. Forster of Firbank, 'How few writers can prostitute all their powers! They are always implying, "I am capable of higher things".' Whether translated onto the musical stage by Sandy Wilson, 'I'd like to spank the white walls of (that shepherd's) cottage', and, of a baby, 'He likes noise and lights – which shows he has social instincts', or the supplicant who 'kissed a cardinal's toe and went on up from there!' – Firbank's wit is extravagant and epicene, and the quivering quips are often inspired by exotic negroes and high church practices . . . 'I hear it's the Hebrew in Heaven, sir – Spanish is seldom spoken.' 'I remember the average curate at home was something between a eunuch and a snigger'; the wonderful 'I know of no joy greater than a cool white dress after the sweetness of confession', and 'Some ninety hours afterwards the said young novice brought into the world the Blessed St Elizabeth Bathilde, who, by dint of skipping, changed her sex at the age of forty and became a man.'

Then there is Madam Rinz in his *Prancing Nigger*: 'A quietly silly woman, Madam Rinz was often obliged to lament the absence of intellect at her door, accounting for it as the consequence of a weakness for negroes, combined with a hopeless passion for the Regius Professor of Greek at Oxford.' Sometimes Firbank's wit is simply precious and unexpected: 'She made a ravishing corpse'; 'His weariness the Prince entered the room in all his tinted orders'; 'She's shy, of the violet persuasion, but that's not a bad thing in a young girl.' Sometimes he goes for suitably lofty dismissal: 'She reads at such a pace,' he complained, 'and when I asked her where she had learnt to read so quickly, she replied, "On the screens at cinemas" ' '*Basta*!' his master replied, with all the brilliant glibness of the Berlitz School'. Or 'But I am so sensitive . . . I seem to *know* when I talk to a man the colour of his braces! I say to myself: "Yours are violet".'

A couple of amusing Scott Fitzgerald sentences on allied subjects serve to point up the heady virtues of Firbank – they come, more haltingly, from *This Side of Paradise*: 'She had once been a Catholic, but discovering that priests were infinitely more attentive when she was in process of losing or regaining faith in Mother Church, she maintained an enchantingly wavering attitude'; and 'Monsignor was forty-four then, and bustling – a trifle too stout for symmetry, with hair the colour of spun gold, and a brilliant, enveloping personality. When he came into a room clad in his full purple regalia from thatch to toe, he resembled a Turner sunset.' (Some of James Elroy Flecker's *Hassan* sounds like pastiche Firbank: 'Plunge not the finger of enquiry into the pie of impertinence, O my uncle,' for example).

Nearer to the true Firbankian style is a sentence of Kenneth Tynan's which stays vividly in my mind though I cannot trace the source. (It is not good to get a high camp sentence *slightly* wrong. I hope that I have remembered accurately.) Tynan was writing about Stanley Parker, a great Oxford character, especially in the fifties, and compared his striking appearance to a 'strawberry ice-cream loudly proclaiming, "No! I will not be eaten with a plastic spoon".' Then there is Robert Farquharson's vision of an elderly actress at the BBC surrounded by quivering males – a fag-hag, holding court – 'Look at her – a moth entirely surrounded by candles'; and James Lees Milne's memory of Harold Acton, confronted by a backwoods peer with the accusation, 'You don't look as though you'd be much good doing things under a motor car', and replying, 'That would depend on who was under it with me.' One anti-homosexualist joke is ascribed to almost everyone at some time or another: 'If God had meant us to have homosexuals, he would have created Adam and Bruce.' Marty Feldman's apologia for this particular appetite was, 'Comedy, like sodomy, is an unnatural act'; and Woody Allen's, 'I'm a practising heterosexual, but bisexuality immediately doubles your chances for a date on Saturday night.' And then there is his dismissive line from the movie he wrote with the witty Mickey Rose: 'Nobody would wear beige to rob a bank.' N.F. Simpson's wonderfully blinkered, 'You should have thought of all this before you were born', makes a different point, and Diaghilev's verdict, like so many of his ideas, was far ahead of his time: 'Tchaikovsky thought of committing suicide for fear of being discovered as a homosexual; but today, if you are a composer and *not* a homosexual, you might as well put a bullet through your head.'

I cherish the predicament of an American friend whose odd name consisted mainly of consonants. Out of a job he went for an interview – a bundle of nerves. (This is wit by accident.) 'Where does that name come from, Mr Sthlittps?' (or consonants to that effect), asked the interviewing body. 'Oh,' he panicked, 'it's partly German and partly Swish.'

I have always admired an embittered remark by an out-of-work American dancer. 'There are more boy dancers in America than there are people.' Another dancer's pinprick, more specific, lingers. Both object and subject were old and distinguished classical dancers, more on view by then as actors, and one of them seemed to have little vocal power. 'Of course not,' said the other, 'he's had his face lifted so many times, he can't afford to raise his voice.'

Noel Coward was intolerant of sentimental approaches to the subject. In his diaries he assailed Mary Renault's novel *The Charioteer*, 'Oh dear, I do, do wish well-intentioned ladies would *not* write books about homosexuality. This one is turgid, unreal and so ghastly earnest. It takes the hero – "soi disant" – three hundred pages to reconcile himself to being queer as a coot, and his soul-searching and deep, deep introspection are truly awful. There are "queer" parties in which everyone calls everyone "my dear" a good deal, and over the whole book is a shimmering lack of understanding of the subject. I'm sure the poor woman meant well but I wish she'd stick to recreating the glory that was Greece and not fuck about with dear old modern homos.' In private he always rejected the idea of 'coming out' – 'A lot of old ladies in Woking would be very disappointed.'

In America for many years in the 1970s, the anti-gay movement was championed by Anita Bryant – a vigorous campaigner, previously popular as a singer on a TV commercial for orange juice. The gays invented a slogan for her, 'Squeeze a fruit for Anita'; but

233

Miss Bryant's main argument centred around the idea that homosexual teachers would lead the young away from a heterosexual path. Suddenly the words, 'role model', were heard in the land. Russell Baker, in the *New York Times*, was unclear what a role model was – 'Lacking fluency in the sociological tongue, a language almost as difficult as Basque!' As a child he had found the ludicrous concept of teachers having any sex life too difficult to master – 'The idea of a teacher in the coils of rapture was as inconceivable as the idea of Herbert Hoover in Bermuda shorts.' Teachers were assumed to be married, and therefore beyond sex. His two unmistakably homosexual teachers he learned to joke about: '. . . The teacher I most wanted to emulate, however, was single, drank wine and had been gassed in World War I. Of his three admirable traits, there was only one I wanted to copy, and sure enough, to this day, I love the sound of a popping cork.'

It is time to move on to the sound of the popping cork, but before doing so, consider the way James Leverett completes his opening sentence (introducing *Torch Song Trilogy*). 'Gays are to sex what blacks are to music: they lead the way but still they stay behind. The bars, baths, fashions, dances and one-night-stands that heterosexuals have so avidly co-opted are only the superficial signs of a change penetrating all levels of sexual order, hence all order. Gay consciousness hones the edge of this revolution. . .' The influence of 'gay consciousness' on wit appears at first sight to be more traditional than revolutionary but it is significant that the three most brittle, witty lyricists in the first half of the twentieth century, Porter, Hart and Coward, all shared homosexuality as a background to their elegant, funny, febrile inventions. Harvey Fierstein's is the last word on this particular subject: 'I guess a drag queen's like being an oil painting! You gotta stand back from it to get the full effect.'

A collection of homosexual wit, edited by Quentin Crisp, is probably the only satisfactory way of running this particular quarry to earth, so switching the knob on the dial of human comedy we move from the appetite for love and sex to that for food and drink. The two are no strangers. We have already heard Woody Allen on the subject and, forgetting for a moment the tediously intense and absurdly optimistic history of aphrodisiacs, from the table comes American food critic, Gail Green's, 'Great food is like great sex – the more you have the more you want.' Thankfully Errol Flynn, recalling Bierce's debauchee, is on hand to offer a more wholesome comment on the joint pleasures of bed and board: 'My problem lies in reconciling my gross habits with my net income.'

The high priest of excess, the Oscar Wilde of hard liquor, is undoubtedly W.C. Fields:

'A woman drove me to drink and I never even had the courtesy to thank her.'

'What contemptible scoundrel stole the cork from my lunch?'

'I always keep a stimulant handy in case I see a snake – which I also keep handy.'

'We lived for days on nothing but food and water.'

'Anybody who hates dogs and loves whisky can't be all bad.'

Chesterton might have been cautiously re-phrasing a genuine Fieldian sentiment when he said, 'No animal ever invented anything so bad as drunkenness – or so good as drink.' Or P.G. Wodehouse, dealing with breakfast not lunch, 'I was so darned sorry for poor old Corky that I hadn't the heart to touch my breakfast. I told Jeeves to drink it himself', a sentiment which Fields no doubt would have shared. However, he might also have taken Eddie Condon's advice – 'For a bad hangover take the juice of two quarts of whisky' – and he would certainly have sympathized with Chesterton's Noah:

And Noah he often said to his wife when he sat down to dine,
I don't care where the water goes if it doesn't get into the wine.

'I don't drink,' said Oscar Levant. 'I don't like it. It makes me feel good.' Lady Astor, whose antipathy to drink was notorious, abstained for the opposite reason: 'I want to know when I'm having a good time.' Winston Churchill, with whom she frequently crossed swords at the dinner table, justified his own indulgence with the remark, 'Always remember, I have taken more out of alcohol than alcohol has taken out of me.' Thomas Love Peacock had two reasons for drinking: 'One is, when you are thirsty, to cure it; the other, when you are not thirsty, to prevent it.' George Jean Nathan was more desperate, 'I drink to make other people interesting.'

Prohibition took its toll on American stomachs and on American nerves. Don Marquis put the problem succinctly. 'Prohibition makes you want to cry into your beer and denies you the beer to cry into.'

Scott Fitzgerald said of one hopeless drunk, 'When he buys his ties he has to ask if gin will make them run.' Possibly that was the man Thurber had in mind when he wrote of 'Joe . . . perhaps the first great non-stop literary drinker of the American nineteenth century. He made the indulgences of Coleridge and de Quincey seem like a bit of mischief in the kitchen with the cooking sherry.' 'An alcoholic', said Dylan Thomas, speaking with some authority, 'is someone you don't like who drinks as much as you do.'

And George D. Prentice offers an unwitting commentary on Thomas's own fate: 'One swallow doesn't make a summer, but too many swallows make a fall.' Dr Johnson distinguished between drinkers: 'Claret is the liquor for boys; port for man; but he who aspires to be a hero . . . must drink brandy.' Woodrow Wilson once asked F.E. Smith solemnly, 'And what in your opinion is the trend of the modern English undergraduate?' 'Steadily towards drink and women, Mr President', Smith replied.

Two favourite jokes about wine and food are at the expense of the snob. There is James Thurber's classic – 'It's a naive domestic Burgundy without any breeding, but I think you'll be amused by its presumption' – and Lucius Beebe's 'A gourmet can tell from the flavour whether a woodcock's leg is the one on which the bird is accustomed to roost.'

Gerald Asher, who knows too much about food and drink to get trapped into pretension, tells a cautionary story of a distinguished French *chroniquer gastronomique* in his book *On Wine*. 'Those assembled (at a Paris luncheon) were on the point of bringing to their lips glasses of freshly poured young Beaujolais, served at cool cellar temperature, when she leapt to her feet. "Stop!" she cried. Wondering what horror I was being protected from, I put down my glass. She held her own aloft, a thermometer sticking from it, in a pose not unlike Liberty with her torch, and came straight to the point. "The temperature of this wine is only nine degrees centigrade", she said. "We must wait until it reaches ten".' The pedantry, Asher felt, may just have been justifiable, but 'by the time ten was reached, the moment of anticipation had vanished.' I also relished Gerald's comment (in a letter) on the autobiography of Craig Claiborne – the star cookery writer of *The New York Times* – 'He describes, I am told, seduction by his father, with whom he had an affair. The trouble with dishing up a story like that in Chapter One, when the final chapter deals with his salt-free diet, is that if the end and the beginning are tasteless, who can be sure about the middle?'

Seymour Britchky – the most pungent of American restaurant critics – is lethal and funny about his least favourite restaurants. He is particularly sharp on the behaviour and pretensions of restaurant staff – a compendium of witty observation. Of 'Woods' on Madison Avenue – a restaurant where I have always enjoyed to eat, he writes, 'Some of the waiters discuss the menu with you as if they were sharing wisdom picked up in the Himalayas.' Of Mr Chow's, again the New York branch, Britchky writes, 'It is possible that Orientals have been on these premises but no one has stepped forward to testify to having seen one. The host captains are a matched set of six-foot, dark-haired, crew-cut dandies. They drift about like sleep-walkers on roller skates. Their politeness is schooled, right down to the five-degree angle at which they tilt their heads when directing a sad smile at an eager client. You get the impression that if someone turned up their power they would swiftly kill.' A different breed inhabit P.J. Clarke's, 'the durable gin mill' on Third Avenue. 'Though it has all kinds, Clarke's features white-haired, red-faced bartenders. They have been here forever, and they strut along their duckboards affecting the deportment of certified salt of this earth. Their exchanges with their chums across the bar consist principally of sardonic references to regular customers who happen not to be present and to managerial personnel who are out of earshot. Their wit is usually weather-related, treating, for example, of what part of an elephant's anatomy this cold snap could freeze off.' The impression of ambience is instant. So it is with the doubtful superiority of '21': 'Your captain . . . may well answer your questions, if any, with a degree of impatience which is only partly the result of his ignorance of the menu.' Or the crystal chandelier of a restaurant in Central Park, 'The Tavern on the Green', where waiters, as in so many American restaurants, are prone to sing. 'The simple facts are that people in glass houses shouldn't sing "Happy Birthday".' He can 'get' the client too, as easily as he hoists the host. 'Odeon' is a hugely chic and successful, English-run shrine to food, well down on West Broadway. 'To judge by the facial expressions in evidence, the range of emotion of this clientèle extends only from painless boredom to contented passivity. Competition, however, there is. Take for instance, this prize-winning lady in a gentleman's vintage shirt of gossamer silk, its tails down to mid-thighs, which she wears over lacy bloomers that are tied at the calf with blue ribbons; her black, patent leather high-button shoes are equipped with five-inch heels, the points of which could easily pass through the eye of a needle. Certainly, she is competing with this other . . .'; but let that pass. The critic's eye view of the clientèle is as sharp as his summing up of the staff. And compare the girls of the Odeon with the gents at '21'. 'Where else can you see at a table for six, six gray suits?'

Mr Britchky is not only a witty social observer. He writes about food, too: 'Avoid with care the so-called Fresh Spinach Salad. The spinach tastes as if it had been in cold storage since the last war, the mushrooms are tasteless, the zucchini plastic, the bacon over-burdened with responsibility among these sorry partners.' At Alfredo, The Original of Rome, on East 53rd Street:

> The speciality of the house, of course, is fettuccine, all 'Al-fredo-made', if publicity releases mean anything, according to a seventy-four-year-old family recipe. By the age of seventy-four, it must be concluded, even a recipe may not remember so well, for one night the sauce that graces your noodles is barely moist, the ground cheese gravelly, so that the pepper you grind on bounces about on the pasta like jacks on a sidewalk; but on another occasion, the sauce is lava-like, thick and buttery.

Mr Britchky can turn slavering at the mouth on and off in a sentence.

S.J. Perelman used restaurants as a launch-pad for some of his wilder whoops of wit. David Frost and I once had breakfast with him at Brown's Hotel and a piece of prose, plainly based on the encounter, duly appeared in the *New Yorker*. It had nothing to do with the meal or us (more tangy than the former, more amusing than the latter), but it made me read every other Perelman story with an eye to identifying the suitably pedestrian premise which inspired that rich imagination. For example, in Hong Kong, he happens upon or imagines 'a place in Kowloon called Cindy's East'. Reeking of Runyon's Mindy's it is modelled on Lindy's, the famed Broadway restaurant of yesteryear and dispensed the same food: 'Corned beef! Pastrami! Cheesecake!' Perelman meets the manager:

a languid young Englishman . . . Angus Smedwick . . . a Cantabrigian. He informed me that he had stayed up till dawn playing bridge . . . he was so unlike the Broadway hustler I expected that I asked him what had impelled him to open a supposedly ethnic restaurant.

'I didn't,' he returned. 'I won it in a card game from a New York chap, name of Manny Rosemont, who started it. At the time I didn't know anything about this sort of food, but I soon mastered it. Take the dish they call cheese blintzes, for instance. You'd think it was a form of curry, wouldn't you? Well, it's just a hard doughnut garnished with smoked salmon.'

'I thought that was called lox on a bagel.'

He gave me a tolerant smile. 'So do a lot of our customers, but I soon straighten them out . . .

His clientèle is mainly tourist. 'We get a lot of those tribal fellows – I can never remember the word. They hail from some island off the American coast.'

'You don't mean Hebrews by any chance?' I asked, arching my back.

'That's it – from Manhattan. Nice blokes, but it's funny – they only come in once. I can't figure out why.'

Damon Runyon's charming distorting mirror reflecting the real Broadway was just as original and personal. The names he invented for his characters were as wittily inspired. In the Canary Club, he created a playwright, Brogan Wilmington, who is laid out by a lady whose Lobster Newburg he has upset. As he is carried out, a dramatic critic, Ambrose Hanmer, whom the playwright had intended to attack, consoles 'the beautiful' . . . who now seems to be crying:

'Miss,' Ambrose says, 'or madam, dry your tears. Your fresh portion of Lobster Newburg will be along presently.'

'Oh,' she says, 'I am not crying about the loss of my Lobster Newburg. I am crying because in my agitation I spill the little bottle of cyanide of potassium I bring in here with me and now I cannot commit suicide. Look at it all over my bag.'

'Well,' Ambrose says, 'I am sorry, but I do not approve of anybody committing suicide in the Canary Club. It is owned by a friend of mine by the name of Joe Gloze and every Christmas he sends me a dozen expensive ties, besides permitting me to free-load here at will. A suicide in his club will be bad publicity for him. It may get around that death ensues because of the cooking.'

In his musical version of *Valmouth*, Sandy Wilson gave a nun, bound by a vow of silence, the intoxicating release of a 'talking day' during which she could patter along non-stop in witty couplets. Let us imagine therefore an 'eating day' crammed with indulgence, planned for a literary appetite after prolonged fasting. For breakfast, taking anonymous advice, start with 'a grapefruit – a lemon that had a chance and took advantage of it'.

Toast? It can be a dispiriting start to the day, according to James Payn:

> I never had a piece of toast
> Particularly long and wide
> But fell upon the sandy floor
> And always on the buttered side.

An omelette? Another warning, this time from Saki, if we make it ourselves: 'Be content to remember that those who can make omelettes properly can do nothing else.' (Call the cook: 'She was a good cook as cooks go and as good cooks go she went'). But some bread surely, in spite of more advice to the contrary. 'Acorns were good enough until bread was invented', said Juvenal. There are those who think Marie Antoinette lifted 'Then let them eat cake' from Jean-Jacques Rousseau: and those who complain with Thomas Hood:

> My God! that bread should be so dear
> And flesh and blood so cheap!

But Wilde cautions against too many quotations so early in the day: 'Only dull people are brilliant at breakfast.' Back to the eggs, which, on the whole, inspire philosophical rather than witty thoughts: 'I never see an egg brought on my table but I feel penetrated with the wonderful change it would have undergone but for my gluttony', wrote de Crèvecour in *Letters from an American Farmer* in 1782. 'It might have been a gentle useful hen, leading her chickens with a care and vigilance which speaks shame to many women.' A hundred years later Samuel Butler viewed eggs as part of a great conspiracy: 'A hen is only an egg's way of making other eggs.' But when the moment of decision is reached, make a clean break. 'You can't unscramble scrambled eggs', goes the American proverb, which anticipates the one about squeezing toothpaste back into the tube as well as the injunction to dry those tears shed on account of the spilt milk.

A little champagne, mid-morning?

> Here's to champagne, the drink divine
> That makes us forget our troubles
> It is made of a dollar's worth of wine
> And three dollar's worth of bubbles.

And worth it. Perhaps it precedes a stroll to the Oyster Bar. People were making 'jests' about oysters back in 1611. A Mr Tarlton even collected them: 'Oysters are ungodly, because they are eaten without grace; uncharitable because they leave naught but shells; and unprofitable because they must swim in wine.' A regular little Touchstone, Mr Tarlton was. You can hear the oyster eaters falling about. Swift considered oysters 'a cruel meat because we eat them alive; then they are an uncharitable meat for we leave nothing to the poor.' Was it Byron who first found them 'amatory', in *Don Juan*? A deal of anonymous wisdom has been preserved on the subject:

> Than an oyster
> There's nothing moister

and,

> An oyster is a fish, built like a nut.

And, one sinister suggestion, still anonymous: 'The great object in the life of the oyster is to convert the whole world into oysters.' 'Secret and self-contained', wrote Dickens, denying that theory of world domination in *A Christmas Carol*: 'Solitary as an oyster'. And then came Lewis Carroll and Cole Porter and Ira Gershwin:

> You say oysters
> And I say ersters . . .

Let's call the oyster thing off, in time for lunch.

241

Lunch out, at an hotel? 'It used to be a good hotel, but that proves nothing,' wrote Mark Twain. 'I used to be a good boy.' On P.G. Wodehouse's advice, eat carefully: 'The lunches of fifty-seven years had caused his chest to slip to the mezzanine floor.' Perhaps the Ritz? According to Cecil Roberts: 'There is only one form of the simple life – living at the Ritz Hotel and touching the bell.' According to Nubar Gulbenkian, who lived there most of the time, 'The best number', if we may paraphrase him, 'for a luncheon party is two – myself and a damned good head waiter.' Perhaps some rare Irish beef, on George Borrow's advice:

> Ulster for a soldier,
> Connaught for a thief,
> Munster for learning
> And Leinster for beef.

And no bottled additives – no chance to prove Richard Armour correct with his:

> Shake and shake the catsup bottle
> None will come and then a lot'll.

Claret to drink with our beef, not water:

> Full many a man, both young and old
> Is brought to his sarcophagus
> By pouring water icy-cold
> A-down his warm oesophagus.

(How much greater the risk before the invention of the refrigerator when, according to the Duchess of Devonshire at Chatsworth, 'Ice . . . cut from the canal and stored in the ice-house . . . was "full of swan's dirt".')

Then it's time for an afternoon snooze and a meditation on the cycle of digestion with Ambrose Bierce: 'Good to eat and wholesome to digest, as a worm to a toad, a toad to a snake, a snake to a pig, a pig to a man, a man to a worm,' or as E.Y. Harburg rhymed it in *Jamaica*:

> Man, he eat the Barracuda,
> Barracuda eat the Bass,
> Bass he eat the little flounder
> 'Cause the flounder lower class.

> Little flounder eat the sardine,
> That's nature's plan.
> Sardine eat the little worm
> Little worm eat man.

Tea? Not if J.B. Priestley has his way. 'Our trouble is that we drink too much tea. I see in this the slow revenge of the Orient, which has diverted the Yellow River down our nostrils.' G.K. Chesterton still had a good word to say for it:

> Tea, although an Oriental,
> Is a gentleman at least.
> Cocoa is a cad and coward
> Cocoa is a vulgar beast.

What is on the evening menu? Perhaps reading Nietzche, a little self-consciously, before dressing for cocktails provides a clue: 'The English diet is a return to cannibalism. This diet I think gives heavy feet to the mind. English women's feet.' In defence of cannibalism there is Swift's modest proposal: 'I have been assured by a very knowing American of my acquaintance in London that a healthy young child, well nursed, is at a year old a most delicious, nourishing and wholesome food, whether stewed, roasted, baked or boiled: and I make no doubt that it will equally serve in a fricassée or a ragout.' Voltaire disapproved, but did not go so far in counselling Frederick the Great: 'Cannibals have the same notions of right and wrong that we have. They make war in the same anger and passion that move us, and the same crimes are committed everywhere. Eating fallen enemies is only an extra ceremonial. The wrong does not consist in roasting them, but in killing them.' No human flesh for him, then.

But who shall cook? It is important. 'What is literature compared with cooking?' asked E.V. Lucas. 'The one is shadow, the other substance.' Shall Virginia Woolf be the one to slave over the hot stove? 'And now, with some pleasure,' she wrote in her diary, 'I find that it is seven; and must cook dinner. Haddock and sausage meat. I think it is true that one gains a certain hold on haddock and sausage by writing them down.' She may 'gain a hold' but she doesn't make them sound inviting. Seneca said, 'It is no wonder that diseases are innumerable – count the cooks.' And a collector of proverbs in 1542 agreed: 'God sends meat; but the Devil sends the cooks.' Perhaps the

French chef Brillat-Savarin is our man. Not only could he tell you what you were if you told him what you ate, but he had the right attitude: 'The discovery of a new dish does more for human happiness than the discovery of a new star.'

While the cook busies himself in the kitchen, cocktails? Not for French composer Paul Claudel: 'A cocktail is to a glass of wine as rape is to love', but perhaps for the other guests, to an old recipe:

> A little whisky to make it strong.
> A little water to make it weak.
> A little lemon to make it sour.
> A little sugar to make it sweet.

There is controversy about how much liquor will make the evening go with a swing. According to a Scottish proverb, 'When drink's in, wit's out', but Harry Hill's Clubhouse door on Houston Street in New York in 1867 advertised:

> A bumper of good liquor
> Will end a contest quicker
> Than justice, judge or vicar.

Settled at the table, grace for a literary occasion, written and spoken by the Rt Rev Mervyn Stockwood: 'For the edible and the readable we give thanks to God, the Author of Life.' And then we must not forget Maugham's advice in his notebook, 'At a dinner party one should eat wisely but not too well and talk well but not too wisely'.

Soup? Of course, on Fuller's advice in the *Gnomologia*: 'Of soup and love, the first is the best.' But sip warily, for according to Beethoven, 'Only the pure in heart can make a good soup.'

A salad? A Greek proverb held that 'Eating cress makes one witty.' No cucumbers if we go by Dr Johnson: 'A cucumber should be well-sliced and dressed with pepper and vinegar and then thrown out as good-for-nothing.'

Mayonnaise? In Bierce's view it is 'one of the sauces which serve the French in place of a state religion'. A better state of affairs perhaps than that judgment on English cuisine: 'There are in England sixty different religious sects, but only one sauce.'

Fortunately, we are not dining with Anthony Powell's Huntercombes: 'Dinner at the Huntercombes possessed only two dramatic features – the wine was a farce and the food was a tragedy.' The conversation flows, the guests have been selected on A.A. Milne's advice: 'It is only the very young girl at her first dinner party whom it is difficult to entertain. At her second dinner party, and thereafter, she knows the whole art of being amusing. All she has to do is listen; all we men have to do is to tell her about ourselves.' (A brief conversational diversion to listen to a young girl's account of an early night out – Antonia Fraser remembering, not a dinner, but a Drag Hunt Ball at Oxford: 'If sexual experiences were theoretically minimal, social expectations were on the contrary great. Once there was a Drag Hunt Ball, just outside Oxford, to which I had un-accountably failed to be asked. I asked God to do something about it, and God recklessly killed poor King George VI, as a result of which the Hunt Ball was cancelled'.)

The fish course? John Dory, perhaps, in order to admit George Lassalle's witty description: 'Note the expression of utter surprise and disillusionment in the eyes. It is as if, at some early revolutionary stage, realization had come to its fishy brain that it had been duped into taking an irrevocable step in the wrong direction; originally designed to fly but now forever condemned to a liquid element.'

As we enjoy the John Dory, along with the writer of Numbers, 'we remember the fish which we did eat in Egypt freely: the cucumbers and the melons and the leeks and the onions and the garlic'. Oh! the garlic – and the English proverb comes to mind, 'Garlic makes a man wink, drink and stink.' Nevertheless, take a little with the meat; but not too much meat for, again on Fuller's advice, 'much meat – much malady'. Sydney Smith would not, however, agree with that sentiment: 'If there is a pure and elevated pleasure in this world it is that of roast pheasant and bread sauce. Barn door fowls for dissenters, but for the real churchman, the thirty-nine times articles clerk – the pheasant, the pheasant!'

Then comes the ticklish question of how to prepare the potatoes. The tasting of the first was a great moment, wittily celebrated by Brahms and S.J. Simon in *No Bed For Bacon*.

> From the banqueting kitchens of the Guildhall arose a smell. A smell unlike any of the smells known to Londoners. And Londoners were connoisseurs of smells. It was a soggy smell, a flat and depressed smell, a smell which was trying to warn you not to expect too much. The quick-witted in the crowd nudged one another.

'For my part,' Burghley was saying, 'I intend to bite my potato most carefully . . .'

Elizabeth of England sighed . . . 'Bring on the potatoes,' she ordered.

The Flower of England was looking at its plates with a mixture of doubt tinged with awe. In front of each one of them lay a soggy island of white mush, shaped rather like a warped egg, only larger.

The potato! This was it!

'Well, well, well,' said the Master of the Revels, in a resigned voice.

Sir Philip Sidney would not permit his doubts to show on his face. He was making up his mind not to let old Walter down. 'Delicious,' he was going to say, whatever it tasted like.

The Earl of Southampton picked his up and experimented. The potato turned over quite easily, and seemed to be the same on the other side.

In spite of the evidence of his eyes, Burghley showed no relaxation of his vigilance. He had picked up a knife, and was pricking it most delicately.

'I shall bite it most carefully,' he asserted stubbornly.

But Elizabeth of England showed no such daintiness. Forthright and purposeful, she dug her spoon into the potato, collected half of it and carried it firmly to her mouth.

The Flower of England waited.

Sir Walter Raleigh gripped his seat under the table. He had sailed half way round the world to find this root, he had faced great perils to bring it back, he had withstood the blandishments of the most expert cajolers at Court, and had not even hinted at the secret of its flavour, he had changed his chef six times, and now Elizabeth of England was tasting it.

He looked at her.

Elizabeth of England spat.

'Not enough salt,' she said.

And pudding? Even out of season, why not 'a smell like an eating house and a pastry cook's next door to each other, with a laundress's next door to that'? That was the pudding in *A Christmas*

Carol. Or an apple pie?

> An apple pie without some cheese
> Is like a kiss without a squeeze.

And cheese by itself? – 'Milk's leap towards immortality', said Clifton Fadiman, in direct contravention of John Ray's seventeenth-century proverb:

> Cheese it is a peevish elf
> It digests all things but itself.

After-Eights? Clive James once came down strongly in favour of After-Eights before joining the Ladies:

> What proper man would plump for bints
> Ahead of After-Eight thin mints?
> True pleasure for a man of parts
> Is tarts in him, not him in tarts.

That's it; along with Alphonse Karr we have to agree that 'even the great Napoleon couldn't eat his dinner twice', and settle for Sydney Smith again:

> Serenely full, the epicure would say
> Fate cannot harm me – I have dined today.

Intimations of mortality prompt guilt about gluttony – never, as Orson Welles observed, 'a secret vice'; in Joseph O'Kern II's more formula phrase, 'obesity is really widespread'. (Exercising some moderation might help. On the other hand there is Robert Quillen's advice, 'Another good reducing exercise consists in placing both hands against the table edge and pushing back.')

Before leaving the subject of human appetites, however, we cannot neglect those two other motive powers that are so inextricably bound up with the sating of our physical and emotional demands – success and money.

There are many formulae for success. Einstein, who knew about both, suggested, 'If A is success in life, then A equals X plus Y plus Z. Work is X, Y is play and Z is keeping your mouth shut.' For Don Marquis success was also a matter of keeping out of trouble, though this time by the art of delegation: 'The successful people are the ones who think up things for the rest of the world to keep busy at.' Then there is L. Grant Glickman's analysis that, 'Behind every successful man is a woman – with nothing to wear' – not quite as amusing as the author's name.

Whatever the route to success, there is unanimity in the verdict on those who reach the summit. Again Ambrose Bierce draws together the threads with a characteristically terse definition: 'Success is the one unpardonable sin against our fellows.' Rilke offered a worthy partner with his assessment of fame: 'The aggregate of all the misunderstandings that collect around a new name.' While Anon, Jr. resorted to rhyme:

> There is a famous family named Stein –
> There's Gert, and there's Epp, and there's Ein;
> Gert's poems are bunk,
> Epp's statues are junk,
> And nobody understands Ein.

At the root of such broadsides lurks another seething passion, gnawing deep inside us with as much vigour as appetite – jealousy; made all the more acute by the equivocal efforts of those who have soared above the millstream to reimmerse themselves in it. Fred Allen, writing in *Treadmill to Oblivion*, took a swipe at this hypocrisy: 'A celebrity is a person who works hard all his life to become well known, and then wears dark glasses to avoid being recognized.' This hints at a rich store of ammunition. It used to be said of T.E. Lawrence that he was 'always backing into the limelight'. Mary Wilson Little had the satisfaction of striking home with a double-barbed dart: 'The penalty of success is to be bored by the attentions of people who formerly snubbed you.' According to Jules Renard success can backfire: 'The reward of great men is that, long after they have died, one is not sure that they are dead.' And *vice versa*, 'Because my name appears in history books, most children think I am dead,' complained Sir Edmund Hillary, one of the few who could claim to have reached the top.

Better targets for the sniper are those still sweating through the foothills with their eyes riveted on the upper slopes of glory. 'Those whom the gods wish to destroy they first call promising', wrote Cyril Connolly. Fellow-critic, Christopher Wordsworth, scored a memorable knock-out when he dismissed the sporting journalist,

Clifford Makins, as 'a legend in his own lunchtime'. And Jean Gammon neatly sums up the present-day cult of achievement and accountability with: 'If at first you don't succeed, you're fired.'

There's nothing like watching others striding towards a glittering horizon for breeding envy; which explains why, in a Russian on-looker's words, 'Next to reading somebody else's love letters, there's nothing quite so delightful as being privy to the facts of his financial life, especially if they tend towards the disastrous.'

W.C. Fields had tasted wealth, and the lack of it: 'A rich man is nothing but a poor man with money.' So did Margaret Chase Harriman, chronicler of the Algonquin: 'Money is what you'd get on beautifully without if only other people weren't so crazy about it.' For H.L. Mencken it wasn't so much the cash as the cachet that counted: 'The most valuable of all human possessions, next to a superior air, is the reputation of being well-to-do.' Walter Freeman detected a divine right to wealth, certainly 'in the western world', where, 'the idea still lingers that the wages of righteousness is prosperity'. But in a society where atheism now is keeping time with indifference, observers can afford to be franker and the wealthy more philosophic. And the formula men have a field day. 'True you can't take it with you,' acknowledged Brendan Francis, 'but then, that's not the place where it comes in handy.' Bill Vaughan was even more pragmatic: 'Money won't buy happiness, but it will pay the salaries of a large research staff to study the problem.' Raising his hand to the heavens Maurice Baring adopted a more censorious stance: 'If you would know what the Lord God thinks of money, you have only to look at those to whom he gives it.' And with a similarly sombre air Logan Pearsall Smith shrugged his shoulders in his *Afterthoughts* and reminded his readers, 'Those who set out to serve both God and Mammon soon discover there is no God.' Not that it's those without it that get worked up about money. Vic Oliver gave a graphic account of the dilemma of wealth – do you hang on to it, or do you enjoy it? 'If a man runs after money, he's money-mad; if he keeps it, he's a capitalist; if he spends it, he's a playboy; if he doesn't get it, he's a ne'er do well; if he doesn't try to get it, he lacks ambition. If he gets it without working for it, he's a parasite; and if he accumulates it after a lifetime of hard work, people call him a fool who never got anything out of life.'

Interest in money isn't limited to those who have a surfeit, it is just that in their case interest takes the form of income not outgoing. 'In the midst of life we are in debt,' sighed Ethel Watts Mumford. Ned Preston peered mournfully into his wallet and moaned, 'A dollar may not go as far as it once did, but it makes up for it in speed.' Anon also looked back over his shoulder to the time when he first started working and, 'used to dream of the day when I might be earning the salary I'm starving on now.' George Clark tried to blame inflation, both fiscal and physical: 'The only thing that continues to give us more for our money is a weighing machine.'

Inevitably we are driven to the depressing conclusion that when it comes to money, human nature is still dragging its feet, as Jack Richardson points out: 'Whenever dice are thrown or cards are shuffled the Dark Ages get another turn on this planet.' And, to return to my opening remarks, judging from the rest of the short-comings thrown up by this catalogue of human weakness, we are still at the crawling stage in most other respects, at least as far as western man is concerned. I leave you to Dick Gregory for the final word on the subject: 'You gotta say this for the white race – its self-confidence knows no bounds. Who else could go to a small island in the South Pacific where there's no poverty, no crime, no unemployment, no war and no worry – and call it a "primitive society"?'

7

CONSIDERED TRIFLES

'If there is one man more deeply hated by his fellow men than any other it is the witty man,' said Oscar Wilde, with some feeling. The burden on the Wildes and F.E. Smiths grows heavier with each tired repetition of jests which once dropped spontaneously from lip or pen – or were polished and presented in the context of a perfect comedy like *The Importance of Being Earnest*. And a reputation for wit means that a dozen willing Boswells follow the wit about, eager to pass on the latest gem. What of the unrecorded wits, 'born to blush unseen'? Everybody is supposed to have one novel inside them. What of the irregular wits who see an opportunity 'because it is there', launch their shapely jest and watch it disappear? This last chapter is a game reserve for the preservation of endangered quips which I have relished and which may otherwise join their extinct brothers in oblivion. It is a sad thought that if any find favour, and suffer repetition, they too may eventually bring disfavour on their originators. Many are puns, and the punster is readily and frequently condemned.

The once-for-ever witticism is a favourite of mine. I cherish the (non-punning) episode in which Frank Muir and Denis Norden coped with BBC bureaucracy. Commissioned to write a programme about Paris in the heyday of radio comedy, they were paid a sum of money to go there for research. Before they could set off, the programme was cancelled. The BBC Accounts Department asked for its money back. Muir and Norden spent a genuinely collaborative morning wracking their brains for the correct disarming reply. Eventually, they found it – phrased wittily in a language common only to accountants: 'Dear Sirs, we are afraid we have no machinery for returning money.' They were not asked for it again.

In another broadcasting context, Eamonn Andrews was the subject of a magazine profile. The conscientious journalist called many of his colleagues. She asked one if he could supply an amusing anecdote. 'Oh no,' said the colleague, 'I don't think Eamonn would get involved in anything as risky as an anecdote.' Paddy O'Neil (Mrs Alfred Marks), something of a closet wit, is on the verge of

251

becoming a cult. For many years the Marks family lived in a splendid house in North London and for all I know, still do. Next door, their neighbours maintained a discreet silence. Neither family exchanged a word for some ten years or more until they saw a removal van taking away the neighbour's furniture. 'Oh,' she yelled, flinging wide the casement, 'was it something I didn't say?'

Then there was the unknown American admirer of the central European operetta stars, Jan Kiepura and Marta Eggert, who went round to see them after they had performed *The Merry Widow*, in translation, in New York. He praised their singing, but the accents had been all but incomprehensible. 'Do you think,' asked Kiepura, anxiously, 'that I polish up my English?' 'No,' said the defeated fan, 'I should English up your Polish.' Sometimes the wit – especially the punster – if really dedicated, has to wait. David Climie, a witty English revue writer, was one of the principal contributors to a revue called *Intimacy at 8.30*. In the cast was an effervescent Scandinavian actress, Aud Johannsen. Climie waited for weeks until one night Aud (pronounced 'Owed') looked downhearted – Climie's cue to rush round to her dressing room and inquire sympathetically, 'Aud, dear, what can the matter be?' Dick Vosburgh has cherished for years an ambition to produce an LP starring the American comedienne, Imogene Coca, singing the songs of Ted Kohler, who wrote the lyric for 'Stormy Weather' among others, simply so that Vosburgh could call it 'The Coca-Kohler Song Book'. I was very fond of an explanatory line, suggested by Tony Geiss, for introducing in *Side by Side by Sondheim* a sequence from the musical *Pacific Overtures*. 'This is not', Tony's intro ran, 'a show about foreplay in a Malibu beach house.'

Genuine moments of embarrassment in the theatre can produce spontaneous examples of barracker's wit. In the 1940s, the late Phyllis Robins had a great success on the wireless and risked a top-of-the-bill appearance at the Met in the Edgware Road. She was unused to music-hall and had only one hit song for which she was known: 'How Much is that Doggie in the Window?' However, she put together an act with her big song as the climax. For the early part of the week, she got away with it; but the Friday night house was different. As her rather genteel performance proceeded the gallery grew restless until one rough voice erupted in as kindly a shout as it could muster, bellowing paternally, 'Come on, Phyl, give us "the Dog" and piss off!'

Burt Shevelove and Larry Gelbart, who together wrote *A Funny Thing Happened on the Way to the Forum*, arrived in London for the opening of the show and were promptly wined and dined in the homes of their producers. On the first night Mrs Tony Walton (at that time it was Julie Andrews) did the honours. Social breast-feeding was becoming fashionable in the early '60s, and after dinner Mrs Walton helped her baby daughter to a public feast. The next night the writers visited Mrs Richard Pilbrow – the wife of the other producer. She too had just been delivered of a child. She too fed it after dinner. The following morning, Gelbart called Shevelove in his hotel room: 'Hey, Burt, are we booked in for any breast-feedings tonight?'

And then there are those instant puns – the three Spaniards having trouble with a revolving door: 'Too many Basques in one exit'; Noel Coward changing hotels in Italy: 'I had to move, I was coughing myself into a Firenze'; Herbert Kretzmer reviewing the interminable *Shogun*, a television series which ended with 'almost everybody except Richard Chamberlain being killed in the city of Osaka. *Moral* – Never give Osaka an even break.' Then there is the Victorian pun inspired by the mudlarking chimney sweep's attempt to get into the Palace and see Queen Victoria. Apparently he succeeded not once but three times and Palace staff nicknamed him 'IN-I-GO Jones' before sending him off to join the Navy. In a Victorian pantomime at Oxford, Brian Brindley produced a rhyme which, once again, was uniquely suited to the occasion. The Babes – lost in the Wood – discover a letter pinned by Robin Hood to a forest oak. They are not impressed:

> It would have been less heterodox
> If he had put the letter in the letter-o-box.

One more 'once-for-ever' witticism – it would be too expensive to repeat the premise. The clever and versatile BBC producer, Ernest Maxim, produced, directed, wrote, composed and choreographed a stage musical which was badly mauled by the critics. The subject was Dr Barnardo and his charity scheme. The flop was resounding, the losses were enormous and the rumour spread through the BBC that Barnardo's were starting a collection for Ernest.

Wit should be encouraged in unlikely places. In the TV listings, for example: the evening *Standard* previewed a Des O'Connor show like this; '9.55 DES O'CONNOR with Max Bygraves as chief guest; it looks like overkill night, charmwise.' On the TV screens, for example, especially in documentaries: a vivid phrase-making punk on a CBC documentary shown on BBC Television explained his extravagant haircut; 'I'm a ratcatcher, see, scares the shit out of 'em when I tread on their 'eads.' On the doorstep for example: a canvassed American barber was greeted during the early stages of a recent US Presidential campaign by a friendly man with out-stretched arm and the words, 'Hi, I'm Mo Udall. I'm running for President.' The barber replied, 'I know, we were just laughing about it this morning.'

And, in the new political climate there are new political obser-vations wittily to be made. In America, Senator Lawton Chiles skewered the problems of investigative journalism for a politician: 'Half the reporters in town are looking on you as a Pulitzer Prize to be won.' Julian Critchley voiced an English reaction to the same dilemma: 'The only safe pleasure for a parliamentarian is a bag of boiled sweets.'

Running witticisms in politics are fun – reworkings of a once proved formula are on the increase as radio, television and news-paper reports of speeches proliferate. Just as the old time music-hall act had to recycle the set-piece sketch to satisfy the omniverous television screen, so politicians can no longer stump the same strong words up and down the length and breadth of Midlothia. Denis Healey, with or without a scriptwriter, is the most conscientious of the political formula men. He came to fame on his original defin-ition of a debate with Sir Geoffrey Howe – 'like being savaged by a dead sheep'. Since then he has observed that Margaret Thatcher is 'a bargain basement Boadicea'; and fired triple grapeshot over her advisers. Prof. Alan Walters – economics – is 'The Doctor Who' of that craft; Sir John Hoskyns became 'The Rich Man's Frances Morell'; and Sir Anthony Parsons (Falkland's blest) 'The George Smiley of the Foreign Office.' But Healey reveals an adroit instinct to respond to an 'ongoing situation'. Geoffrey Howe's debating prowess may be at a standstill, but Healey's phrase-making must keep pace with change. A year later, being 'savaged by a dead sheep' became 'being nibbled by a hearthrug'.

Improvising on, bringing up to date or disputing an old saw is a rewarding springboard for wit:

> How odd
> of God
> To Choose
> The Jews,

inspired Leo Rosten to answer:

> Not odd
> of God
> Goyim
> Annoy 'im.

But let me finish by picking up three stitches hitherto dropped. Groucho Marx's favourite poem is 'the one that starts "Thirty days hath September" because it actually tells you something.' W.C. Fields thought that Jeanette Macdonald's face reminded him of an Aardvaark's Ass'. And Alan Bennett once said: 'Arianna Stassinopoulos is so boring you fall asleep halfway through her name.' All considered trifles, I agree, but I wanted to get them into the pattern.

INDEX

Index

Index

Molnar, Ferene, 25
Monroe, Marilyn, 64–5, 210
Montagu, Lady Mary Wortley, 222
Morgan, Charles, 74
Mozart, Wolfgang Amadeus, 118–19, 126
Muir, Frank, 31, 251

Nash, Ogden, 41–3, 96, 209, 213, 224
Nathan, George Jean, 72, 75, 76, 135, 148, 235
Nevill, Dorothy, 57
Newman, Ernest, 124
Nicholson, Harold, 61, 225
Nietzsche, Friedrich, 1, 44, 243
Nixon, Richard, 147–8, 153–4, 175
Nobbs, David, 211–12
Norden, Denis, 251

O'Connor, M. D., 218
Oliver, Vic, 249
Olivier, Laurence, 58, 70
Orwell, George, 9, 207
Osborne, John, 21–2, 60–1, 94–5

Paderewski, Ignace, 130–1
Parker, Charlie, 131
Parker, Dorothy, 2, 40–1, 50, 51, 71–2, 73, 76, 97, 98–100, 102, 153
Patterson, Floyd, 204
Payn, James, 240
Peacock, Thomas Love, 47–8, 235
Pepys, Samuel, 169
Perelman, S. J., 238–9
Pétain, Marshal Henri, 56
Peter, Laurence, 27, 147
Pinter, Harold, 195
Poe, Edgar Allan, 28
Pope, Alexander, 1, 4–6, 10, 12, 19, 24, 28, 32, 222
Porter, Cole, 131, 134–5, 234
Potter, Dennis, 202
Potter, Stephen, 214–5
Powell, Anthony, 244
Prentice, George D., 236
Presley, Elvis, 129
Preston, Ned, 250
Priestley, J. B., 56, 243
Prior, Matthew, 29

Quillen, Robert, 247
Quinton, Anthony, 112

Randolph, David, 114
Ravel, Maurice, 117
Ray, John, 247

Reagan, Ronald, 98, 153–4, 170, 175
Rembar, Charles, 27
Renard, Jules, 248
Richardson, Jack, 250
Richardson, Justin, 33
Rivers, Joan, 62
Roberts, Cecil, 242
Robertson-Glasgow, R. C., 193–5
Rodgers, Richard, 134, 212
Rodriguez, Chi Chi, 201
Roosevelt, Franklin, 179–80
Root, Henry, 215–17
Ross, Amanda, 28
Rossini, Gioacchino, 114
Rosten, Leo, 255
Rowland, Helen, 218–19, 221
Royko, Mike, 211
Runyon, Damon, 191–2, 239–40
Ruskin, John, 119
Ryan, Ralph, 190

Saki (H. H. Munro), 224, 240
Salinger, Pierre, 180
Sandburg, Carl, 30, 34
Satie, Erik, 71, 117
Saxe, J. G., 13
Schlesinger, John, 60
Schnabel, Artur, 115, 123, 125
Schonberg, Harold, 120
Schwartz, Arthur, 136–7
Scott, Sir Walter, 31–2
Shankly, Bill, 206
Shaw, George Bernard, 2, 3, 12, 64–5, 76, 80–3, 94–5, 96, 114, 115, 119, 122, 124–5, 147, 202, 220, 223–4
Shelley, Percy Bysshe, 148–9, 223
Sheridan, Richard Brinsley, 5, 12, 149, 155–6, 222
Simon, John, 75, 127
Simon, S. J., 1, 70, 220, 245–6
Simple, Peter, 17
Sitwell, Edith, 9
Smith, F. E., 2–3, 236
Smith, Patti, 128
Smith, Red, 189–90
Smith, Sydney, 5, 30, 124, 245, 247
Sondheim, Stephen, 43, 138
Soper, Lord, 177
Sousa, John Philip, 131
Steinbeck, John, 212–13
Stephen, J. K., 121–2
Stevenson, Adlai, 12, 13, 21, 146–7, 150, 174, 178
Stevenson, Michael, 208
Stewart, Jackie, 211
Stocks, Baroness, 177

259

BIBLIOGRAPHY

In addition to the works listed under Acknowledgments the following anthologies greatly assisted my research:

Beecham Stories by Harold Atkins and Archie Newman (Robson Books, 1978)

The Book of Sports Quotes by Jonathan Green and Don Atyeo (Omnibus Press, 1979)

The Book of Political Quotes by Jonathan Green (Angus and Robertson, 1982)

A Dictionary of Contemporary Quotations by Jonathan Green (Pan Books, 1982)

Violets and Vinegar by Tom Hartman and Jilly Cooper (George Allen & Unwin, 1980)

The Book of Hollywood Quotes by Gary Herman (Omnibus Press, 1979)

Dictionary of Quotations by H.L. Mencken (Collins, 1982)

The Macmillan Treasury of Relevant Quotations edited by Edward F. Murphy (Macmillan Press Ltd., 1979)

The Oxford Dictionary of Quotations

The Penguin Dictionary of Quotations

The Penguin Dictionary of Modern Quotations

No Turn Unstoned by Diana Rigg (Elm Tree Books, 1982)

The Encyclopaedia of Quotes About Music – edited by Nat Shapiro (David and Charles, 1978)

The Book of Theatre Quotes by Gordon Snell (Angus and Robertson, 1982)